Japanese Lessons

Japanese Lessons

A Year in a Japanese School
through the Eyes of an
American Anthropologist
and Her Children

GAIL R. BENJAMIN

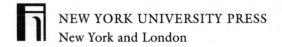

NEW YORK UNIVERSITY PRESS
New York and London

NEW YORK UNIVERSITY PRESS
New York and London

Library of Congress Cataloging-in-Publication Data

Benjamin, Gail.
Japanese lessons : a year in a Japanese school through the eyes of
an American anthropologist and her children / Gail R. Benjamin.
p.   cm.
Includes bibliographical references and index.
ISBN 0-8147-1291-6 (cloth : acid-free paper)
1. Education, Elementary—Japan—Urawa-shi.   2. Students, Foreign—
Education (Elementary)—Japan.   3. American students—Japan
4. Elementary schools—Japan—Urawa—Sociological aspects.
5. Comparative education.   6. Benjamin, Gail.   I. Title.
LA1314.7.B46   1997
372.952—dc20   96-35698
                   CIP

Manufactured in the United States of America
10 9 8 7 6 5 4

for Samuel Rhian Bobrow
Ellen Elizabeth Bobrow

intrepid colleagues

Contents

Acknowledgments

I want first to acknowledge my greatest debt for the writing of this book, the one I owe to my husband, Davis Bobrow, for supporting me during fieldwork and after our return from Japan. Only he knows in how many ways he has accomplished this. My children, Sam and Ellen, also bore burdens caused by this project and showed consideration and forbearance.

My colleagues at the University of Pittsburgh have listened apparently patiently to my stories about school in Japan and have heard the ideas presented here as they were developing. Paula L. W. Sabloff and Jeremy Sabloff as constant lunch companions probably bore the brunt of this, along with Steven J. C. Gaulin. Students in several classes at the University of Pittsburgh also listened to these stories and ideas, and their reactions were valuable to me.

My friend Judith Capen brought her intelligent insight to bear on my writing in progress, and her architect's eye on the details of editing was invaluable. Her encouragement helped keep me going at several points.

In Japan the Graduate School for Policy Sciences at Saitama University, under the leadership of Dean Toru Yoshimura, gave me a helpful academic home. Our neighbors and colleagues at the graduate school, James and Kimie Rhodes, helped us with daily life and gave us relief from being always foreigners. The principal of Okubo Higashi Elementary School, Takeshi Kano, and the students and teachers there, especially Akemi Ohshima and Eiko Kuroda, welcomed our children, made them feel like real members of the school community, and enriched their lives forever.

Toshiaki and Sumiko Ohi and their children Kyo and Susumu offered us their friendship: help and concern as well as companionship. I miss them.

1

Getting Started

Every morning, six days a week, the streets of Japanese towns and cities are full of lively groups of children converging on neighborhood schools. Elementary school children wearing leather backpacks for books and junior high school students in dark uniforms carrying briefcases, all meeting friends and calling gaily to each other, give the residential neighborhoods a sense of bustle and excitement, which emphasizes the quiet that follows during the school day.

What would it be like to be one of those children? Are the backpacks heavy? What can be in them? All of us were excited and scared at the prospect of Sam and Ellen's becoming part of these large groups of seemingly identical but animated and happy school children.

We were coming back, really. Our family's plan to spend ten months in Urawa during 1989–90 meant that we would be returning to the city where we had spent nearly a year during 1982–83. Our experiences during that year certainly colored our expectations of how we would spend the coming year, what we could look forward to, what we worried about, and our feelings about taking two children, ages seven and eleven, to Japan.

Both my husband, Davis Bobrow, and I would be affiliated with the Graduate School for Policy Sciences at Saitama University in Urawa.

My plan was to do research on language patterns in schools and other educational settings, and Dave had a research grant from the Fulbright program to study Japanese national security policy. My work could have been done anywhere in Japan; Dave's required that he be near Tokyo with easy access to government officials and records.

There were several factors that made our affiliation with Saitama University attractive. First, we had made good friends there in 1982–83, and knew the school to be a congenial and helpful host to visiting foreign scholars. Second, the school is located within reasonable commuting distance of the government centers, but far enough away from central Tokyo to make a significant difference in the cost of housing. Furthermore, the school had available an apartment that we could rent on the university grounds. The disadvantages were the distance from central Tokyo, which meant more commuting time for Dave, and being at least two hours away from any elementary schools where English was the language of instruction.

I had read a lot about Japanese elementary education, William Cummings's book *Education and Equality in Japan* (1980) and John Singleton's *Nichu* (1967) among others, and had a generally positive impression of what life for children would be like in Japanese schools. But I think that without our previous experience with a day care center and a kindergarten, we would have been much more reluctant even to consider dropping two American kids into a Japanese elementary school.

On our first visit Sam had been four and a half, and Ellen six months old when we arrived in Urawa. Sam had needed to be in a kindergarten because he needed to be with children, and Ellen had needed to be in part-time day care because both her parents were doing research. We had no particular plans about how to manage this when we arrived, but by great good fortune we ended up living in a small apartment building with wonderful neighbors. The Li family lived two floors below us. They were Koreans, Mr. Li a businessman, who had been in Japan for about four years. They were members of the Urawa

Episcopalian Church and sent their five-year-old son to the church's kindergarten. Through their intercession Sam was able to enroll in the school also.

We didn't realize at the time what a stroke of good luck this was. Not only was this school one of the most prestigious and oldest in Urawa, but it was also small and very friendly. The members of the church included both Japanese and Korean families, and the minister had studied in England. Though there had never been a Western child or family affiliated with the school, the teachers and families seemed to have no hesitation in inviting us into the school. Most students did not come from Christian families, so our being Jewish was no barrier and only made us even more exotic.

Sam arrived at this kindergarten able to say "good morning" and to count to five in Japanese. After the first day his teacher told me that they had taught him how to say "Give it to me" because the other children didn't like it if he just took toys, and so he needed to be able to ask. After that I didn't hear about any explicit Japanese lessons, only occasional reports that "gradually" he was getting used to things. He was always eager to go to school, and in time my apprehensions gave way to admiration for the school and its teachers and for the students and their families.

I was particularly impressed with the way in which Mrs. Li and a circle of mothers cooperated both to incorporate me into activities with them and to protect the time I needed for my work. They were supportive of both my roles, as mother and as researcher, and made life easier and more enjoyable for me.

Arranging care for Ellen was a bit more of a problem; it was through our landlady's efforts that we succeeded. She was not only the wife of a local politician and real estate developer, but also a pharmacist of traditional medicines with a business of her own and two grown children. She first took me to several private businesses that take care of small children, but we discovered that they would take children only on a full-time basis, six full days a week. I wasn't prepared to leave Ellen for that long. We then went to city hall to inquire about municipal facilities, and it was that office that directed us to the university's own day care center, where I was able to enroll Ellen for three days a week.

Here, too, we were very favorably impressed with the individual, loving care that children from six weeks to three years received. And here, too, the caregivers seemed neither daunted nor rigid about the prospect of dealing with a foreign family.

These two very positive experiences with our children were the deciding factors in our decision to live in Urawa again and to send the children to the local Japanese school. We also shared the feeling of many American parents that what our children would miss in a year away from American schooling wasn't too important, that it could easily be made up. We believed that the immersion experience of a year of life in a different culture and language would in itself be valuable education for the children and ourselves, valuable enough to offset the inevitable frustration and despair of having to deal with an unknown language and a strange conception of school, children, and life. Such a dramatic change can be hard for both parents and children, though there's no doubt that the major difficulty is faced by the children, who have to spend more than forty hours a week in the school environment. The year was not always easy, but we have had no reason to regret the decision.

Urawa is a typical Japanese city in many ways. It is an old city, the capital of the prefecture, a center for administration, agriculture, and industry for several centuries. It is now also a bedroom community for families of Tokyo workers; its main train station is about an hour from central Tokyo. The university was moved from the center of town to its fringes after the war, but the city has grown out around it in the haphazard "mixed use" way of Japanese cities. The neighborhood of the university also includes farms, commercial areas, temples, light industries, and some heavy industry, along with housing for families of all economic levels.

On their daily walk to school the children passed homes, shops, small apartment buildings, a kiwi orchard just behind the auto repair shop, and a big old *keyaki* tree fenced off from the surrounding paddy fields and marked as a Shinto shrine by the straw rope with paper streamers around it and by the plaque saying it had been recognized as a shrine by the Taisho emperor. Farther on, past the paddy fields where we could see the whole process of growing rice as the year went on and hear the frogs that lived there when the fields were flooded, a Buddhist temple with its graveyard provided an oasis of green. Gardens around the older houses also held trees, the noisy cicadas that are an integral part of Japanese summers, and an occasional Inari shrine. Right across from the school a small shop sold school supplies and snacks to students and to people who waited for the bus there.

Coffee shops and small restaurants crowded together on this major street and on the four-lane street closer to our home where the traffic also supported a number of fast-food chain stores. It soon came to seem perfectly normal to us to see a shop, carved out of a paddy field, selling small electrical appliances, next door to an old farm house, across the street from a six-unit apartment house and a small factory making aluminum window frames and doors.

We decided not to have a car, so I rode my bicycle to the supermarket about a half mile away several times a week to shop; I was glad to join a food co-op that would deliver some foods, once a week. For other shopping we took the bus downtown from the university stop about three blocks from our building. We rented a car for weekend trips a few times.

Our own apartment was in a building owned by Saitama University and used for housing the foreign students and their families who were at the Graduate School for Policy Sciences. These are primarily mid-career level civil servants from Southeast Asian countries who come to Japan for two years of study. Many of them have young children who attend the local kindergarten and elementary school. That makes these schools among the most cosmopolitan in Japan; at least our children would not be the first non-Japanese students encountered by the school, the teachers, and the students.

Our apartment was the largest in the building, because Dave was the most senior resident, and at 700 square feet was considered very spacious. It had a small entryway for storing shoes, umbrellas, and other outside gear, two bedrooms, a bathroom, a large (comparatively speaking) kitchen-dining-living room, and a balcony for hanging laundry. Perhaps the greatest luxury in the apartment was its view of Mount Fuji a hundred miles away to the southwest, visible during the clear winter days.

ENROLLING IN SCHOOL

Even though our research prospects seemed ideal, even though our housing situation seemed good, even though we felt comfortable making our way around Urawa, and even though we liked our neighborhood and felt confident the year was going to be a good one, we were still a bit apprehensive about school. Would we find that the congenial friendliness of preschool in Japan had given way to a regimented and strictly academic atmosphere, as suggested in some American media depictions of Japanese schools? Would the social pressure for conformity prove to be stronger than in American schools and uncomfortable for foreigners? Just the process of getting our children enrolled and ready for their first day of school provided answers to some of these questions and brought us face to face with differences in approaches to education that became clearer as the school year passed.

Almost immediately after moving into our apartment at Saitama University, we went to Urawa City Hall to apply for our Alien Registration cards. (Sam and Ellen like the term *aliens* better than *foreigners*, though not all foreigners feel that way.) With the help of a colleague from the university we were able to arrange a meeting with the city board of education officers responsible for enrolling children on the same day we picked up the Alien Registration cards. We were surprised that such a high-level meeting would be required. Our colleague went with the four of us to this meeting. The principal of the school was present along with two or three officials from the board of education.

The discussion covered several points of concern. The principal and the officials stressed that our children would be expected to participate fully, as Japanese children do. We were warned that no instruction in Japanese as a foreign language would be provided, that they followed the total immersion, "throw them in and see if they swim" philosophy of language learning. The principal said he would, however, assign a few children to guide ours around, play with them, and help them get started. Everyone looked relieved on hearing that Sam had been to preschool in Japan and seemed to think this would make things easier for us and for them, a feeling we shared.

Japanese are always very concerned that Japanese food is so unique that foreigners will find it inedible, and these officials said our children would have to eat the school lunches—as though they felt this might be a major problem. They did ask if there were foods our children couldn't eat; they recognize that some children have allergies, and many of the Southeast Asian children in this school are Moslems who do not eat pork or some of the seafood found in Japanese school lunches, but our children had no restrictions.

The next part of the discussion centered on the grades in which the children would be placed. In Japan the school year runs from April 1 of each year to the following March. The rules about grade placement are rigidly followed: a child must be six years old by April 1 to begin first grade and must begin on the April 1 following the sixth birthday. Sam, born in April, had just finished fifth grade in the United States, and Ellen, born in March, had just finished first grade. The correct grade placement for Sam was thus fifth grade in Japan. The principal and the officials felt this was the best placement for him. We agreed, and we had discussed this possibility with him beforehand. We knew that much of the material covered would be different from the curriculum at home and that any repetition in Japanese would be useful. Following the principal's recommendation, we agreed that Ellen should be put in the first grade, though according to her birth date she belonged in second. This made her one of the oldest first graders instead of the youngest second grader. First grade is a beginning, and it seemed reasonable that she also begin there.

We agreed with the principal on a day in the next week to bring the children to school to meet their teachers and join their classes; we left the meeting feeling excited and nervous. It was all becoming very real.

THE SCHOOL

Our school, Okubo Higashi Shogakko (Okubo East Elementary School), is unusual in Japan only because it has some foreign students. It is a public school, free, part of the compulsory education system in Japan, run by the city board of education in compliance with guidelines from the national Ministry of Education, and funded by both local and national taxes. Only 1 percent of elementary school children in Japan are in private schools, so this kind of education is what is experienced by virtually all Japanese children.

Okubo Higashi's students come from the immediate neighborhood. It has students from first grade through sixth grade in twenty-five classes, about one thousand students in all, including the ten or so foreigners. This is a very ordinary size in Japan, where population densities in the cities and towns are such that this many children all live within easy walking distance of the school. There is no special transportation for students, and they are not allowed to ride bicycles to school, though most children have bikes and use them on other occasions. Think of nine hundred or so bicycles converging through narrow lanes on the school and the problem of where to put so many bikes during the school day!

The front of the school lot is the playground and athletic field, mostly open space but with some simple equipment for games and skills training around the sides. Old tires embedded in the ground serve as hurdles; there are some iron bars for simple gymnastics and some bells hung at various heights for children to try to ring by jumping. One end of the playground has elaborate sets of swings, jungle gyms, climbing poles, ladders, and slides—the same complex we saw in schools all over Japan.

Around the main buildings are some small sheds used to house animals and birds, some storage sheds, a few straggly plots for flowers and plants, the swimming pool and dressing rooms, and the gymnasium/ assembly room in a separate building.

The buildings of the school follow a standard pattern, three stories of concrete construction looking very institutional if not prison-like. The two classroom buildings, joined by a short hallway section, are both one room and a hallway deep, so that each classroom has a long southern or western wall that is mostly windows, leading to a balcony outside the classroom. Most buildings in Japan are built this way, to capture sunlight and heat.

At the front there is a large staircase to the ceremonial entrance near the school office, the principal's office and the teachers' room on the second floor. Children, however, usually use a ground-floor entrance near their classroom, going into a large entry hall where there are shelves and cubbyholes for each person to leave outside shoes during the school day and to store school shoes while one is away from school. There are also sinks for washing hands and gargling outside these entrances. The hallways leading to the classrooms are clean and light, decorated with projects done in class.

In each classroom there is a rack for hanging book bags during the day, and each student has a desk. Shelves under the windows hold classroom supplies. There is an electric organ in each room. The walls are decorated with posters, the school motto, the classroom schedule, and student work. The windows have curtains used to regulate the sunlight, and each classroom has a gas stove for heat. This sits away from the walls near one corner and is used sparingly during the coldest months; the hallways and other areas of the school are not heated at all.

At least at Okubo Higashi, children are encouraged to wear long pants during the winter months. We were told by parents that at other schools in Urawa children who wore long pants instead of skirts or the very short shorts Japanese boys usually wear were subject to ridicule by their teachers. Stoically enduring cold has long been a means of character building in Japan.

The motto found in every classroom, in the hallways, on school publications, over the stage in the auditorium, and which makes its way into many public speeches is

Thinking Children
Bright Children
Strong Children

At first glance this did not seem to be remarkable in any way, except that I particularly noticed the word "Strong." Interpreting it to mean physically strong as it usually does, I was a little surprised to find this as a goal in school. Only later did I think to ask my friends what the phrase "Bright Children" might mean, to confirm my suspicion that it did not refer to intelligence. They said it meant children who were lively and eager to participate in activities and life, not hanging back out of mistrust or selfishness or idiosyncrasy. These answers sent me back to the booklet about the school prepared for parents of first graders, which we were given as a new family in the school.

The motto is explained in the booklet and turns out to be shorthand for a complicated set of ideals for children. "Thinking Children" is explained as children who can consider well, making correct judgments about actions. "Bright Children" are those who are rich in cooperativeness, full of fresh and lively vitality. "Strong Children" are children who, being healthy in mind and body, are able to make the judgments needed to carry out the responsibilities of their own individual lives.

As the year went on I decided that this motto accurately reflected the goals and practices of the school, more than mottoes sometimes do. It suggests that action, not merely abstract academic learning, is the test of education; it suggests that children are active agents in their own education, not passive recipients; it suggests that education and action are embedded in a world of other people and that individual judgment, cooperativeness, and physical and moral strength are what children should be learning in school. It doesn't mention math, reading, and science. They seem to be both components and by-products of the larger goal.

THE FIRST DAY AND THE EQUIPMENT

On the appointed day we went to school with our colleague, the last school meeting he would be required to attend. We met with the principal, the assistant principal, Sam's teacher Ohshima *sensei* and Ellen's teacher Kuroda *sensei*. *Sensei* is a Japanese word that means "teacher," and teachers are addressed either by their family name followed by this title or, more commonly, by the title alone. Because of the honor attached to this role, the same title is used for other people to whom respect is given—medical doctors, religious leaders, and some politicians.

There was a sense of ceremony surrounding the introduction of the children to their teachers and the presentation of backpacks for the children. These were the standard ones we had seen worn by elementary school children all over Japan. They are made of heavy leather, black for boys and red for girls, designed to survive 240 round trips to school each year for six years. They have several compartments and attachments, and all the school equipment sold in Japan is sized to the dimensions of this pack. Sam and Ellen's shy grins as they tried them on showed that they too felt this was an important moment.

The school gave these packs to our children, a gesture we appreciated on both a symbolic and a practical level—they cost a minimum of one hundred dollars each, usually closer to two hundred dollars. Later in our stay as we watched Japanese children prepare to enter first grade, we became more aware of the importance of the packs. They are bought after much discussion within the family about price and quality and are often a present from grandparents. They are the badge and uniform of a child's status. Just as other occupations are marked by appropriate clothing and accessories, the occupation of schoolchild in Japan is announced through the wearing of the backpack. Though public school elementary students do not wear uniform clothing, this backpack is as much a marker of status as a blue suit and white shirt for salaried employees, split-toe boots and gaitered baggy pants for construction workers, or briefcases for professionals. Sam and Ellen could now be identified by anyone in Japan as proper elementary school students, especially when they also had the official school name tags they were to wear each day pinned to their clothes, giving their name, the school name, and their grade and class.

Next, each teacher gave them their textbooks. Sam received fifteen, Ellen ten. Besides the ones we expected for mathematics, social studies, and Japanese, there were texts for physical education, music, morals, art, and calligraphy, among others. Ellen also had a communication notebook, which a parent had to sign each day, used for sending individual messages between parents and teachers as well as notations about special things needed the next day at school and homework assignments. I was familiar with this concept because the preschool and day care centers had also used such booklets.

The textbooks are free and do not have to be returned to the school at the end of the year; only replacements for lost ones must be paid for. The books themselves are attractive, nicely illustrated paperbacks, smaller than most U.S. textbooks, most of them nine by five inches or ten by six inches, 100–130 pages. They are light in weight and all of them are supposed to come home every night, the idea being that if there's no assigned homework, students should still review and study. It turned out that Ellen's teacher was much stricter about this than Sam's, as she was about many things.

Besides the backpacks and textbooks there are other materials required for school that must be provided by parents. The next part of the discussion took us through the list of these items and where to purchase them. First there were the sorts of things we expected—pencils, erasers, crayons, and exercise books for each academic subject. But we didn't expect that the hardness of the lead in the pencils would be a matter of concern, as it was, or that there would be instructions about the kind of erasers to buy.

In the case of uniform erasers, however, the school is fighting a losing battle. Because of the nature of the writing system, people in Japan seldom use typewriters and make a fair number of mistakes when handwriting. So they use a lot of erasers, which have become something of a minor art form. They come in many colors and elaborate designs, from flowers and flags to cars and cartoon characters. Children much prefer these fancy erasers to the plain white ones we were told to buy, and almost no one at school follows the eraser guidelines.

The clothing requirements, which we learned about next, were also more elaborate than we expected. Most important are the shoes for school. Outside shoes are not worn in Japanese schools any more than they are in Japanese houses. Slippers are provided for visitors at school; we were all wearing those for this meeting. (Somehow, getting dressed up to look serious for such an important meeting and then wearing sloppy bedroom-type slippers during it struck us as incongruous.) In the school building children wear special shoes, white canvas slip-ons with rubber soles. The soles and trim are colored, and each grade at the school is assigned a different color. Ellen's first-grade color was green, Sam's red. These are washable shoes and indeed are supposed to be washed each weekend and taken back clean on Monday. Again, it turned out that Ellen's teacher was more strict and made sure this happened every week, while Sam often left his shoes at school for weeks on end.

There is an outfit for physical education: white shorts for boys and blue ones for girls, with white T-shirts and a reversible red and white cap for all. The T-shirt must be marked with the crest of Okubo Higashi Shogakko, and a large patch must be sewn on the front of the shirt. This patch has a colored strip corresponding to the grade of the child and is also marked with the child's last name in very large writing. These clothes are brought home in a drawstring bag for washing each weekend. For swimming, a part of the physical education program, there is an ugly navy blue swimsuit for girls and navy blue briefs for boys, and a cap in the class color, both to be marked with the child's name.

The children wear protective clothing at lunch, consisting of a white smock apron with sleeves, a white cap to cover hair, and a surgeon's face mask that is worn while serving food or going through the line. Our kids called these their "doctor clothes." They too, are brought home for laundry each weekend in their own drawstring bag, along with a place mat, a napkin, and chopsticks. Finally, there is a triangular white head scarf to be worn each day during the cleaning time.

I came to resent the necessity of doing this laundry each Saturday afternoon or Sunday morning no matter what other weekend activities might be planned, worrying about the weather and whether things would get dry on time, coordinating the drying space school clothes needed with other laundry needs. In the telling, it seems like a minor thing to be bothered by, but for me it was one of the irritations of life in Japan. Clothes dryers are expensive and not very effective in Japan. Having to rely on a limited amount of outdoor drying space for the laundry did make me more aware of and attuned to the weather and the "natural world"; that was some compensation.

The next topics covered in our discussions were the monthly fees for lunches, PTA dues, and special purchases of supplies made by each teacher, finally, there was the walking group. Each child is assigned to a group of children living close together, who meet at a specified place each morning for the walk to school. A mother from this group is in charge of gathering everyone together, and one child is designated by the school as the group leader. The route they will follow to school is also laid out, and where several groups converge on the way to school the roads are marked with a sign telling drivers that the road is a school path. Children from our apartment building joined with those in the next building to form a walking group of about fifteen children led by a sixth-grade girl. The meeting time was forty minutes before the beginning of school, and the walk took about twenty minutes, guaranteeing that everyone would not only be on time, but have time to play before school began. This also gave the mother in charge time to round up any children who did not appear on time. The first day Sam and Ellen were sick, she came to our door looking for them. After that I went down to notify her if they were not going to school.

Then it was time for Sam and Ellen to join their classes. The principal asked if they knew what to say or do, and we said they had practiced bowing and saying *"Bobrow desu. Dozo yoroshiku onegai shimasu."* This is a standard phrase said on introduction, meaning approximately "I am Bobrow. Please be kind to me." So they were hurried off by their teachers to confront their new classmates for the first time, and Dave and I went home. We felt as though we were abandoning them.

I also felt I had been plunged rather abruptly into the world of the *kyoiku mama*—part of my plan for the year, but startling nonetheless. *Kyoiku mama* is a slightly derogatory job description for modern mothers. Literally it means "education mom," and it points to the intense involvement of many Japanese mothers with the education of their children. There is a hint in the use of the term *mama* that this is a new phenomenon, since *mama* is a term for mothers that has been borrowed from Western languages, replacing the native *okaasan* in some families.

The job of the *kyoiku mama* is a complicated one, revered, accepted, gently ridiculed, and sometimes resented by Japanese mothers, children, and families. The term indicates the widespread feeling in Japan that education for children is of crucial importance to their lives and that children cannot succeed in the job of getting educated for adult life without significant help from their mothers. Effort, persistence, and commitment are required of both mothers and children in the business of education. Mothers' efforts encompass the physical health of their children, loving support, willingness to have them place school responsibilities above family ones, willingness to absorb the frustration and rebellion that school demands often engender in children, and the ability to cajole children into the homework, study, and drill that school success requires. The modernity of this role has two aspects. First, only very recently have many mothers had the leisure, the release from more directly productive economic activities, to pursue this job. Relatively low employment rates for Japanese mothers of school children, and most strikingly the move away from farming, are necessary for mothers to have the time to make these efforts.

Second, calling a mother *mama* instead of *okaasan* imparts a sense that the motivations operating in the relationship between mother and child that induce a child to accept a mother's guidance and control have changed. The children of *okaasan*, children in a "traditional" Japanese family setting, are motivated to cooperate by love mixed with respect for the mother's rank and power. A modern *mama*, most often found in the context of families that depend on salaries for their livelihood, must depend on love alone, without much rank or power, to entice children into the desired paths of education and socialization. The emotional intensity of the relationship between mothers and their one or two children in this situation inspires some ambiguity in contemporary Japanese.

In spite of a popular media image of modern Japanese mothers as totally absorbed in their children, however, it is not clear that this is a wholly accurate picture. First, nearly half of the elementary school students in Japan in the 1990s have mothers who are employed full time or part time. These women, by all reports, work for money as well as personal fulfillment, and the jobs they are most often found in certainly do not seem likely to be very enjoyable in and of themselves (Kondo 1990; Roberts 1994). There is no reason to doubt that their earnings make either crucial or significant contributions to the family quality of life.

At the same time, it is true that one of the culturally acceptable reasons a woman can offer when she seeks full- or part-time employment is that her earnings will contribute to the educational success of her children, by making available to them the supplementary schooling called *juku*, commercial tutoring for elementary, junior high, and high school students. Many students attend these schools to receive the supervision, help, and emotional support to accomplish drill work and study imposed by school. Their mothers' jobs both make it impossible for mothers to do all of this and make it possible to pay someone else to do it. Some women openly acknowledge this tradeoff; others I think make it but less openly. Some women decide that they will sacrifice the income they might make and the satisfaction they might find in jobs for the sake of a personal investment in their children's education. Several of my friends, though, were quite aware of the implications of this choice for their own lives; they had not been brainwashed into thinking it was the only available path for Japanese women.

One of the questions I wanted to be able to answer after this year as an observer and participant in Japanese elementary education concerned the relationship between school and home and how each one was implicated in the academic performance standards reached by Japanese children and in the quality of life for Japanese children and mothers. I wanted to see just why "it's hard to be the mother of an elementary school child," as one of my Japanese friends put it. Although I had her as an example to watch (and she was much better at the role than I), I was already well on my way to finding out through personal experience.

2

Why Study Japanese Education?

I have several purposes as I write this book. It is an attempt to put together in one package my concerns with Japanese education as a parent and an American citizen observing and participating in American education in the 1980s and 1990s, and as an anthropologist interested in modern Japanese culture and society.

The research on which the book is based is a combination of two approaches. A growing body of observational research on Japanese education has recently been developed in English and in Japanese. This has enriched our potential for understanding the implications of Japanese education beyond the spectacular headlines about school suicides, bullying, and the rat race for entrance to the best kindergartens that have been featured in the popular press. That research informs the observations reported here. Second, the data that really bring this material to life are those gathered from living and doing research in Japan for three years and having two children enrolled in Japanese educational institutions: being an observer and participant in the Japanese educational setting as a parent and anthropologist during that time.

As an American parent and citizen concerned about the education of my children and others in America, I share the ambivalent feelings of many about education here and now. I think public education has been a positive integrative force in American society in the past; I worry that it is no longer so. I favor public education in principle but worry that it might not be the most effective way to achieve the goals it seemed to achieve in the past. I worry about the great disparities in education and opportunity that the public schools offer different children in America. I am concerned about the quality of teachers and curriculum in the United States, and about the unofficial lessons in life that children learn from the social and institutional settings of education. I look at the international achievement test comparisons, and I think the United States shouldn't rank so low. I teach college students, and I find their brightness and interest hampered by their ignorance.

The newspapers and magazines of contemporary America are filled with fixes for American education—longer school days, a national curriculum, vouchers for private schools, jail terms for the parents of truant children, more centralized control, more local control, fewer functions for schools, more community functions for schools, funding equity, more individualism, more discipline, and on and on. A central but less articulated question asks what schools can do in the face of societal breakdown, the unemployment, poverty, and unstable family situations that seem to many to be characteristic of this era.

In Japan, by contrast, there is general public satisfaction with the educational system. No one regards it as perfect or beyond improvement, but people generally regard it as academically effective, psychologically healthy for children, and supportive of Japanese society and culture and of Japan's economic needs. There are social problems in Japan, which find their expression in schools there, too, but the public, the parents, and the children in Japan are generally satisfied with the education system. Public elementary schools in Japan enroll 99 percent of the school-age children (*Japan Statistical Yearbook* 1989:646), and there is no movement for changing this pattern. In the ubiquitous public opinion polls, which reach even elementary school children in Japan, high proportions of Japanese children assert that they like school. They are happier with this part of their lives than Japanese adults are about most aspects of their lives, and happier than American children are with school. During high school almost 30 percent of Japanese students are in private schools, but this is because the public schools don't have room for everyone, not because private schools are generally preferred. They are usually a second choice (James and Benjamin, 1988; Rohlen 1983).

According to international comparisons of achievement, Japanese students do very well. Mathematics and science seem to be the subjects most amenable to testing across different languages and cultures, and in these areas Japanese students have been at the top or near the top in every international study since the 1950s (Lynn 1988). I don't want to labor this point too much, but it is important to understand that we are not talking about schooling that is only marginally more effective in Japan than in other countries, but education that is dramatically more effective. The charts below, adapted from figures in Lynn's summary of the comparative achievement tests that have been given in Japan and other developed countries periodically over the last several decades, show clearly superior achievement levels of Japanese children, not subtle statistical differences. Table 1 shows the test scores for ten-year-olds and fourteen-year-olds in science in Japan and in the United States. Both countries have compulsory universal schooling for children at these ages, so neither school population is an elite one. At ten years of age the Japanese are ahead of Americans, but there is great deal of overlap in the range of scores. By the age of fourteen, however, the overlap has diminished considerably; almost half of the Japanese score above the eighty-fifth percentile of American students.

In a mathematics comparison reported by Lynn, based on the American High School Mathematics Test given to fifteen-year-olds in Japan and Illinois, the Japanese lead has increased so much that the two distributions do not even overlap: the lowest-scoring Japanese do better than the highest-scoring Americans.

TABLE 1

Science Achievement, Ten- and Fourteen-Year-Olds

	Ten-Year-Olds		Fourteen-Year-Olds	
	U.S.	Japan	U.S.	Japan
Mean	17.7	21.7	21.6	31.2
Range, ±1 SD	8.4–27.0	14.0–29.4	10.0–33.2	26.4–46.0

SOURCE: Adapted from Lynn (1988:10).

TABLE 2

Mathematics Achievement, Fifteen-Year-Olds

	U.S.	Japan
Mean	16.72	34.35
Range, ±1 SD	9.00–24.44	27.56–41.14

SOURCE: Adapted from Lynn (1988:14).

One of the best and most recent studies of achievement in Japan and the United States is that done by Harold Stevenson and his colleagues at the University of Michigan and Tohoku Fukushi University. They compared achievement levels, as measured on tests based on common elements in the curriculum, in a number of different classrooms and a number of different schools in Minneapolis with achievement levels in a matched set of classrooms and schools in Sendai, a similar city in Japan. In each country there is variation within each classroom; the Japanese classes show perhaps more variability than the American ones. In first-grade, there is considerable overlap in the achievement of classes in the two cities, though it is striking that all the bottom classes are American ones. By the fifth grade, however, there is no overlap in the average levels of achievement in the two cities; the lowest-scoring classes in Japan score above the highest-scoring classes in the United States (Stevenson et al. 1986:201–16).

Because comparisons between Japan and other countries show the relative superiority of Japanese students increasing more and more as the number of years of schooling increases, it is not unreasonable to suppose that it is their schooling that gives them their advantage.

Attempts to measure achievement in reading and social studies show that, again, Japanese students do very well. Test scores in these subjects show less variation among students of similar grade levels in Japan than in the United States. More students in Japan are found to be close to grade level, neither very far behind nor very far ahead, than in the United States (Stevenson et al. 1986:227). The appendix, "Reading and Writing in Japanese," shows why this is an expected result of the writing systems and will also dispel any thoughts that it is easier to learn or to teach reading in Japanese than in other languages.

In physical education, art, and music, the general levels of Japanese children's performances are less easily measured but easily observed, and they are very impressive. These are also important parts of the curriculum, approached in much the same way as "academic" subjects, learned and practiced with gusto.

Some of the suggestions for improvements in American schools come from the Japanese example, so it is important to look closely at how that system really operates. This book combines a down-to-earth, day-to-day ethnography of what happens in a Japanese school with a description of the structural institutional base for the system and an appreciation of the cultural understandings that permeate the actions and structures of Japanese education. No one knows better than anthropologists that cultural features taken out of one context and inserted into another are more often than not altered beyond identity in their new setting. But anthropologists also know that cultures are constantly changing and adapting, reacting to stimuli within the culture and imported from outside. Examples from outside can often, with care, become the medium for effecting changes desired within a culture. And Americans do seem to desire changes in their present education system.

As a parent and a citizen, then, I undertook this study to find out what really happens in Japanese schools that is different from what happens in American schools and how those differences in practice affect differences in outcomes. I hoped to find paths for improvement in American education.

As an anthropologist I am interested in Japanese culture and Japanese society, without necessarily wanting to do anything more than understand it, in itself and in comparison with other cultures and societies (a modest goal!). One of the important ways in which anthropologists try to obtain cultural understanding is by asking the question, How do they get to be that way? This is the question of socialization, of how infants who arrive at their birthplace with no culture, no language, and no social patterns become socialized, encultured members of their group, passing on the thoughts and behavior patterns they have learned to new generations.

Although our individual experiences result in unique individual histories, personalities, and selves, anthropologists have seen that cultural groups have certain ways they view and treat children that are relatively the same for all individuals in that cultural group and relatively different from the patterns found in other cultural groups. Anthropologists have long felt that in order to understand cultural groups, and the individuals who grow up in cultural groups, we have to pay close attention to socialization practices.

It seems to all of us that childhood experiences have a lasting effect on our lives and that if we want to understand the lives of other people we need to know something of their childhood experiences. In most modern settings school is a major component of those experiences. Education, in the sense of formal schooling, is only one aspect of socialization, and we understand that in some senses socialization continues throughout a person's life—there are some things about how to behave effectively in work situations that we don't learn until we finish school and find ourselves in that situation, and there are some things about being a grandparent that we don't learn until we reach that life stage. Many Western people, however, share a feeling that the most important socialization takes place in infancy and childhood. For these reasons, derived from our own cultural and scholarly frameworks for understanding individuals and groups of people, the study of Japanese education is important. By learning about the experiences that Japanese encounter as children, we expect to learn something important about the kinds of adults they turn out to be.

These inclinations on our part as Westerners intersect nicely with Japanese notions of the importance of education. The Japanese approach socialization with a particular view of individuals in mind, the view that experiences are more important than innate differences in shaping personalities and adult characteristics. They do not seem to have a strong feeling that the very earliest years, say up to age five, are of overriding importance in forming permanent characteristics of individuals. Because in Japanese thinking, experiences, including those of older children, are important in forming individuals, education, what happens at school, is important enough to be of great cultural concern to them.

In the context of this orientation toward the importance of educational experiences, the regimentation that so struck us in our first encounter with our elementary school takes on a different meaning. Instead of being, as we tended to feel, the arbitrary imposition of authoritarian power, it becomes the expression of a concern for fairness and equality of opportunity.

American conceptions of personality and development tend to focus on the differences inherent in different people, to see life and education as fostering tendencies that are inborn in each individual and unique to each individual. Japanese conceptions of personality and development tend to focus on experience as the source of both the unique characteristics of the individual and of the qualities that all people have in common. Individuals are not inherently very different, so it follows that by having common experiences, they will all learn the same things and develop the same characteristics. If they are given different experiences, they will turn out to be different kinds of people.

In premodern Japan this view of individuality and education was used to support a social system based on hereditary occupations. There was no problem with sons and daughters simply following in their parents' footsteps, so that the sons of farmers became farmers; the sons of craftsmen, craftsmen; the sons of political leaders and rulers, the political leaders and rulers of the next generation. All were educated to their tasks, and no one was expected to show any great talent for his destined job. Everyone was educated to become the right kind of person for the job he would inherit. But with the great leap into modernization that Japanese society took about the middle of the nineteenth century, hereditary occupations could no longer supply the education needed: there were too many new kinds of jobs, and the skills and personal qualities they required were different from those embodied in the older social structure.

A new and modern universal education system was instituted, based on models from the United States and France, but the cultural understanding of education did not fundamentally change: Japanese still feel that education, not unique inborn differences, is the key to individual development. What is required for a well-functioning and fair modern social system is to give all children, at least at the elementary school level, the same education, so that they have the same chances for success in the modern world, where hereditary occupations are much less important.

Education in this sense is given a wide meaning in Japan. For children to have the benefits of the same education for all, they must experience even the details of school life in the same ways. Within a class, within a school, within the country, many aspects of life that in the United States are treated as inconsequential are regulated, because regulation ensures that everyone has the same experiences and that each child will have a fair chance to succeed in education. Perhaps the most fundamental expression of this approach is a taxation and funding system for public elementary education that guarantees that schools throughout Japan have the same resources for their students. The feeling that it is right for them all to use the same textbooks, wear the same physical education uniform, and carry the same backpack is simply another expression of the same philosophy.

In examining Japanese education, we are looking at an area of life that the Japanese themselves have thought about deeply and at practices that they also consider to be both formative and revealing of their cultural values. This is not to say that teachers and others involved in education do not act most of the time in ways that just seem "natural," because no one can be introspective all of the time. However, a great deal of thought has gone into setting up schools as institutions where behaviors that seem "natural" to the socialization agents, teachers and parents, will be "naturally" adopted by the pupils.

Modern Japan is presented to the West as a very homogeneous nation, a nation without important internal ethnic, religious, language, or class cleavages. Modern Japan is experienced by most Japanese as that sort of place, too. Nevertheless, the modern education system was conceived and set in place soon after a major political upheaval, the Meiji Restoration of 1868. This political revolution in favor of modernization instead of isolation, a "beat them at their own game" approach to the impending threat of Western colonialism, established Japan's course in the modern world. Some scholars have compared the impact of the political and military struggles leading to the new Meiji government system in Japan with the Civil War in the United States. The sympathies, allegiances, convictions, and divisions of that period did not disappear overnight. Like many new nations, Japan was faced with the prospect of solidifying a disparate population into a coherent modern nation-state, and like most countries in that situation, Japan's government expected the education system to be a crucial agent in the change.

Decisions about the academic content of education, about the target populations for education, and about the nature of experiences at school were made quite self-consciously by the government of the time and by succeeding generations of governments and educators. Though the Japanese education system certainly incorporates many features that are simply taken for granted as "natural" by Japanese, it is not a system that just grew haphazardly, an amalgam of uncoordinated local or special interest groups patched together into a somewhat coherent national system at a later time—a description that can be applied to the education systems of most English-speaking countries.

The plan of this book is to use ethnographic observations to explain how Japanese elementary education takes place, in order to understand how Japanese children become Japanese adults and how they achieve high levels of academic learning, then to examine what aspects of educational practice—together with the cultural underpinnings of such practices—might be usefully adapted in order to improve American education.

No one would suppose that observations in one American school could adequately represent understandings of elementary education in America. We are all too aware of the range of cultural worlds to be encountered in the United States. It is legitimate to ask whether such an objection is not valid for Japan also. One stereotype of modern Japan is that it is a "homogeneous" nation. To what extent, in what ways, is this true or untrue, particularly with regard to the topic of this book?

To some degree the two related cultural hallmarks of modern Japan, that it is homogeneous and that its central defining value is harmony, are inaccurate. Outside observers of Japan in the social sciences have by and large come from countries like the United States, even less homogeneous than Japan, and so they may have been too susceptible to the view of Japan as a relatively uniform, relatively undifferentiated population. To some analysts the notions of unity and harmony are simply malicious propaganda, foisted on Japan and the rest of the world by a governing elite intent on its own political ends. Many Japanese social scientists and historians have documented the political rhetoric and actions that support the notions of homogeneity, common interest, and harmony, and the importance the ruling class places on maintaining these fictions. In English, work by Mouer and Sugimoto (1990) and by the journalist Jon Woronoff (1991, 1992) are easily accessible analyses in this vein. Certainly no serious look at the history of Japan over the last two hundred years can escape the conclusions that there are and have been many groups with disparate interests, overt and covert conflicts, and suppression of dissidents. It is obvious that Japan as a unified nation-state has been and is a political creation.

Still, there are fashions in emphases on diversity and unity, and it is equally inaccurate to magnify cultural differences within Japan, especially in comparison with many other nations. Political and economic conflicts within a nation are not the same as cultural differences within a nation. Many of the tactics designed to reduce diversity in Japan—political, economic, religious, linguistic, and cultural—during the last hundred years have been successful, and in the field of education in particular, reports from ethnographers in many areas of Japan and in many contexts support a high degree of consensus on cultural understanding and practices throughout Japan.

There are even serious reservations as to whether the two most frequently cited minority groups in Japan, Koreans and *burakumin*, should be considered culturally distinct or simply people who are culturally Japanese but discriminated against. Surely, recognition of the different life experiences of these people, or of women, or of the handicapped, or of people in different occupations, does not require us to assume they are not culturally Japanese. To hold that Japanese culture encompasses a multiplicity of thought, practice, and experience is different from saying there is no common ground of thought, practice, and experience in being Japanese.

Ethnographic truth lies in two dimensions, great underlying generalizations and nitpicking, consequential details. This book offers both. It is focused around the experiences of a school year in Japan, as our family participated in all its everyday concrete reality and as we used our increasing encounters with Japanese culture to relate the experiences of school to life in Japan.

Most chapters of the book are organized around particular recurring events in Japanese school life. Some are annual events, for example, Sports Day. Some are frequent events like daily reading classes. In each case close attention is paid to the organization of time, to the talk and activities of students and teachers, to the physical accoutrements of education such as textbooks, uniforms, space, and equipment. Relationships between what happens in schools and what happens in life outside schools in Japan are made explicit. Often our American and personal reactions to events at school are contrasted with Japanese reactions. The work of other scholars is presented to augment our experiences.

A few other chapters offer new theoretical insights on some issues in Japanese ethnography, for instance the structure of groups and group memberships. The book ends with an overview of the role of education in modern Japan and the history of Japanese education. I offer some suggestions about what might be borrowed into American schools and in what form.

The ethnographic bases for the conclusions presented in this work are the time I spent in Okubo Higashi School as a parent and as a recognized researcher; the written materials and communications from school collected over the course of the year; reactions to school events we experienced; reports on "what happened at school today"; interviews with Japanese parents, teachers and other adults, including some whose children had been in American schools; what we learned and experienced when our children were younger in Japan; participation in other Japanese groups; and friendships with Japanese people.

Working as an anthropologist in Japan is not like being dropped onto a newly discovered small island; every scholar who works in Japan benefits in ways that cannot be adequately acknowledged from the work of previous scholars. This is certainly true in the fields of anthropology and education. Many previous works are cited in this book, but some understandings have become background to the thinking presented here, and although that debt is not easily cited, it is nonetheless real.

I alone wrote this book and am responsible for interpretations made here, but there were two other field-workers involved in the project: my children, Samuel and Ellen Bobrow. I observed Japanese elementary education and experienced it as a parent, but they underwent the life of Japanese school children in its unrelenting ordinariness. Their reports and reactions are an integral part of what is presented here. Their cooperation, fortitude, and openness were essential to learning much of what I have learned and tried to convey.

3

Day-to-Day Routines

DAILY SCHEDULE

Now that Sam and Ellen were fully equipped for school, belonged to a walking group and a classroom, and were prepared to begin the life of a Japanese schoolchild, we all wondered what that life would be like, how the hours of school would be spent, just how different a classroom in Japan could be from one in America.

Our first hint of the answers to these questions came from the class schedules. Though there are of course variations in the routine, the basic format of the school week is laid out in a schedule established by the teacher at the beginning of the year. Sam and Ellen each brought home a printed weekly schedule to keep in a special pocket on the flap of the book bag.

The teachers have taken some trouble to make the schedules look nice, and the first-grade schedule is written almost exclusively in the syllabary that almost all children can read when they enter first grade but can certainly read by the end of the first term of the school year. The same schedule is written on a poster in each classroom; it doesn't change over the course of the school year.

There are a number of interesting features in these schedules. First, although school begins at 8:30 and children are required to be at school by that time, most of them arrive earlier because the walking group timetable assures it. The schedule begins at 8:50, except on Tuesday, when there is a school-wide assembly each week. Second, Ellen's schedule, for first grade, shows an irregular dismissal time, anywhere from 2:00 to 2:45. This is common in Japanese schools; the dismissal time of 3:40 for older students is felt to make too long a day for first graders. Thus, first graders officially spend thirty-three hours per week in school, fifth graders forty hours and fifty minutes. This includes the Saturday hours for everyone and a required hour for club activities on Wednesday afternoon for students in fourth grade and older.

Despite what looks like a full schedule during those hours, Sam's startling observation that there is a lot more time to play in school in Japan led us to look at the schedule more closely. He was right; there is much more time not given over to formal classroom instruction in this school than in the American schools with which we were familiar. To begin with there's the twenty minutes between 8:30 and 8:50. On Ellen's schedule this is marked "individual preparation," a time for children to get organized for the day, to finish up homework, to move their supplies from their book bags into their desks, to greet friends, and to prepare for the day. It's time when the classrooms are noisy with talk, laughter, and play, when teachers are probably not in the room, so that the children are not being subjected to close scrutiny.

Bells ring throughout the day to signal breaks between periods. There is a five-minute break between the first and second and between the third and fourth periods and a ten-minute break between the fifth and sixth periods. These breaks are truly breaks; children can play, talk, and move about during them, going to the bathroom or into the hall for drinks. Teachers don't seem to feel a need to keep the noise down during these periods, and the children are livelier than would be tolerated in many American schools. On the other hand, neither students nor teachers move to other classrooms during this time, and so the confusion of gathering up school materials and going from room to room is eliminated. (There are very few special teachers in elementary schools, and they come to the children's room for their classes. The students don't move except to the gymnasium or outdoors for physical education or to the science lab once or twice a week.)

The whole school has a twenty-minute recess between the second and third periods. Most days everyone goes outdoors for free play. In bad weather the gym is used along with the hallways and one or two special playrooms in the building. This is generally a recess for the teachers too; only a few are on the playground. (There were five teachers on playground duty for a thousand students, the days I counted.) Children are not considered to be in danger during play time nor to be dangerous to others. On days of some wonderful snowfalls, I saw students throwing snowballs at each other and at teachers who returned the favor. Other pupils ran into the fence to knock down avalanches of snow on friends who crowded close, yelling at the joy of it all.

The playground equipment itself would not be found in U.S. playgrounds because it would be regarded as too dangerous. The slides and climbing apparatuses are quite tall; it would be easy to fall from them, and the ground underneath is hard dirt. The swings are wooden, and there are no guard rails to keep other children from running in front of them. The hurdles in the ground around the edges of the playground are not fenced off; it seemed as if children playing tag around them could trip.

Despite the apparent physical dangers of the playground and other areas Japanese children frequent, such as city streets, and despite their use of fireworks and other dangerous toys, they don't seem to get hurt very often. It's not a perfect measure of accident rates, but United Nations World Health Organization data show lower death rates from accidents, including traffic, drowning, and others, for Japanese children than for American children.

The most noticeable time-out is lunch time—one hour and twenty-five minutes. This includes time for eating, a recess period, and daily cleaning. Lunches are prepared in the kitchen by professionals but are eaten in the classrooms. (Like rooms in Japanese houses, classrooms are used for many purposes.) Students are assigned on a rotating basis to bring the carts of food from the kitchen, dish it out to everyone, clean up, and return dishes and food to the kitchen.

There are no janitors in schools in Japan, so students and teachers take care of cleaning everything except the kitchen. This means classrooms, hallways, stairs, bathrooms, and grounds; they also take care of the school's animals and their houses. Cleaning in a Japanese building means primarily cleaning the floors. All the hallways, stairs and classrooms are swept and polished every day, with desks and other furniture moved aside to ensure a complete job.

The work is divided into different chores, and work groups are assigned chores on a rotating basis—no one much likes doing the bathrooms. Some jobs can be done more playfully than others. Nor is this frowned on. No one minds if a group of five whose task is to polish the classroom floor turns this into a race while pushing the polishing rags across the floor. Cleaning is required school work, but it's surely closer to play than sitting at a desk being talked to by a teacher.

Since we have returned home, Sam and Ellen have complained about the cleaning, though they didn't voice any objections or even think it was worth talking about while we were there. They now say it was hard work and sometimes distasteful. Cleaning the toilets, even with plastic gloves on, was "gross" and "disgusting." The other jobs were also not fun but serious work, in their view. But they have never expressed the idea that it was inappropriate for students to do this, whereas most American children who hear about it immediately suggest they would expect to be paid.

Training children to take on responsibility in a group, for the group, is a legitimate task of schools in Japan, and cleaning is a major tool for teaching this. It's not part of a "hidden agenda"; it's part of the curriculum. It also encourages children to think of the school as theirs, as a place they each have a stake in. Cleaning is not play, but it's different from instructional class time.

Finally, dismissal from school may not mean the end of playtime. Everyone lives within walking distance of school, so no one is being picked up by a school bus or a car pool and whisked away; many children either stay on the playground (it's the biggest open area in the neighborhood) or walk home with friends slowly—Sam and Ellen took up to an hour to make it home. I worried, but that's because I'm American. A common family rule among my friends was that their children should be home by 5:00.

Japanese parents realistically do not worry about their children being kidnapped, accosted, or molested, either by adults or by older children. They do not worry about their children doing inappropriate activities when they are not under close supervision, and children seem welcome in stores and snack shops. They get modest allowances to spend as they please, usually on food and toys. Japanese parents also seem not to worry about their children getting hurt in traffic, though three years of living in Japan has not been enough to make me feel safe about adults walking or bicycling around, let alone children. This is a misperception on my part, though; pedestrian accident rates are low.

The academic part of the school schedule is largely determined by the Ministry of Education, which issues guidelines on the number of class hours that should be devoted to each subject each year. In Ellen's case those specifications take up twenty-four of the twenty-nine class periods each week. The teacher can decide how to allocate the rest of the time. In Ellen's class and in most classes, one period a week is devoted to a class meeting. Ellen says this time was usually spent talking about problems, but sometimes class meetings were fun and included games or play.

For Ellen's first-grade class, Japanese (the name under which reading is taught) gets eight periods a week, mathematics four, social studies two, science two, music two, art one double period, morals one, and physical education three. The textbooks are chosen from a small number of series approved by the Ministry of Education; teachers supplement these with commercially available materials geared to the textbooks and with materials they prepare themselves.

Sam's fifth-grade schedule includes five periods a week for Japanese, five for math, three for social studies, three for science, two for music, one for morals, three for physical education, two for home economics, a double period for art, and one for calligraphy. Wednesday afternoon there is a club meeting, and that still leaves four periods a week at the teacher's discretion.

There is a morning assembly for the whole school on Tuesdays from 8:30 to 8:50, sometimes held outdoors and sometimes in the gymnasium. Its main feature is usually an address by the principal on a theme of his choosing. Each class marches in as a group and lines up as one of the older students in charge for the day issues commands for students to stand at attention, dress their lines by extending arms to the side and to the front, bow to the principal, and then stand at ease for his talk. All the students sing the school song before the talk. At the end of the meeting the student in charge again gives the commands for coming to attention and bowing, and then classes march around the room or the area and back to their classrooms.

Just as there is a weekly routine, there is also a routine that establishes the modes of behavior for each class period. Each day there are two children in each class who together are in charge of issuing the verbal commands that get pupils ready to be taught and help them move through their day. In the morning these children report the attendance to the teacher. They take care of getting all the desks in the proper order for the kind of class coming up. Sometimes desks are arranged in rows and lines, sometimes pushed out of the way altogether, sometimes gathered in groups of four or five facing each other. At the beginning of each period the leaders announce the subject and the page in the textbook and ask everyone to get ready and be quiet. This is all done in standardized verbal formulas. They look around to be sure that everyone is in proper order and may sometimes tell one or two children to sit up straighter or stop talking. They then announce to the teacher that all is ready and call on the class to stand and bow. Everyone says, "*Sensei, onegai shimasu*" "Teacher, do us the favor (of teaching us)." The teacher then begins to teach.

All of this happens very quickly, taking perhaps two to three minutes, with the beginning and end of each class also marked by school-wide bells. The bells are treated as signals, but the classroom routines are more important. Students don't assume that they should immediately be released at the first vibrations of the bell. In general I was struck with two contradictory feelings as I observed these routines. First, the routines are followed very easily and quickly; the whole pace of movement in this school feels very lively. Second, the routines and the schedule are treated as a comforting set of guidelines. There is no sense of hurry or compulsion about getting things done exactly on the button, but the end result is that things are accomplished very smoothly and on schedule.

A FULL-TIME OCCUPATION

Like other occupations in Japan, being an elementary schoolchild is considered a full-time job. This seems a reasonable assessment of the role school plays in the lives of children. Consider the days and hours that elementary school occupies. Elementary school is in session 240 days a year, for forty-one hours each week (less for first graders). The forty-one hours include Monday through Friday from 8:30 A.M. to 3:40 P.M., 8:30 to 12:30 on Saturday, and one hour of required club meeting on Wednesday afternoon. Japanese children go to school 1,640 hours a year. American elementary schools vary but are typically in session 180 days a year, thirty-two and a half hours a week, or 1,070 hours a year.

By comparison, U.S. Civil Service employees are considered to have a working year of 2,080 hours per year, only 440 hours more than Japanese children put in. American children are "at work" about half time compared with these American adults. Adults, of course, don't have homework at night and during vacations, as Japanese and American children do. If we compare schooltime for Japanese and American children in terms of school days, then the Japanese children spend the equivalent of twelve more weeks a year in school than American children. They spend the equivalent of seventeen more weeks in school in terms of hours at school.

But as we have seen from Sam's and Ellen's schedules, not all school time in Japan is class time. For Sam about eleven hours a week was taken up with recess, lunch, cleaning, and other nonclass activities. These are all considered educational in the wider sense in Japan, but they are not class hours. In the United States we might reasonably estimate that one hour a day, or five hours a week, is spent in recesses and lunch periods. In terms of class hours, then, Japanese students have about 1,200 hours a year, Americans 890 hours. This translates to a difference of almost ten weeks more class time for the Japanese students.

School, then, simply takes up more time for Japanese children than for American children. The importance of school, defining the Japanese child's status and occupation, is reflected in other ways too. One is that children are seldom identified by age but rather by grade in school. Parents say, "My son is a third grader" instead of "My son is nine years old." Adults scold children by saying, "That's not how a sixth grader should behave." Strangers ask a child, "What grade are you in?" not "How old are you?"

A second sign of the importance of school and the occupation of being a schoolchild is all the equipment and specialized paraphernalia required for elementary school children, different from that used by older students or adults. Besides the materials mentioned in the first chapter, a desk and study space are provided for each student in even the most cramped and crowded house. Each winter as the preparations for a new school year in April get under way and stores begin major promotions of school materials, there are special sales on these desks. They cost about Y50,000 ($355) for the desk, plus Y15,000 ($100) for the chair. The desks all have a place to hang the backpack, a light, a timer for practice tests, a place to put the weekly schedule, and a buzzer. Everyone knows that the buzzer will be used to call Mother to bring a snack or to help with homework or just to offer encouragement and sympathy.

CLASS TIME

When we hear about the high achievement levels typically reached in Japanese elementary schools and the discipline and social pressure for conformity that are often said to characterize the Japanese, it is easy to imagine what Japanese elementary schools must be like. Usually Americans expect them to be quiet, disciplined, tightly controlled environments with teachers in charge who manage the social and academic activities so that a minimum amount of "wasted time" interferes with a learning program that requires great concentration from students and intense teaching from teachers.

I was able to observe the classes of several teachers at first-, second-, fifth- and sixth-grade levels, in the subjects of music, science, physical education, morals, and reading, and I talked with Sam and Ellen about other classes. There were differences among teachers and among classes in different subject areas, but there were also common approaches and techniques that were different from those usually found in American classrooms. Like other observers, I was struck by the easy, relaxed discipline, the quick pace, and the high degree of student participation in these classes. The students seemed to be engaged, active, lively, and anything but downtrodden.

At Okubo Higashi, as in most urban schools in Japan, class sizes vary from thirty to about forty-five students, drawn from the immediate neighborhood and not grouped or tracked by ability; the purpose is rather to give each class an equal mix of abilities and characteristics. Since Japanese neighborhoods are less economically segregated than those in many other countries, there is usually a wide range of socioeconomic backgrounds represented in each classroom also. In less densely settled areas of Japan, classes may be smaller and more homogeneous. This is generally seen as a disadvantage.

The rooms at Okubo Higashi are standard issue classrooms. There is a wall of windows on the south side, the major source of heat and light. At one end of the room is a blackboard, and bulletin boards are found on the other walls, though there are also windows into the hallway on the north side of the room. Access to the outdoors is from doors in the window wall; classrooms on the upper floors open onto a balcony. Each student has a cubbyhole where the backpack and personal belongings are kept during the day. Each room has a desk for the teacher, a desk for each child, an electric organ, and some bookcases. Each room at Okubo Higashi also has a gas heater in one corner for use in the winter. For the younger grades there is a flimsy guard fence around this stove. The stove is an immovable object, because of its venting system.

Children have all their classes in the same room except for physical education and, for the upper grades, science labs. Music, art, and science all involve the use of equipment in the classroom, brought out for use and then stored again. Like Japanese houses, the classrooms give the impression not of being cluttered so much as being packed full of useful things. They are also liberally decorated with work done by the students, as are the hallways. These are not specially chosen pieces of work. If drawings from the expedition to the park are exhibited, the drawing of every student will be included. If the calligraphy exercises are being shown, everyone's is there. The school motto is displayed in each room as well as admonitions about behavior, changed from time to time (sample: "Let's all listen when someone is speaking") and the class's weekly schedule. Children are expected to take home most of their books and equipment such as pencils, crayons, and so forth each day, not leaving them in their desks or cubbyholes. Teachers, too, remove many belongings each day, in their case to a permanent desk in the teachers' room.

Because there are times during the day when children stay in the classroom but teachers leave to go to the teachers' room, there is a sense in which the room belongs to the students, the class, more than to the teacher. The children's imprint on the classroom in terms of paraphernalia and decorations is much stronger than the teacher's.

In Japanese houses, the furniture is movable, and it is often moved. In nearly every Japanese home, for instance, the room that is used for eating, watching TV, and most other activities during the day is also used for sleeping. Beds (soft mattresses and quilts) are stored in large cupboards during the day, and the daytime furniture is shoved aside each night to make room for sleeping. Even if there are separate bedrooms for some members of the family, the bedding is seldom left in place all day; it is stored away and the room used for play, study, and other activities until bedtime. (Bedding left on the floor all day is a sure sign of immorally sloppy housekeeping, and besides, they say, the bedding will get moldy if it is not put outside to air every sunny day.) The notion of a fixed arrangement of furniture that remains constant is not part of usual Japanese life at home, and certainly not at school. I would guess that the furniture in Japanese classrooms gets rearranged four to six times a day for different activities. This means moving all the movable elements—the teacher's desk, the student desks, the organ.

For some classes the desks are in parallel rows facing front. There is an assigned seating order for this arrangement. In some classes two rows are pushed together with a boy and a girl sharing each pair of seats. In other classes, though the boys and girls are not separated, the arrangement is somewhat looser. Rows of desks face the front for classes such as reading, when everyone in the class is doing the same thing and not working in small groups. Sometimes in Sam's class, he said, there would be two long rows of desks facing two more rows on the other side of the room with the teacher pacing the middle area.

Another pattern, all the desks in a circle around the edges of the room, is used for large group discussions. When small work groups (*han* groups; see chapter 4) are engaged in activities together, the desks are placed in clusters, with each desk facing the others in its group. Such study groups might be formed for almost any subject.

One common U.S. classroom practice that does not occur is to have a portion of the class interacting with the teacher while other members of the class work individually on other subjects or assignments. In other words there are no reading or math groups divided by ability level, no times when some members of the class are separated from the others to receive different instruction. In Japan all students are working on the same class material at all times, sometimes as individuals, sometimes as a large class group, and sometimes in small groups.

Classrooms are multipurpose rooms, and Japanese elementary school teachers are multipurpose teachers, too. Teachers are not specialists but teach all the subject areas. Guidelines imposed by the school and the Ministry of Education regarding how many hours should be spent on each subject each year prevent teachers from idiosyncratically emphasizing their favorite subjects or slighting areas they do not like teaching. The prevailing philosophy, that everyone can do everything if they try, applies to teachers too, who as a matter of course teach art, music, physical education, mathematics, reading, social studies, morals, home economics, and everything else that elementary school students are expected to learn.

The various ways of arranging the furniture of the rooms give some indication of the variety of teaching formats that children will encounter during a day—all, however, with the same group of fellow students and the same teacher. In many if not most schools, students in a given class remain together for two years with the same teacher.

In America Sam and Ellen have always been in schools that prided themselves on the number of specialist teachers they were able to provide, for art, music, physical education, foreign language, and computer skills. They have also had rather complicated methods of providing specialist teachers for academic subjects. Some schools have grouped the children in a grade by ability, and had each homeroom teacher teach one or two subjects to several different groups at different times; some also have provided special teachers for enrichment or remedial work. The upshot of these efforts to give students well-qualified teachers, teaching to each child's level of achievement in a small group of similar students, is that an individual child has to deal with the personalities and teaching styles of as many as six different teachers each week or even each day, and with the personalities and group dynamics of as many groups of fellow students.

I would find it difficult to work in such circumstances; I have always thought that this typical mode of classroom organization places great burdens on American students. It may also help to explain why American teachers feel psychologically overloaded. They often complain that it is difficult to know many students well and say that problems are created when children do not have adequate opportunities to become adjusted to an individual teacher's style. The disadvantage of the Japanese system, of course, is that occasionally a student and a teacher experience a real antipathy, with no relief. Teachers say this is a relatively rare occurrence, however.

Japanese students are faced each period of the day and week with a fairly constant schedule. Each class's program for accommodating the required hours of study for each subject remains the same for an entire year. Sometimes this is disrupted, as when preparations for Sports Day involve some activity every day during September; in addition, four whole days are given entirely to preparation for this event. Generally, though, life is predictable.

The course of a class is predictable, too. Teachers work hard at the beginning of the year and during the first years of school to teach students to manage the routines of classroom procedures, so that the teachers can be uninvolved in activities that are not teaching. Because the class leaders are responsible for getting everyone ready for class, teachers can begin classes not having had to tell anyone to be quiet, nor urge anyone to get ready, nor scold anyone for slowness. The teacher's job is teaching, not classroom management.

Much of the class time in Japanese schools looks familiar, consisting of a period of teacher explanation or teaching, a period when the teacher asks questions and members of the class raise their hands to respond, and a summarization period. On closer observation, however, there are some striking differences from American practices. One is the way every student who volunteers seems to be given recognition, and another is the role of the teacher in judging student responses.

Teachers appear to have several techniques to make classes feel more participatory. In one sixth-grade reading class students seemed to be reluctant to take part in a discussion of a new story (I think my presence made a difference). When several students did raise their hands to respond to a discussion point, the teacher called on one, who gave an answer. Then he gave each of the others a chance to respond also. Many of them simply said, "The same," which seemed to be treated as a legitimate response, and both students and teacher appeared to feel the contribution was constructive. The students were apparently not striving for uniqueness. Sam said one of his teacher's techniques was to ask everyone who had volunteered to stand at once. She would then choose one student to give an answer, and those who had planned to say the same thing would all sit down, leaving those with different responses to offer still standing until their answers had been requested. This pattern of giving every volunteer recognition, even for a response such as "the same," prevailed in all the classes I watched, and student responses were not commented on by the teacher, either positively or negatively. They were assumed to be correct, unless students objected.

I did see teachers use questioning of specific students in a controlling way a few times. In these cases the teacher would call on a child who had not volunteered by name. The child would stand in the usual way and sometimes give the required answer, but more commonly would look at the floor and mumble *"Mo kangaete iru,"* "I'm still thinking about it," a formula for avoiding an answer that still is less self-denigrating than "I don't know" or some other alternatives one can imagine.

One of the most startling sights for me the first time I saw it was what happens when a student gives an incorrect answer. Other students immediately raise their hands, calling out loudly, "*Chigaimasu!*", "That's wrong!" One of those who called out would then be chosen to give another answer. Or, as Sam reported, in his class if you were the one whose answer was wrong, you got to call on someone to correct you.

It was seeing this happen that led me to focus my later observations on the practice of teachers in evaluating student participation. It became clear that teachers routinely and emphatically refrain from giving either positive or negative evaluations of students' answers to questions or other responses to academic material. Those responses are evaluated, but only by other students. If no one objects to what you've said, you can assume, and the rest of the class can assume, that it was right, at least for the time being; it doesn't need to be said or restated by the teacher for it to have validity and authority.

I don't mean to suggest that teachers can't or don't manipulate a series of questions to lead to conclusions or points they want established, nor that their tactics necessarily are ones that kids can't figure out. But I am saying that teachers do not use their authority as masters of the material or as adults to establish the correctness of answers or responses made by students. Instead, peers are the source of validation or correction of a student's responses.

Students are often sent to the board, singly or in groups or as representatives of their groups to write answers to math problems or science problems or for other activities. It is a common practice for these students, either individuals or groups, to be applauded by the entire class for successful performance. Students show by smiles and bows that they appreciate this approval. The teacher may sometimes initiate the applause, but her role is subordinated to the class's; it is the class's applause that students acknowledge, not teacher praise.

Nor is the value of student responses solely a matter of their correctness. When leading class discussions, teachers are careful to list and acknowledge all the positions and arguments contributed during the discussion. Offering an idea that eventually is rejected is still seen as worthwhile, because the reasoning that leads to its rejection is a way to learn. Students, at least in science classes, do not seem so attached to the ideas they individually have proposed that they are not willing to change their minds.

Several classes that I visited, in reading, science, and morals, ended with individual writing as a summary activity. In these cases the teacher handed out small, unintimidating pieces of paper with an illustration and a lined space for writing. Each child was to answer a broad question concerning the lesson on the paper. The teacher wandered through the class as this was going on and watched what was being written. Either by marking the paper as he went through the class or by calling on a number of pupils at the end of the allotted time, he chose a group of different responses, and the authors read to the class what they had written. No teacher comment was made—none, either positive or negative.

Similarly, at the end of a second-grade science laboratory class on materials that do or do not conduct electricity, the last activity involved making a switch to turn on and off the current from a battery to a light bulb. The teacher moved through the class as the students worked. At the end she asked six children to come to the front of the room and demonstrate their switches. The switches were all different and all successful, but no comments were made about which were "better." There seemed to be some expression of delight from those watching. The teacher's only action was to choose the examples shared with the class; she made no comments or compliments.

Not only do Japanese teachers, then, stay in the background as far as the social management of the class and the classroom goes, but they try to do the same when it comes to academic material as well. Evaluation by one's fellow students is focused on more than evaluation by the teacher, by teacher design.

Of course, Japanese teachers do not just let incorrect responses stand, nor do they fail to exercise discretion in the written selections that are read out loud, but they do use manipulation of further discussion or follow-on questions to get to the points they want clarified, without relying on out-and-out correction of student responses. They do not act in authoritarian ways, as academic authorities, as much as teachers do in many other systems.

Most Americans expect that in a classroom students should encounter new materials or ideas and incorporate those materials and ideas into their existing mental frameworks, thereby changing them, and "learning." If we think that this process entails playing around with ideas in an experimental mode, then an important function of teaching is to provide feedback on the efforts of learners to use the ideas. They must try out the ideas, present the results of their trial thinking or use of the materials and ideas, and then get some evaluation of their efforts.

In American classrooms teachers are the evaluators. Through their assessments of student responses as right or wrong, acceptable or in need of additional work, they let students know about their progress in learning. Teachers are supposed to know and understand the materials they are teaching, and they serve as the authorities on thinking and operating with that material; they decide who has mastered it. It is considered important classroom practice to give students timely feedback about their responses, feedback that lets them know whether they are on the right track or not. We reasonably expect this judgment to come from the teacher, who is after all the one with the most knowledge, the one who can make the judgments accurately; she is the authority.

In the Japanese classrooms that I observed, teachers almost completely delegated this teaching function to students. Teachers almost never corrected or praised student responses. Students did this, and some student responses, usually at the end of a class session, were left without any overt evaluation. A set of attitudes about evaluation of schoolwork is being conveyed by these practices. One is that teachers are not available arbiters of correctness, because they fail to act as judges. Another is that one's peers are a reliable guide to academic correctness. If one's peers are capable of being reliable authorities, then one is oneself likely to be reliable. Third, this custom of peer evaluation implies a contract according to which each student must to be willing to correct fellow students and to accept their correction. Calling out "*Chigaimasu!*" "It's not that way!" involves some danger to one's own face—after all, the other guy may be right. At the same time it is a challenge to the fellow student you have accused of being wrong. I think children become more sensitive to this dilemma as they grow older, comparing my time in fifth- and sixth-grade classes with the time I spent in first- and second-grade classrooms. That may be why in the upper grades a challenged student is allowed to choose a corrector. Fourth, students learn that evaluation need not always be explicitly formulated or made public. Confronted with the writings of a number of classmates in the setting where no comments are made, one may make one's own judgments, or withhold judgment altogether, and do so privately. No one else intervenes to judge your judgments. One effect of this standard procedure is to emphasize that each person's judgment is valid and can stand alone. But it also teaches children that others may be judging their actions and work even when nothing is said openly.

Perhaps the ultimate realization of how independently Japanese elementary school classes can operate both socially and academically was brought home to me the day Ellen reported at supper that her teacher had been absent that day. To my routine query about what the substitute teacher had been like, she replied that there was no substitute. I asked somewhat anxiously how they had managed and what had happened, and she replied, "Oh, Kuroda *sensei* wrote on the board what we were supposed to do, and sometimes a teacher looked in the room." There were no riots, and they did their work, she said. Sam said his teacher had been gone that day, too, and they did the same thing. I later asked other parents about this and learned that it is routine practice. When I questioned the principal sometime later, he confirmed that several teachers had gone to a training course for two days and that no, they didn't get substitute teachers unless a teacher was absent for a long time—a month or more. Some parents nowadays object to the absence of a teacher, not because they worry about discipline but because they are concerned about their children falling behind academically, so schools are starting to use more substitutes. I still can't decide whether it's more extraordinary to be able to leave thirty-five first graders with no teacher for two full days, or to be able to leave forty-five fifth graders in the same situation. Sam did say the fifth graders didn't work as hard as usual.

REPORT CARDS, *JUKU*, AND EXAMINATIONS

There are some other contexts in which teachers make very overt judgments of student work. Homework is often corrected by the teacher and is used as a monitor of student progress. Report cards also reflect evaluation by teachers. Because there is a standard curriculum and a timetable for getting through it, the report card for each marking period, three a year, lists specific areas of competence, such as "addition and subtraction of numbers through 100" in the third term of first grade. Students are graded as average, high, or low. There are schoolwide criteria for assigning the grades: 15 percent of the students get "high," 75 percent "average," 10 percent "low" at Okubo Higashi. These grades have few or no consequences. Passing a grade does not depend on grades—everyone passes, as a matter of national policy. Being a student of a certain grade is a process of life, not an accomplishment. After all, no one fails to pass from being nine years old to being ten years old, and similarly it is impossible to fail to become a fourth-grade student after a year as a third-grade student.

There are two other arenas, very different from the institutional elementary schools, in which children and parents get "authoritative" feedback on academic performance. One is *juku* and private testing services, and the other is the high school entrance examinations. *Juku* are private, commercial tutoring schools. They range from in-home tutoring of a few students by a housewife, through neighborhood operations that enroll enough children to support a family, though probably modestly, to nationwide chains with hundreds of branch offices. They divide children by achievement levels and provide remedial help for those who are falling behind, additional practice for those who are keeping up, and accelerated or enriched programs for the academically advanced. They have smaller classes and a more overtly competitive style of teaching than are found in schools. They are cram schools of different levels, geared toward improving students' performances on the high school entrance examinations. After-school classes that children take in sports or art are also called *juku*.

The willingness of most parents to pay noticeable amounts of money for tutoring in commercial establishments, which make extensive use of repeated, indeed tedious, testing and ranking, indicates that parents think this activity is important. The crucial importance of placement in high schools as a determiner of the options available to students for the rest of their lives is well known to all Japanese parents and adults. Grades and teacher recommendations have nothing to do with the process, only the results of the high school entrance examinations. High schools are ranked by the test achievement levels of their entering students, which in turn are directly linked to the university entrance success or the employment success of their graduates. In one sense, looking at the situation from outside, it seems that gaining admission to a particular high school only predicts, more or less, a student's success in gaining admission to a particular college later on, or in obtaining employment with certain employers. Japanese participants in the process, however, act as though getting over the high school entrance barrier definitely determines their ability to get over the next college or employment entrance barrier.

The issue of high school admission is complicated, and it varies somewhat from one part of Japan to another, but it can be briefly described as follows: high school is not part of the compulsory school requirement in Japan; the legal school-leaving age is after finishing ninth grade. However, about 95 percent of Japanese children do enter high school, and nearly all of them graduate. About 30 percent of high school students attend private schools; the rest are in public schools. Both public and private schools charge fees, and both require students to take entrance examinations. There are several vocational curricula, as well as general academic and college preparatory academic programs. Within a school jurisdiction, which may be as large as a prefecture, there are no residence requirements for attending a particular high school, so schools choose entrants on the basis of their examination scores. The result of this process is that all the students in a high school are academically very similar—in strong contrast to students in the untracked compulsory levels of school. Because the student bodies of individual high schools are academically very similar when they enter, it is not too surprising that they are academically very similar when they graduate. The ranking of public and private high schools in terms of the examination scores of their new students, and in terms of the college and employment placements of their graduates, is widely known by the general population and by teachers and parents.

There is a contradiction between the importance of authoritative evaluations of academic performance in *juku* and in entrance examinations and their absence in the institutional setting of elementary schools. The situations in which "authorities," either the *juku* and testing services or the high schools in giving entrance examinations, evaluate student performance are resolutely separated from the elementary school context itself; I think they are viewed as antithetical to the social values and relationships that schools are entrusted with teaching. Schools and teachers feel, and say, that *juku* are inappropriate for children, unhealthy and unnecessary. The examinations for high school entrance (and later university entrance) are felt to be like an external foe, against which students and teachers alike struggle for success. These evaluations and rankings are not something imposed by teachers on students. Teachers teach; they do not evaluate, and they do not hold their students' fates in their hands directly.

4

Together at School,
Together in Life

HAN GROUPS

To most foreign observers a striking aspect of classroom organization and class time activities in Japan is the division of the class into *han* groups. *Han* means a platoon, a squad, a working group. It has implications of being the smallest operational group in a joint endeavor and of being a group that operates with little or no hierarchy. In Japanese classrooms each *han* includes five to eight children, depending on the size of the class, and in order to be an efficient teaching and social environment, each class should have six to eight of these groups. Both social and academic activities are carried out with *han* groups as the basic work unit.

Teachers decide on the grouping of children into *han*, and usually they change the groupings at the beginning of each term of the school year. Teachers have several goals in mind when forming groups. The foremost goal is to make each group heterogeneous in terms of personalities, abilities, previous friendship patterns, and previous *han* groupings. Ideally, the result will be groups that can all operate on the same level in many different activities. Life after school will not be spent in homogeneous groups, so it is important to learn to cooperate and draw the best from each member.

Japanese teachers use a number of different methods to decide on the composition of *han*. One fourth-grade teacher, talking to Catherine Lewis (1995:92), said that at the beginning of the year, when she didn't know the children well, she simply used the seating order, based on height, to form groups. For the next term she chose leaders who had not yet had a chance to be *han* leaders and let the children themselves decide who would be in the groups led by these students, subject only to the constraint that there be three boys and two girls in each group. She was available to help resolve difficulties if they arose. At another reorganization she choose leaders who were kind, who took care of others, and who were fairly good at mathematics. She had decided to emphasize math in the coming months, the subject in which there were the greatest differences in achievement among her students. In groups led by students who were good at math, slower students would have a chance to learn from the leaders, a process they would probably find "more fun" than learning from her. Other teachers told me they sometimes put all the leaders together in one *han* so they could learn how to manage among themselves and so less dominant children would have a chance to become leaders in their groups.

Han groups are used as units for many activities, and teachers often address the groups rather than addressing individuals by name. The same small groups are used for music, physical education, lunchtime preparation, and cleaning, as well as for math, social studies, and other academic subjects. In both academic and social activities students are responsible as a group for accomplishing their goals. In cleaning, for example, if the *han* that has the responsibility for dusting in the classroom does not do a good job, the whole *han* will be criticized when doing chores is the subject of a class meeting. When a *han* is given an arithmetic problem to solve, the solution is treated as a joint product. When a social studies question has been discussed and the issues presented to the whole class, it is the *han* group that is credited with the ideas expressed by the reporter.

Americans invariably ask about freeloading in such a situation. What keeps members of such groups from simply letting others do their work? When there are no sanctions that apply to individuals, why don't some people do their best to get out of the work? Why don't some people take advantage of the efforts of others and get "credit" for work they have not done?

Japanese also recognize that such problems can arise, but they nonetheless often treat these questions as puzzling, the sort of thing foreigners ask about—reasonable questions, but not ones they themselves worry about much. I got the same reaction to this question that I got when I asked why children compete so wholeheartedly in Sports Day, when there are no prizes. The underlying feeling was that it is natural and fun to join in the activities of *han* groups, that it is obviously self-defeating behavior to "get out of" those activities.

Sam and Ellen, too, said that freeloading was not a problem in *han* activities in school in Japan, though it happened sometimes, and both think such behavior is a noticeable aspect of group activities in the United States. As observers, we are left with the problem of analyzing why participation seems natural in the Japanese context, and freeloading seems natural in the United States.

The most general answer to this question lies in the role of socialization agents—teachers, parents, and other adults. Absolute conviction is very convincing. When children spend most of their time with adults who have firmly internalized the notion that participation in group activities is natural and rewarding, they become convinced of the same thing. After all, an appetite for social interaction at some level of intensity is a part of the nature of humans as a species, and everyone is susceptible to having that part of their nature nurtured and emphasized. At a less general level, however, we must look at specific social mechanisms that encourage this view of social life rather than the equally natural one that leads to freeloading and the suspicion that others will freeload.

How do Japanese children learn in school that the best course of action to adopt is the one of cooperative participation? How do they learn not to exploit others and not to be exploited themselves? These are not lessons learned only in school, but school is one of the places where they are taught. Lois Peak, in *Learning to Go to School in Japan* (1991), has written the most extensive study of how teachers impart these attitudes to students. One part of the technique involves making few demands on young children. That is, a large part of their time at preschool is spent without much teacher supervision or intervention in free play. The initiative of free play should come from children themselves, and it is important that teachers not dampen the enthusiasm and zest with which children engage in play they have chosen for themselves. Thus, teachers make no attempt to control the number of children using sets of equipment during free play, or to ration the time that is spent on a single activity, or to determine the kinds of play children engage in. Teachers know that playtime is successful if it is very noisy and lively, filled with exuberance and physical activity. Teachers intervene most often to help individuals negotiate entry into a play group or to encourage solitary children to be more sociable. Most of the time that children spend in the preschool group is time that is fun, that is self-generated activity, not regulated by teachers and not solitary.

Fighting and arguing during these periods is seen as inevitable, an immature but valuable social interaction between children. As children learn to understand, they will become more skillful at social interactions and abandon these inappropriate activities. This will take years of effort, but isolating children from interaction is not seen as a way of effectively teaching interaction techniques. It is important that children accept some constraints on their behavior because they want to, because it leads to more fun, more pleasure. All children want to play with other children, and Japanese preschools and schools are organized to make that play as rewarding as possible. Japanese educational philosophy explicitly recognizes this as a ploy for socialization.

Peak tells how she was taught to take this approach at a school she was observing. One of the four-year-old boys developed a pattern of approaching her during outdoor playtime and hitting her, then running away. This soon escalated to kicks strong enough to leave bruises. She tried to ignore these attacks, waiting for the teacher to intervene. Finally, one day the teacher made an opportunity to talk about the play styles of different children. Some, like a charming little girl whose invitations to "come to my house for tea" Peak always accepted, were verbal and sophisticated in their approach to social interaction. Others, like the boy bothering Peak, were equally friendly but less skilled, instead acting like puppies, wanting to be chased and using direct action as an invitation to play. The next day, acting on the insight of the teacher, who felt that Peak's unresponsiveness was the problem at issue, Peak chased after this boy making monster noises, to his delight (Peak 1991:163–64).

The reason children may sometimes seem to pull back from participation or to act in ways that could be interpreted as aggressive or selfish, according to the Japanese, is that they "do not yet understand" why such behavior is inappropriate. It is not because they are selfish or aggressive; they are simply not skillful enough or mature enough to act otherwise. Actions that teachers should take in these cases are those that explain how children should behave and those that teach social skills, not punishments or reprimands.

At the same time children are allowed long periods of great freedom, they are also asked to learn to participate in shorter periods of very controlled, ritualized group activities. These are the periods in preschool that require children to carry out certain activities as a unified group: the morning greeting period and the protocols of eating lunch or snacks and of saying goodbye at the end of the day. These activities must be done by the group in unison. It is not sufficient that each child individually carry out the right behaviors; all must simultaneously perform a reasonable approximation of the right behavior. As children get older, they are capable of longer periods of controlled group behavior, so by the time they reach elementary school, the time devoted to controlled activities is much longer than the time spent in free, unritualized play, although some periods of (alarmingly) free play remain available to children all through elementary school.

Not infrequently, especially at the beginning of their school life, individual children show that they "do not understand" group activities and rituals. Teachers extravagantly praise those who do cooperate, and they wait patiently for the others to comply, not scolding, but explaining over and over that it is necessary to be part of the group. Otherwise, the next set of activities, playing or going home, for instance, simply cannot take place. The teacher waits for other children to tell the laggards to participate and then seconds their calls, often more politely. Other students bring pressure to bear on those who are reluctant, because they do not want to be constrained any longer than necessary in these formal situations. Peak reports incidents in which the frustration of waiting for reluctant classmates leads to "letting off steam" behaviors such as loud, inarticulate screaming, carried out by the whole group. Teachers interpret this as evidence that unanimous group action is intrinsically rewarding to children, evidence that they can be led to appropriate unanimous behavior "naturally." Though it may take a while, all eventually conform, and it is either because their peers persuade them or because they all want to move on to other things, not because teachers eventually resort to force to resolve an issue. Children are persuaded to cooperation and participation, not forced into it. (I must say that the relentless efforts at persuasion sometimes seem to me more underhanded and nastier than an outright imposition of power and authority. I also think this is a very American reaction on my part.) A lot of time is spent in this way, especially at the beginning of school, but it is not time wasted; it is the curriculum of preschool.

Preschools also start the practice of rotating leadership roles among the members of the class. Each child is routinely, not as a reward or a punishment, given a turn to be the leader. Children seem to like this, because it increases their individual interaction with the teacher by a small amount, because they get a chance to tell other children what to do, and because they become the center of attention for several important rituals during the day. As teachers often point out, being a leader is a good way to learn how to be a follower. The difficulties children have in getting each other to follow directions and prescribed behavior patterns are meant to teach them the importance of compliance when they are not the leaders. Teachers articulate this lesson over and over and cite it as one of the important things children learn at preschool.

There are also some activities at preschool that seem to fall between the unrestrained and chaotic free play in groups, which occupies most of the time, and the ritualized, required group performances. An example is the time at the end of the day when the group is assembled for leave-taking. Teachers call children individually to get an attendance sticker placed in their book, then run through the class list again to hand out the communication books and notices to be taken home. At this time teachers do not enforce strict silence and patient waiting; they allow some quiet play and talk as the routine is accomplished.

Preschool group activities, then, are predominately unorganized, child-initiated free play for the greater portion of the day, interspersed with other group activities that are either relaxed or very ritualized. But everything is done together. No distinction is made between doing what you want individually and having to do what the group requires when in a group. All the time is spent in a group, and most of it is fun. The predisposition to find group activities desirable is fostered by making sure they are desirable most of the time, and children learn to expect time in a group to be rewarding.

By the time they reach elementary school, most children are well on the way to sharing the conviction of fully socialized Japanese people that group activities are good and that participation is both desirable in itself and what one freely chooses. Elementary school patterns continue to emphasize this message; it is regarded as something still incompletely learned that needs to be reinforced by enjoyable group activities, in order that children internalize fully the group-oriented understanding of the nature of a truly human life. Japanese children do like most activities at school, many of which are undertaken simply because they are fun.

At still another level, we need to look at the rewards and sanctions for participation and for freeloading. In the school context, the reward for participating in the *han* activities is intrinsic, not external. There are no awards in terms of higher grades or overtly marked status, except for fairly frequent applause from classmates. If these activities will help you learn, and you know learning is important in the long run, and you have a good chance of gaining applause and recognition for yourself and your group by cooperating, and if the activities are "fun" in the short term—and why not, since they are done with your classmates—what do you have to lose by participating? What can you gain by freeloading except isolation and boredom? These seem to be effective motivators for participation; more authoritarian punishments do not seem to be necessary.

In contrast, group activities in the United States often result in individual grades. Sam reports that in U.S. groups some students want to get A's, whereas others are happy with C's. There is conflict and resentment about the amount and quality of effort contributed. When group activities are instituted for learning purposes, not grading ones, a different dynamic comes into play.

For many non-Japanese it is difficult to visualize how social groups can be used for truly academic learning activities, since learning is something that takes place in each individual's head. American observers have reported numerous ways this takes place. Catherine Lewis (1995:77) describes a Japanese first-grade science class that was meant to teach conservation of material and concepts of measuring. Class began with each of the children individually showing a plastic bottle brought from home, explaining what it had held, and at the teacher's encouragement, making comments about the bottles. "This one is a vinegar bottle. I love vinegar, just like my Dad." The teacher announced that they would try to decide which bottles held the most. But first, he displayed two glasses of water on the front table, one tall and narrow, the other short and wide. Which one of these, he wondered, held the most water? Many children called out answers, and he then asked each *han* to consult with each other and prepare to report to the whole class their conclusions or their thoughts about how to determine which held more water. As they worked, he strolled through the class, commenting on which groups seemed to be talking well together. "It's all right to have more than one answer. It's also all right to say you can't think of an answer."

At the end of the discussion period, one person from each *han* gave the group's ideas. Some reported that their members thought you could tell by looking which glass held more, others proposed measuring the water in identical containers, and one group suggested weighing the glasses. The teacher formulated the basic dispute between those who were in favor of looking and those who proposed measuring. "Let's give Group Four a hand; they were the only ones who thought of weighing the glasses."

The teacher took note of the glass that looked as if it held more water, then poured the contents of the two into identical containers. They turned out to have exactly equal quantities of water, an unexpected outcome that prompted loud comments from both groups; some children rushed to the front of the room to check more carefully.

As the excitement died down, the teacher asked each *han* to consider the bottles its members had brought in. They were to reach a decision as to which held the most water and prepare to explain how they found out. Each group was given a pair of measuring containers, and one group went looking for scales. At the beginning of the lesson, the teacher had cautioned that he hoped there would be no floods during this lesson, but if there were, then he hoped they would be cleaned up without fighting about whose fault it was. The period for measuring the water held in each child's container did proceed with only one spill, and at the end the teacher asked each *han* to choose one member to report. As each group displayed its bottles, the teacher encouraged class members to call out predictions about which held the most; then he let the *han* representative explain their procedures and announce the results.

Academically, what activities did each *han* participate in? During the first *han* period, they had to pool the ideas of five children and have one member formulate these for presentation to the class. The teacher's recognition of group four's unique contribution, strongly validated by the applause of the rest of the class for this *han*, illustrates some of the pressures put on *han* groups. Because of a unique suggestion, the whole *han* was rewarded by applause. Had they not been skillful enough to remember or incorporate this suggestion, initially made by an individual, or had they rejected it because they didn't like the child who made it or because some *han* members didn't understand it or thought it implausible, they would have missed being applauded. (Children unmistakably show that they like being given this recognition.) But in this interaction validation was given (1) to the individual who first offered the suggestion to the *han*, providing the opportunity for the group to be applauded and gaining the respect of the other *han* members who participated in being the objects of applause, (2) to the *han* reporter, who included it in the report of *han* deliberations, and to the *han* as a whole for accepting a unique contribution. The teacher and the class applauded group four, not an individual, and on this understanding it was a group effort that brought the suggestion to the class. The suggestion was clearly a relevant, substantive contribution to the material of the class, not a "social" contribution. Japanese teachers suggest that some shy children may be more willing and able to offer contributions through their *han* than individually to the whole group.

During the second *han* work period, each group had to use the principles established for the teacher's two containers to evaluate their own unique collection of five different containers. There is a distinct step in intellectual complexity from evaluating two objects to evaluating five, and none of the containers they brought from home resembled the teacher's glasses. They had to talk among themselves about how to do this, carry out together several steps of comparison, and prepare an explanation that would make sense to other children who had not worked with their set of bottles. This, too, is academic learning.

Mathematics is one of the most individual subjects in the elementary school curriculum, but here, too, *han* activities become important. Features noted by several observers of Japanese math classes include the emphasis placed on as many ways as possible to solve problems and the importance of the analysis of mistakes. In this context *han* groups can be effective. A common format for classes is for the teacher to present a concrete problem to be solved and to solicit strategies for solution. These are usually multistep problems, and often more than one strategy will work. When teachers ask *han* groups to offer potential solutions, two goals are accomplished. A number of different suggestions can be gathered efficiently, each *han* set to work trying one of its suggestions, and then each group can present its solution to the class, being required to discuss the reasoning the group used in trying it or to explain why they now know it was not a correct solution. No individual alone is responsible for either successful or unsuccessful approaches, and several can be tried out. Teachers do not pass over mistakes but regard them as teaching opportunities, bringing out the reasoning that made them seem reasonable to start with and then pointing out where the reasoning went wrong. Even groups that offer wrong answers, then, contribute to the ongoing discussion of the class, and no individual gets singled out for poor performance. Often the group itself discovers its mistake, and they then get public credit for doing so. Again, the social framework provides for academic learning.

Even during the *han* activities that consist only of group discussion of a problem in social studies, for instance, a student who spends twenty minutes discussing with four other classmates has a chance to say more than most students will be able to in a twenty-minute discussion with thirty-five or forty participants. Many students may be more willing to participate in the smaller format than in full-group contexts. Fellow students, who have the incentive explained above for listening to all their members, are less intimidating than teachers. At the least, it is probably more difficult to "tune out" what is going on in the small group situation.

Han groups, then, are involved as stable configurations for both academic and nonacademic activities in Japanese classrooms. The stability of the groups, giving children a genuine opportunity and incentive to learn to work at various tasks together, is an important factor in their success. The ongoing experience that Japanese children have in such groups, starting in preschool, where they are developed primarily as social, nonacademic units, is the key to making them effective as academic units, along with the teachers' practices in formulating academic tasks that are truly group activities, not just masks for individual performance and grading. In contrast, in most U.S. school settings, group projects usually involve short-term groupings of students, often cooperating only for one task, for which they will be given individual grades. In these circumstances shirking and taking advantage of the efforts of others becomes a rational course of action, a "natural" thing to do.

Though for adults from outside, the constant use of *han* groups is very noticeable, for Sam and Ellen it was an unremarkable feature of school life in Japan. They were neither enthusiastic nor unhappy about this aspect of school; it seemed to them to be just part of the way things were. Even though they were probably the most incompetent members of their *han*, they didn't feel left out or resented, and whatever they could do was accepted and appreciated. Both students and teachers seemed to think that of course they would do their best, and the assumption didn't feel unreasonable to Sam and Ellen.

One of the strengths of Japanese education, it seems to me, is that behavior patterns learned in school continue to be useful in life after school. The values and interaction patterns fostered in *han* groups in the classroom are among those carried over into adult situations. The fundamental idea that solutions to problems arise from the cooperation of groups and not just from inspired individuals, the noncompetitive joint evaluation of proposals, the notion that often more than one solution might be found, practice in not taking others' suggestions as challenges to authority or competence, the idea that a group has a goal to accomplish and each member contributes whatever he can and whatever needs to be done, rather than following a detailed job description: all these habits of thought and practice emerge clearly in ethnographic descriptions of how employees (and bosses) behave in work settings in Japan. So, too, do the ideas that social ties and entertainment, "having fun," make work groups more effective and that rituals help bind and focus work groups.

Rohlen, in *For Harmony and Strength* (1974), describes how the members of a branch bank staff begin each day with a meeting to recite the company's goals and principles, to follow the radio exercises together, and to drink tea and talk about the day's activities. Periods of new or increased work patterns are likely to be initiated with a group meeting, where the branch leader will listen to suggestions and objections and elicit a plan to be adopted. An after-hours but compulsory party follows. Company evaluations of performance (monthly counts of bookkeeping errors, for example) are by branches, not by individuals. Employee morale is an important factor in the evaluation of branch chiefs.

Even for workers on the line in factories, the expectations that members of a group will help each other and that their production is a matter for the group to accomplish through cooperation are fairly strongly felt (Kamata 1982; Roberts 1994). This is not necessarily a benevolent notion; from management's point of view, such social cohesiveness increases productivity and reduces labor costs. It's not hard to think that exploitation is occurring when employees are reluctant to take their earned vacation time because their fellow workers will have to cover for them. Nonetheless, Japanese workers do find compensation for their hard lot in the social relationships of the small work groups and in the generally nonantagonistic relationships with foremen and management, who in turn are not inclined to regard suggestions from workers as challenges. The very effective (from a management point of view) development of quality control circles in Japanese workplaces depends on the ability of workers to want to improve their work, to cooperate to identify problems and solutions, and to be able to present them to management without being seen as insubordinate.

Han groups in Japanese schools are structured to be groups in which the self-interest of individuals genuinely coincides with the interests of the group. Children are not tricked, in some sense, into subordinating their own goals over an extended period of time to the interests of the group; rather, they are put into situations where in order to satisfy their own needs, they must contribute to the efforts of others in the group. Students are taught, by trial and error and by coaching from teachers, how to make these groups effective social units and goal-oriented units. Skill in functioning in small and larger groups with the same structuring of incentives and rewards is highly valued in nonschool situations in Japan; groups like this are encountered by adult Japanese in both economic enterprises and leisure occupations. Lessons that teach how to succeed in school also teach how to succeed in life outside school.

Groups

The Japanese are group oriented.

The purpose of preschool is to prepare children for group life.

Children study morals in school because a group is the appropriate place to learn about morality,

Sports Day and school trips are undertaken to teach children how to live in a group.

It's impossible to read about or experience Japanese education without encountering persistent references to groups and group behavior.

When a concept is so pervasive in a people's understanding of their own experience and practice, it is a good idea for outsiders to pay careful attention to that idea. They should not assume that the English words have the same meanings for us that the Japanese words have for the Japanese.

Much of what is written about the Japanese being group oriented is true, I think, but Japanese groups are not necessarily like those in other societies, and they're not all like each other. They're not all formed the same way, they don't all function in the same way, and they don't all demand the same attitudes and behaviors from their members.

In this section I want to discuss generally Japanese and Western approaches to issues of the individual and the group, to describe two contrasting ways in which groups operate in Japan, to consider the feelings about group life that Japanese express, and to suggest how the demands and pressures of groups are made tolerable for Japanese.

The many philosophers and social theorists who have thought about the issue of the group and the individual in Japan, like those in the Western traditions, have been sophisticated thinkers whose ideas about this complex relationship are not simplistic. Still, I think it is fair to say that, although there is not a stark all-or-none differentiation in the elements of their thought, there are different emphases and tendencies in how the two traditions approach this issue.

In broad outline, the Western tradition has seen the group as posing a threat to the virtue of the individual, holding that people in groups are less likely to behave morally than individuals are, that one must resist the seduction of the group and the abrogation of individual responsibility. Our moral and ethical training is geared toward helping people "think for themselves," to be individually responsible for their behavior, not to be misled by the attractiveness of following the group. We also worry a lot about protecting individual rights and liberties from intrusions by the group. At the same time, of course, Western philosophy has recognized that groups are an essential part of human life and that human fulfillment depends on belonging to groups.

In contrast, starting from their perceptions of infants and what goes on in child rearing, Japanese have tended to see people as isolated individuals who through great effort are able to become members of groups and thus live a fully human life. Individuals left to their own inclinations are likely to act in selfish, immoral ways. The danger according to this mode of thought is that individuals will fail to see the necessity of giving up their own selfish impulses to achieve the social life that is essentially human.

We see infants as dependent and all too connected to other people; they need to become independent and capable, to trust their own perceptions and become strong enough to act on their own moral judgments. The Japanese see infants as isolated, with only their own interests to guide them, needing to be brought into social relationships in order to appreciate and accept the moral behavior that groups entail. For us independence is hard to achieve but desirable; for the Japanese integration is hard to achieve but desirable. This is a rough caricature of subtle thinking in both traditions, but I think it captures some significant differences between Japanese and Western social orientations.

Japan is famous for a mode of group organization that is characterized by clear hierarchy and clear patterns of deference. Japanese and foreign observers are quick to notice the seating patterns, speech patterns, deference behaviors, and avoidance of disagreement with "superiors" that characterize such groups. They stress that these groups are similar in structure to the *ie*, the traditional Japanese family, composed of one household head and the subordinates of that head. Families are not made up of similar or equal individuals, but rather include people of different ages, sexes, ranks, functions, and abilities. Differences of age, sex, and function within the *ie* are, according to this set of observations, resolved into a set of vertical relationships, expressed by the dominance of the head in all decision making and the deference of all members to the head in matters of behavior and thought. In general, elders rank above juniors in the *ie,* and males rank over females. The overwhelming moral duty of the head in such a group is to ensure the well-being of the group as a whole; this is the basis for the acceptance of subordination by the other members.

Nakane Chie (1970), a distinguished Japanese anthropologist, puts forth that viewpoint, partly on the basis of her fieldwork in India. In India, she felt, groups were organized on the basis of characteristics all members held in common (for example, caste membership). Clearly articulated rules governed the areas and extent to which members' actions were constrained by their membership in the group. Beyond those rules individuals were free to act as they wished. To her it seemed that Japanese groups were more demanding, requiring members to accede to the well-being of the group in many more domains of behavior and requiring conformity of thought as well as of behavior.

One of the many examples she gives of the kind of allegiance demanded of group members concerns different schools of *Noh* drama. She says that the followers of one school will not even attend performances of the other schools, though their traditions are very closely related. In the academic world, according to Nakane, real debate and discussion of intellectual issues is hampered by the division of that world into groups, each led by a senior professor whose rank and authority over junior members of his group are so overwhelming that they can never disagree openly and publicly with him. At the same time they are so involved in their own group that they do not readily debate the positions of other groups of scholars. On a much more mundane level, many Westerners have been struck by the usual practice of Japanese groups eating at a restaurant who all order exactly the same meal, usually chosen by the most senior person present. Another characteristic of these vertical Japanese groups is that they tend to become multipurpose groups, not single-purpose ones. One's work group is also the group that fills one's leisure hours; group participation is so encompassing that individual hobbies or interests are pursued only with difficulty. The Japanese family, the *ie,* is the model for other forms of social organization in these aspects.

Many Japanese and outside observers have joined Nakane in finding that a fascination with ranking in many areas of life illustrates and reinforces the importance of vertical ranking in social organization. In Japan people take very seriously the notion that there is a number one *tempura* restaurant in Tokyo; they easily accept the idea that everyone can agree on the criteria that give a particular restaurant out of thousands that rank. Similarly, there is a number one university, a number one school of flower arranging, a number one potter, *kabuki* actor, car, and so forth.

No one can speak in Japanese, even the simplest and most straightforward sentence, without being aware of the vertical social relationships implied by linguistic choices. Hierarchical relationships and in-group versus out-group relationships are implied by choices among vocabulary alternatives and by the verb forms used. English speakers do in fact vary the ways they express themselves depending on who it is they are speaking with and the sort of situation involved. We sometimes say, "Would you like a cup of coffee?" sometimes, "D'you want some coffee?" and at other times, "Here, have some coffee." Every time we speak we have to choose among these and innumerable other possible ways to accomplish the same interaction. English speakers, however, usually avoid thinking overtly about these choices and their social implications. Japanese, on the contrary, are quite self-conscious about the same sorts of choices and interpret their linguistic decisions as socially significant, revealing of hierarchy, and burdensome.

One of the many confirmations that relations within the nuclear family have this hierarchical dimension can be seen in the terms by which family members address each other. Respectful kinship terms are used almost exclusively. Only children are addressed by their given names, and only by older kin. A good friend in Japan reported to me that as a result of their two years in the United States, her eleven year old son had acquired the habit of calling his twelve year old brother by name, instead of "older brother," and that this usage bothered his grandparents and neighbors when they moved back to Japan.

Many groups in Japan are organized quite self-consciously on the model of the family. Such a pattern is called *iemoto*, "family form." Within an organization following this pattern, each member has a strong relationship to the next higher link in the hierarchy. The lower ranking member is bound to show deference to the higher; the higher is required to take care of the lower. In both directions, human factors are supposed to be given at least equal weight with the formal or contractual obligations of the relationship. (In fact, these relationships are subject to abuse in both directions. Sometimes superiors make illegitimate demands on their followers, and sometimes followers demand indulgences that are not justified.) Relationships between equals in these organizations are much weaker than the vertical relationships.

In the bank that Thomas Rohlen described in *For Harmony and Strength* (1974), equals, those employees who joined the bank at the same time, were scattered in work assignments to different sections of the bank, so they really had little opportunity to form strong relationships; outside their immediate hierarchical work groups, they looked mostly to ties with senior members of the bank who had graduated from their own school for support and guidance.

If organizations are structured by reliance on vertical links between members, then the question of what criteria are used to determine the vertical ranks becomes very important. Around the world and for different purposes people have used many different criteria to address this issue. Age, sex, competence, elections, personality, parentage, wealth, and physical prowess all have been used to determine rankings, and each brings with it characteristic problems.

Since the *iemoto* groups we are discussing in Japan are predominately groups formed for economic purposes, and the livelihood of their members depends on the success of the group's endeavors, one might expect that competence would play a major role in determining the hierarchy of these groups. Instead, we find that the overt hierarchical structure of such groups is primarily based on the criterion of seniority. The advantage of seniority as a ranking device is that it is objective and unchanging. The disadvantage, of course, is that other criteria, notably competence, do not always match the seniority ranking, and in groups that require competent performance of important activities it seems that competence should be rewarded with high status.

In actual practice there are several factors that resolve this contradiction, at least to some degree. First, competence often does correspond to seniority; there is not always a disparity. Second, there are ways of recognizing competence without disturbing the overt seniority rankings. If groups use meetings and discussions as ways of coming to decisions, as Japanese groups do, then even junior people can—politely and deferentially—express their views, and those views can be acted on. Third, though ideally the more senior members should have higher rankings, in fact organizations do promote people to levels where they have higher status than more senior members. Such a person should refrain from flaunting success over seniors. Finally, patient juniors will inevitably become seniors, and they will eventually be given the deference they deserve. Ronald Dore (1987:87) and other observers of Japanese behavior in groups have said that they think subordinates or juniors can have more freedom to express their views or opinions in Japan than in Great Britain or the United States because their opinions are seen as input to group decision making, not as challenges to the hierarchical order.

The analysis of Japanese groups just given is one that most writers about Japanese society would accept; it is part of the standard understanding of Japan that has been developed over the last fifty years or more. But when I think about my participation in Japanese life and the groups I observed, both from outside and as a participant, a very different sort of group structure is dominant. Perhaps this form of organization could be characterized as amorphous and leaderless. These groups operate as collections of peers without hierarchies. Like the vertically structured groups, they are functional groups, meant to accomplish some goal or set of actions; they are not merely friendship groups or gatherings. Reflecting on my experiences and rereading various ethnographies, I find evidence that amorphous, leaderless groups are found in many situations and at all age levels in Japan.

I remember two specific incidents from Sam's kindergarten. One occurred on a parents' visiting day, when we watched a school project of making cookies. There was a clear educational agenda in doing this, namely, following the recipe, measuring the ingredients correctly, and putting them together in the proper manner. It involved weighing dry ingredients and measuring liquid ones in measuring cups, as well as mixing and stirring the dough.

One teacher talked about the recipe and led the group through the actions necessary. The fifty children were divided into groups of six or seven at small tables, each making one batch of cookies. There were only three teachers in this school, and one was leading the demonstration. The other two seemed to spend most of their time loosely supervising the three-year-olds. That meant that each table of children had to divide up the work—or participation opportunities—by themselves. They did it with no discussion, no arguments, no overtly stated rules, no instruction from the teachers, and no perceptible unhappiness with results.

At some tables they took turns by going around the table, with the next child doing whatever came next in the process. At some tables someone just took on the next task without being "in order." There was no noticeable jostling for especially desired tasks, such as breaking the eggs, which American children always vie for. At one table, when it came time to stir the batter at the end, the first girl counted a number of stirs and passed the bowl on to the next child, who counted the same number of stirs before passing it on, and the bowl continued around the table in this way. But none of the other tables showed even this amount of overt structure. At no table was there an apparent leader, either appointed by the teachers, self-selected, or chosen by the group.

Another incident involving amorphous, leaderless groups that I observed concerned the swings. At some point in the early spring the daily communication book started coming home with comments that Sam was "crazy about the swings." These comments continued for a couple of weeks. During this time I happened to stop in at school during a free-play period, and I watched the play on the swings. There were two swings, and about ten boys were playing on them. They had organized themselves into two lines and were taking turns. One boy would swing a while, get off, and go to the end of the line as the next boy took his place. After a while he would get off, and so on. There was no talk about how long a turn each boy had. No one was counting or timing, no one was urging the swinger to hurry up, no one was complaining about not getting a sufficient turn or having to wait too long. No teacher was watching, or even present on that part of the playground. The contrast with boys in America, who even at that age argue a lot about the rules for group play, was striking. Maybe the teachers helped them institute some procedure when their joint infatuation with the swings began, but when I asked about it they didn't seem to be aware of having done anything.

In the ethnographic literature, Johnson's study (1975) of a village boys' club provides striking evidence of how with almost no hierarchy elementary and junior-high-school-age boys can carry out both purposeful and recreational activities free of adult supervision. Not only do these boys manage the weekly meetings, the weekly baseball games during the school year, the summer camping trip, the raids on watermelon patches, and the endless baseball games that occupy much of summer vacation, but they also fulfill their village responsibilities, which include carrying out certain festivals, cleaning temple grounds and paths, and delivering New Year's mail. A mild hierarchy of senior boys over junior ones is found, but junior boys don't "follow orders," and senior boys don't give them. Boys stop being members of this group after they finish junior high school, and all boys in the last year of junior high are officers of the club, however many offices that takes.

Three groups of adults I participated in seemed to operate in much the same way. One was an English conversation group at the local community center. This group had been established, with a changing membership, for about twenty years. It contained both men and women, ranging in age from the mid-thirties to eighty, from a variety of educational and occupational backgrounds. They met once a week to study and speak English and hired native English speakers to attend and lead their meetings once a month. I met with them for about nine months and also attended a couple of parties they held.

The procedure for classes was pretty straightforward, but there was some organizing to be done. Often the tables and chairs in the room needed to be rearranged, the heater turned on, the water for tea put on to boil, the cups and supplies gotten out, and announcements about activities and plans made. There was no consistency as to who did these tasks and no planning for them. Whoever got there early did them, and someone always got there in time. But there wasn't a roster, or an organized way to take turns, or anyone who was responsible for a given evening or chore. It all just happened.

Flower arranging classes were a second arena in which this sort of organization was the mode. Even though the two classes I attended were very different in some ways, they were alike in this. There were certain things that needed to be done, and someone did them, both before and after classes.

The international cooking group also operated in this loose way. Someone was in charge of the menu, the recipes, and the shopping for each meeting, but beyond that it was free form self-sorting-out of participants to different tasks, with no discussion as to how it would all get done. Everyone kept doing something until everything was done. It didn't seem as though anyone was excluded or that anyone ended up doing a disproportionate share of the dirty work. Even the foreigners in the group, who were somewhat at a loss for how to proceed sometimes, were never directed to certain activities, or any activities. Not only I, but also foreigners from Brazil, Taiwan, Indonesia, and the Philippines felt a little bewildered on occasion, and maybe even excluded, because no one suggested to us ways to participate. Either you did or you didn't find something to do, and either way seemed acceptable.

Other anthropologists have also reported on groups, even hierarchical ones, that acted as though they were amorphous and leaderless. Leaders seem very reluctant to assume authoritarian roles, preferring to spend time getting group consensus on goals and procedures, even when those will turn out to be the ones insisted on by higher levels of the formal organization. Thus Rohlen (1974) describes how branch chiefs at a large bank work hard to get the group's assigned tasks done by willing subordinates without giving abrupt orders or appearing to impose their will without consultations. Even those with clear authority should not act as though they have a superior position; they are more effective if they do not behave in a domineering way. Those who are promoted to positions of authority are men who do not overtly exercise authority but instead can get group members to work without invoking hierarchy and power.

Dore (1978) describes in lengthy and human detail the thoughts and actions of the residents of the village of Shinohata in maintaining village harmony—carrying out actions for the good of the community without resort to authoritative decisions or orders from the supposed authorities. The personality of the village headman and his skills in handling social relationships make a difference in what the village accomplishes as a social unit, and that makes a difference in people's feelings of how good a place Shinohata is to live. The most effective headmen are those who by example, persuasion, and social skills are able to make others feel good about contributing effort to community activities, and who are able to organize these activities without giving orders or being high-handed.

In the midst of metropolitan Tokyo, Bestor (1989) found community organizations that operated in the same way. In one memorable dispute in a neighborhood of about twenty-five hundred people, the young men wanted the community organization to buy a new portable shrine for the annual festival at the local temple. The older men favored a more practical expenditure of any available funds on improvements to the community hall. When one of the young men lost the election for president to one of the older men, there could have been open conflict and division in the community organization. Instead, the younger men simply formed a new ad hoc group to raise money for a new shrine and then presented it to the community. Their initiative, effectiveness in raising money, and tact in avoiding a full-scale challenge to the older men had the result of validating their claims to leadership, and in the next elections a young man was chosen to be president, the community organization accepted ownership of the new shrine and responsibility for its maintenance, and a tacit recognition that leadership was passing into the capable hands of a new generation of leaders could be felt in the community.

When Japanese talk about school as the place to learn about group life, I think they really have in mind learning to live in these leaderless groups composed of peers. Many practices in schools and preschools do in fact give children this experience, without glossing over the disadvantages for individuals involved. To return to names and language again, all members of a class use names that are appropriate for equals: mutual given names, mutual last names, or nicknames. They use familiar, nondeferential language forms with each other, also. Teachers consistently refer to everyone as *tomodachi*, "friends"; they address students in groups more often than as individuals.

There's little doubt that Japanese themselves feel that being a member of a group is oppressive to some degree, that it definitely involves giving up independence and freedom, and that this is a cost.

"The nail that sticks up gets pounded down" may be the proverb most frequently quoted by Japanese themselves, and it doesn't have the meaning implied by "The squeaky wheel gets the oil."

When rules are imposed on group members from above, they sometimes rebel. For example, most junior high schools and high schools require students to wear uniforms and style their hair in certain ways; they enforce those rules. Some students object and make their objections a civil rights issue, sometimes going to court to assert their right to choose their own hair style, for instance. At times they are supported by parents, fellow students, and teachers. The more usual situation is for schools to use students to bring pressure to bear on the nonconformists, making these rules ones that are imposed by peers and thus harder to resist. Most students feel that such constraints are necessary. In this and many other contexts, Japanese do feel that their peers in a group are an unwelcome constraining force. Individuals must contend with a general cultural bias that says that individuals are probably wisest in most cases to accept the judgment of the group about their behaviors and thoughts.

Certainly among the major concerns the Japanese themselves have about their schools is a problem known as *ijime*, "bullying." This occurs when children are singled out for mistreatment by their classmates. Almost always the reason given for such mistreatment is that the victim is "different." There is a general feeling that difference would naturally call forth aggressive behaviors from other members of the group, that the simplest way to resolve the problem would be for the "different" child to stop being different. Often, however, even a child who is willing to conform is not able to. One can't change the fact that one's parents come from a different part of Japan or that one has lived overseas, for example. In some cases children seem to try hard to conform but find their efforts rejected.

Since by Japanese thinking both kinds of group structure, vertical and amorphous, are in some ways "unnatural," or difficult for human beings, something must be done to make participation in groups and subordination to groups palatable. The notion of *amae* is invoked to characterize the emotional ties and behaviors that make a vertically ordered set of dissimilar individuals into a tolerable group for its members. *Amae* is the feeling of being lovingly dependent on someone else and the behaviors that such a feeling produces. The prototype vertical group is the *ie*, the family, with its members of different ages, sexes, and responsibilities. In the family a new member, an infant, learns to appreciate the advantages of membership in the group through learning *amae*. The feelings of being recognized as an individual with one's own likes, dislikes, and propensities, of having a will that counts and is not arbitrarily thwarted, of having the power to give back these feelings to other members of the family or to withhold them, become the grounds on which individuals are believed to come inevitably to prefer group membership, even with its demands and disadvantages, to solitary independence and isolation. It is in the nature of human beings to respond in these ways, according to Japanese thinking. *Amae* is often expressed as dependence, as letting someone else take care of you, letting someone else make decisions for you, feeling that what someone else wants for you is indeed what you want for yourself.

To Western observers the process by which modern Japanese mothers teach their children *amae* seems like indulgence. They teach children that their desires will not be ignored by giving in to children's desires, when persuasion seems ineffective. They teach children about their power over other members of the family by letting them exercise that power, even hitting, kicking, and yelling at their mothers. Adults who have to handle a child throwing a temper tantrum are likely to offer candy as a bribe, or cajole and persuade children to stop, or simply give in to the child's demands. These actions are not seen as spoiling them, but as pulling children into the human relationships that are important in life.

Only when they are convinced that human relationships are essential to their well-being and happiness can children face the inevitable constraints on their individuality that being a member of a group entails.

It is at preschool and school that one confronts both the joy and the pain of a group of peers, a nonhierarchical group.

(This is an idealized version of child rearing approaches in modern Japanese families, especially those of wage and salary earners. By all reports, household heads in *ie* that were economically central were less hesitant to invoke authority and power to induce members to behave as the head decided. Mothers and caretakers who were economically busy or overworked had less time and fewer resources for indulgence of children.

I would also like to stress that in my experience Japanese toddlers and children are not less well behaved than Americans, either. In the areas of behavior that are important to their parents, they are at least as compliant as American children. I don't see more temper tantrums in the grocery stores in Japan than at home. I'd rather take a Japanese toddler along to do a series of errands than an American one. Japanese children learn polite greeting behavior, learn to say "thank you" and to follow rules of deportment in public places—how to handle their clothes, bodies, and voices—very well.)

Amae is not appropriate behavior within a peer group, but the experience of *amae* and the ability to learn *amae* are seen as indispensable in preparing children to adopt the behaviors of a peer group. *Preschool in Three Cultures,* by Tobin, Wu, and Davidson (1989), outlines the connections Japanese make between *amae* behavior and the behaviors appropriate with peers. Their book details the approach taken to one child at the preschool described. This boy, Hiroki, appears to the Western observers to be a problem, a troublemaker. He ignores teachers' instructions and consistently tries to draw attention to himself through joking, storytelling, and sexual and scatological antics. He is aggressive toward other children, taking toys, interfering with their play, and hitting and kicking them, and he does not cooperate in chores. He is also lively, inventive, and entertaining.

The consistent approach taken by the teachers to this child, as a matter of policy as well as inclination, is to ignore his misbehavior, to do little or nothing to repress it, and to impress on other children that his behavior to them is their problem, to be solved by them. The other children try a variety of approaches, from mediation, to ignoring him, to returning his aggression. Teachers refrain from helping with these strategies or evaluating them.

What is the explanation for Hiroki's behavior? Because his mother is dead, he has not had as much practice in *amae* as other children, he "doesn't know how to receive care and attention" (Tobin, Wu, and Davidson 1989:27), and so he is less convinced that social relationships are worth self-sacrifice and less skilled at self-denial for the sake of the group. Nevertheless, the teachers feel that he is a valuable member of the group, that the others are lucky to have such a lively, interesting classmate, and that the lure of their companionship is the most effective socialization tool available. The other children will benefit from learning to deal with a difficult group member, too. His teachers share the absolute conviction expressed by other preschool teachers that they have never encountered a child who genuinely prefers to be solitary—though some realize this sooner than others. They feel that isolation as a punishment or control technique would be self-defeating in his case: his problem stems from being too isolated. Hiroki has problems in a peer group because he has not sufficiently experienced *amae* in the vertical family setting.

Amae is the sugar that makes the medicine of belonging to a vertical, hierarchical group easier to swallow. For peer groups, the intrinsic rewards of not being isolated and of participating in social relationships are the incentive for belonging. The inherent disadvantages of belonging to a group are offset by the rewards of sociability and also by a certain self-restraint in what the members of the group demand of each other. Restraint in demands ameliorates the intrinsic disadvantages of being part of a group. But things can go wrong in groups that rely on self-restraint to govern themselves; self-restraint mechanisms don't work without a lot of effort on the part of group members and "leaders."

The rotating leadership roles provided in schools are thought to guide children to the conclusion that because they would like others to be cooperative when they are leaders, they should cooperate when they are not leaders. More generally, the empathy gained as a participant in a group is thought to lead children to be tolerant of each other, because each child needs toleration for his or her individuality. Teachers explicitly talk about this interpretation of school life to students, in both formal and informal situations. Westerners are likely to think these are not the only conclusions children could come to and that there is a great danger that some children will use this situation to become too dominant, to tyrannize others. Such children in Japan are seen as "not yet understanding" social life; continued exposure to group life and continued interpretation by teachers and peers will result in their better understanding.

Possibly another reason that Japanese feel groups can be oppressive is that they tend to belong to few groups, but ones that occupy a lot of time and psychological space—groups that have a tendency to become "total institutions." Not all Japanese people belong to such groups, but school groups are ones with these tendencies, and everyone is affected by them for what seem at the time to be many long years. Because school groups and the employment groups of modern white-collar workers, as well as traditionally organized economic groups such as villages and craftsmen's organizations, demand many hours of one's time and become the basis of recreational activities as well as education or work, nearly all of life for many years, for many people, is lived in the context of one dominant group.

One of the ways in which life experiences differ most in Japan is in the extent to which individuals find their lives enmeshed with that of some group. Most women's lives exclude them from all-encompassing group memberships, because they work in the context of their own small families, or perhaps marginally as part-timers, nonregular employees, or temporaries in other outside employment contexts. Many occupations for men are also not carried out in groups that are demanding or enveloping. Some people deliberately seek out such livelihoods, and some fall into them less purposely. In the setting of domineering groups, the self-restraint of the group in terms of how much participation and conformity is demanded becomes extremely important. Japanese seem to rely on the empathy gained as a group member to monitor this: don't demand from other members what you would not like to have demanded from you. This is a fragile mechanism, however, that seems to many Japanese at times not to work as well as it should; it sometimes breaks down totally, as in the case of *ijime*, "bullying."

One can see in Japanese schools certain practices of teachers and children that encourage a laissez-faire, undemanding attitude toward group members' behavior. The case of Hiroki, cited above, who was never isolated or treated as an outsider, no matter what he was did, is one example. The sort of minimal participation required in group calisthenics that I saw in both elementary schools and preschools is another. Teachers' resolute treatment of various activities as group activities that by definition encompass everyone, even when some children are clearly not participating, is another. Even if Hiroki was busy singing TV commercials and acting them out while everyone else was still filling in the pages of the workbook, he was right there with everyone else, a "part of the group."

I never saw teachers delay a class activity while they coerced attention from one or two students, for instance. Those who don't participate simply get left behind, without comment. They "naturally" prefer being with the group and eventually come to participate in a timely fashion. In contrast, it is common practice for American teachers to interrupt a whole class in progress to scold a single child who is late in arriving or needs to leave the room or is doing something other than the teacher-designated task. These children thus become the focus of class and teacher attention rather than something going on at the undesirable periphery of the group. They dominate the group rather than being treated as a marginal part of it.

It is because being part of and managing unordered, nonvertical groups is so difficult that Japanese are convinced so much effort to learn this skill, in the educational settings of schools, is necessary and desirable. It is not because such skills come naturally to children or adults that schools adopt them and teach techniques for living and participating in them, but because they are so "unnatural."

REACTIONS

It is the Japanese who live in Japan, in a social structure that includes both the hierarchical and the amorphous groups described here, with their particular demands and rewards; it is they who make the real judgments about the value of their cultural patterns and the socialization practices in schools, families, and other institutions that reproduce their patterns of thought, feeling, and behavior. For foreigners living in Japan, however, and especially those who are enmeshed in a Japanese milieu as we were, and most especially as Sam and Ellen were, this is an area of Japanese culture where we feel compelled to make judgments, to ask moral questions about how life "ought" to be, and to try to understand what it would be like really to be Japanese and to have to live life in the context of this social structure.

Our reactions to Japanese groups, their demands, and their rewards are determined by an implicit "compared to what?" question. Are Japanese groups more rewarding, more constraining, than whatever groups we are most familiar or most comfortable with? This is not an easy question to answer, nor is it easy to decide how we would go about establishing a reliable answer.

There are certainly indications in Western fiction, biographies, and autobiographies that many people experience Western groups as being demanding, as infringing on individual freedom and self-expression. We talk about the difficulties of responding to "peer pressure" that our children encounter; we reflect on the limitations on our own actions that our families and social situations impose on us, and we long sometimes to be able to be more independent. We sometimes experience belonging to groups in our own culture as unwelcome restrictions. In the literature of the Western world, however, the pain of being excluded from groups is equally evident. Many of us can remember unhappy experiences of being left out, too. On the social level, commentators have written that the loss of community, of encompassing group membership, is the source of many social problems and much individual unhappiness: such groups can cause pain both for members and for those excluded. When our feelings and attitudes about groups in our own experience are so divided, perhaps it is not surprising that our reactions to Japanese groups and "groupism" are ambivalent, too.

Sam and Ellen felt the advantages of belonging to their school groups in Japan. They were treated as members of the group by teachers and students, not excluded from activities or roles either because they were incompetent or because they were foreigners. They both say they were not bullied or discriminated against because they were different. Ellen loved (her word) to be the daily leader for class activities. Sam was expected to participate fully in all activities, even ones like calligraphy in which he had had no previous experience. His New Year's calligraphy was exhibited along with everyone else's. He cared enough to practice a little during the vacation and to produce acceptable samples of brush writing for the class display. He helped write the program for the class performance day and practiced his music enough to be able to play with his group. His abilities at Sports Day were appreciated.

Their experiences of being part of the school group were mostly positive. They were happy to go off to school each morning (well, 95 percent of the time); they lingered with their friends after school and dawdled with them on the way home; they were happy to encounter classmates outside of school. They did not expect to be bullied or to be disliked, and they didn't feel unpopular or that they were picked on. It is only accurate to point out, however, that they knew they were going to be in Japan only for one year and that their friends and teachers knew this too. The pressures to conform were much less than those applied to Japanese who live their entire lives in the Japanese context. Their experience is not a fully accurate guide to what Japanese children are subject to. Sometimes the strain of not knowing the language led them to avoid after-school activities with other children. They always knew that they could escape from Japanese life in the end, and I let them stay home from school on a few days when I knew they weren't really sick. On balance, though, I think it was the positive aspects of being included in school life that made the year a good one for them, not the knowledge that they would only have to tolerate living in Japan for a limited period.

5

A Working Vacation
and Special Events

SUMMER VACATION?

We had arrived in Japan near the end of June and had Sam and Ellen enrolled in school by the first week of July, so they had been in school only for a few weeks when summer vacation began. In Japan, since the school year runs from April 1 until the following March, summer vacation comes at the end of the first third of the school year. It was preceded by a flurry of newsletters from school, several notices from each classroom teacher, and a long letter from the principal himself. There was information about homework assignments, proper leisure time activities, regulation of living habits, suitable clothing, the date of the school meeting in the middle of the vacation, the schedule of swimming lessons, warnings about bicycle and fireworks safety, and for perhaps the first time this year, warnings about small children and the dangers of kidnapping. (There had recently been three disappearances of five-year-old girls near here, one later found dead. People were upset and somewhat at a loss as to how to react. Japanese children had not been taught before this to be wary of strangers.)

I tended to regard the information and suggestions about food, bedtimes, clothing, and so on as irritating and intrusive, probably partly because it was hard for me to read it in Japanese. But I was told by a Japanese friend when I complained about it that this is a sign of the genuine, all-embracing concern that the school feels about its students.

The attitude that seemed to be expressed in these communiqués was that summer vacation is a period of fun, of excitement, and of danger. The danger arises from the possibility that the summer vacation will involve a change of routine and that the goals and habits established through hard work and vigilance in the previous months will be eroded. A change in routine is also felt to be dangerous for one's health, as are going to strange places and being among crowds of people, things likely to happen during the summer vacation.

A number of conditions help to minimize the dangers, however. First, this long vacation is not so long—six weeks, as opposed to twelve weeks or more in American schools. Second, very few families take vacation trips together during this time, since people who are employed full time seldom take more than two or three days in a row off from work, even though they are entitled to more. Families are most likely to take a few days to return to relatives' houses for the mid-summer holiday *Obon*, when the spirits of the ancestors return to their homes for three days.

Third, if one followed the school recommendations for daily living during vacation, children would get up and go to bed at their usual times, eat regular meals, have a scheduled time for homework and other activities, follow a timetable for accomplishing their homework assignments, and generally not succumb to chaos. It was never clear to me how many of these guidelines families actually followed. The school's suggestion that children not get together to play from 8:00 A.M. to 10:00 A.M. did seem to be adhered to; their suggestion that children not play outdoors between 1:00 P.M. and 3:00 P.M. was often not followed; and the admonition to wear a hat when playing outdoors was universally ignored.

The most important device to keep children on the straight and narrow is the homework. I culled out of all the written materials the homework assignments, and they seemed formidable. Had I been faced in America with the prospect of getting kids to do all this during a "vacation," I would have contemplated changing schools. The workload seemed an imposition on all of us. Summer vacation was going to be a major challenge to me in my effort to be a *kyoiku mama*.

Ellen, as a first grader, had the following assignments: First, there was a booklet of assignments in reading and math, with spelling exercises and addition and subtraction problems to do, practice in telling time, and handwriting. Children were expected to read at least three books and do picture reports on them, illustrating something about the book and their own reactions to it. For music there was a book of fifteen songs to practice on the *pianika* (an instrument that is blown into like a recorder but played with a piano-like keyboard). For physical education there were swimming lessons scheduled at the school on fifteen different days; students were required to attend at least five sessions.

For arts and crafts each child was to do a project of constructing some toy or useful object, and the result was to be taken to school for display. One of the newsletters that came home from school gave suggestions for this project. They all involved using a hammer and nails to make such things as a boat, a stand for flower vases, and a simple pinball game.

Each child was to make a collection, label it, and set it up for display. Different flowers, stones, seashells, or insects were suggested, but other choices were encouraged. Children were to draw three pictures of their vacation activities and take them to school to be displayed.

Each first-grade student also had a science project, keeping records on the growth of a morning-glory plant. In fact, it seemed to me that nearly every first-grade child in Japan was nourishing and observing a morning-glory plant, that year and probably every year. Friends would say, "Ah yes, Ellen is in first grade. Does she have a morning glory?" There was a sheet giving the proper format for recording measurements of the plant's growth, weather records, and when buds, flowers, and seeds appeared and how many there were.

Each child was also to do some other "independent research." Every bookstore had helpful materials about this. We bought a book of first-grade project suggestions that outlined twenty-eight different projects with clear instructions and materials lists, all written so that first graders could read it. Most projects, it seemed to me, were within the capabilities of a motivated first grader with a helpful mother willing to tolerate some mess; they did not require much money.

The last major category of activities was helping around the house. Japanese children do few or no chores at home; they are busy, and mothers often feel it's easier to do the work themselves. But during this long vacation, when they have so much free time, the school feels they should help their mothers. For first graders the suggested activities included laundry, especially washing the school clothes and shoes, folding laundry before it is put away, and ironing simple things like handkerchiefs. Cleaning the bathtub was also suggested, as were sweeping the sidewalk, going to the store on errands, and polishing the floor.

The school provided a chart to record one's daily activities in the categories of studying and helping at home; more elaborate and colorful ones are often given away by the bookstores where one purchases the materials needed for the vacation school assignments.

In case your first grader has lots of extra time (unlikely, given these assignments), a number of other worthwhile activities are suggested in the school bulletins. For first graders these include making a *hiragana* (alphabet) game, making a set of musical instruments for the whole family, making mobiles to hang at home, making jewelry from household items, making a map of the neighborhood, and keeping a weather record, along with a report of the emotions and feelings that are stimulated by various aspects of the weather. Then there are various contests children can enter, which involve designing a postcard, writing a letter or a postcard, calligraphy, or writing a composition and drawing a picture inspired by the seaside.

For Sam, in fifth grade, the pattern of summer vacation homework was much the same. There were drills to be done in math and Japanese, a construction project, two science projects, book reports, daily help around the house, swimming lessons, and contests to enter. Again, both the school and commercial publications provided help and suggestions. But there were many fewer communications from the classroom teacher about summer vacation, probably for two reasons: they are less necessary for students and families who have had several years of experience with summer vacation, as first graders have not, and also Sam may have been less conscientious about bringing everything home.

Sam and Ellen and I made some effort to do almost all of these assignments. In addition, the children had some Japanese lessons, and they both learned to read the Japanese syllabary—a total of 103 symbols sufficient for reading anything in Japanese that is written in the syllabary. For Ellen this meant she could read all her school materials, though she often didn't understand what she was reading. By fifth grade the syllabary is augmented with *kanji,* Chinese ideographs, so Sam could not read his materials.

How did we do? First of all, it seemed like a burden and an imposition to all of us. Second, I didn't realize early enough that there were special prescribed formats for a number of these assignments, such as science projects and drawings and book reports, and I also took what I am sure the teachers regarded as a typically careless American attitude toward some of the standardization. I tend to think that if the observations of the morning glory are done, and are correct, it doesn't matter much what kind of paper they're recorded on. This contrasts with a more Japanese notion that if you're doing it you might as well do it right—in a format that ensures nothing is forgotten (and why not a format that someone else has figured out?), neatly, on nice paper, showing the value you place on this effort and showing consideration for the audience. Even children's summer homework is real work, deserving of the best materials and the best presentation.

This was my first experience with summer vacation homework in Japan. Some projects I thought were optional were really "required," and some aspects of the formats for drawings and reports were less open to variation than I took them to be. I could have known more about these if I had asked more questions of friends. At that stage in our visit, however, I was feeling that I had been an incredible nuisance to everyone I encountered in Japan, and I didn't enjoy the feeling of incompetence and childishness that having to ask so many questions gave me. So I didn't ask as much as I should have. Our homework suffered from it.

Soon after the fall term of school started, when the many projects done over the summer were on display in the classrooms, there was a Parents' Visiting Day attended by about two-thirds of the first-grade mothers in Ellen's class. A large part of the banter between mothers focused on how well each mother had accomplished these projects. There was some competition over who had "helped" her child do the best job, some resentment over having had to do these projects, and some discomfort over whether mothers should participate so heavily in children's schoolwork.

Somehow or other, though, we did manage to find vacation time very different from regular school days. Though no one I knew broke the school's recommendation that children not contact each other for play between 8:00 A.M. and 10:00 A.M., children did play a lot during the rest of the day and in the evening. A lot of this play was more unsupervised than many American children enjoy these days. Because of the physical safety of children in Japan and because they are generally welcome in public places, children are free to come and go as they please, without adults feeling they need to know just where the children are at every minute. So a friend's fifth-grade boy, who lives near a public swimming pool, would leave home about ten in the morning to do whatever he wanted until five o'clock. He might spend time at the pool, go to a friend's house, ride his bicycle, and go back to the pool, but until five o'clock no one checked up on his activities or whereabouts. Even younger elementary school children had this freedom.

Sam's favorite play activity was fireworks, sold in many stores in Japan and intended for children to use—even the school only recommends that they be careful in doing so. These fireworks include not only sparklers, but also bottle rockets, fountains, and other delights forbidden to nearly all American children. Almost every night of the summer one can hear and see fireworks going off in Japanese neighborhoods. I let Sam use them, in spite of misgivings about safety and cost. I remembered how much fun it was to set them off with my cousins when I was young, and I'm not sure I could have kept Sam away from such a desirable activity. Fireworks are also part of the summer festivals of many towns and temples. We went to the city of Urawa's display—the best fireworks I have ever seen, better than the one in Washington, D.C., on the Fourth of July during the Bicentennial.

We also went with friends who have children near Sam's and Ellen's ages to their grandmother's house in a rural area of Nagano prefecture. My friend's conversation revealed some of the advantages she saw in a week-long stay there for her children. It was nice to eat vegetables straight from the garden, to go to the dairy farm to buy milk, to work in the garden, to see the stars unobscured by city lights at night, to hear the sounds of frogs and insects, to observe farming activities in the fields, to walk along country roads with no traffic, and to spend time with the family instead of with friends in the neighborhood. Hiking in the mountains was an easy thing to do and didn't involve a long train ride to get to a hiking place. All of us, adults and children, did enjoy these things; the pace of life was refreshingly different from the school term in the city.

The fifth- and sixth-grade boys in this family had the same sorts of homework assignments ours did (and they did them all), but their family found the time to go to Nagano for a week, though the father, a junior high school teacher, was away supervising a trip for his students part of the time. Each of the boys also had an additional trip away from home. The sixth grader's class went to the beach as a school group for four days, and the fifth grader went to a private camp, with horseback riding and other camping activities.

In spite of all the homework, then, this summertime vacation was indeed a vacation in the American sense, a time when daily schedules became more relaxed, when the demands of school were greatly diminished, when children had more freedom, and when their parents encouraged a delight in the moment itself, not emphasizing the serious business of preparing for adulthood.

I couldn't help contrasting this summer vacation with my memories of summer as an American child, however. My (probably distorted) memories are of a long, long, period of time with very little structure, of boredom but also of unlimited time to do just what I wanted. I could read for hours on end, play hide-and-seek until after dark night after night, be at the swimming pool all day with friends, or play the piano without practicing for the next lesson. I could decide on the spur of the moment, without planning, what to do. It was the spontaneous, self-generated, unsupervised aspect of these activities that made summer vacation so wonderful.

Japanese adults, too, remember periods of time like this in their childhood. Even Japanese educators remember them and feel that Japanese children have lost a valuable part of life in having so many aspects of it controlled by home and school. They recall a vision of village life in which unsupervised groups of children of varying ages spent their leisure time "playing," doing activities they invented, at their pace, with their own rules. Not only were these times fun, but looking back, adults feel that important lessons about inventiveness and independence, getting along together and tolerance for individuals, were learned.

In 1967–68 Thomas Johnson (1975) studied the peer group activities of the boys in fourth through ninth grades in a village about sixty miles west of Tokyo, including their summer activities. These boys all automatically belonged to the village boys' club, which had an official existence with government funding, a clubhouse, and an official adult advisor. (He came to one club meeting in the eighteen months Johnson was an observer of the group.) This context seemed to make the parents feel the boys were safe. The boys were very concerned to behave well enough that they did not attract any adult attention to themselves or their activities, and they succeeded very well. Parents reported that sometimes their boys would be away from home for two or three days at a time, at the clubhouse, eating and sleeping there, sometimes stopping at home or at a friend's house for food.

The boys planned and carried out an elaborate three-day camping trip but spent most of their time in more mundane activities like baseball and raiding watermelon patches. Ten to twenty hours of preparation would go into a foray to get two watermelons to share, watermelons that would have been given had they asked, or which they could have bought with club funds. They kept track of whose gardens had been stolen from, in order to be "fair" to the owners. Homework was a minor activity, apparently confined to frantic efforts the last two or three days before school started.

This degree of freedom is difficult to achieve in the urban settings where most Japanese children now live, and the school homework seems deliberately designed to make such a loose structure impossible. Feeling they cannot have their urban children just wandering around the neighborhood for days on end as village children do, parents are amenable to the lure of more structured activities, whether they are academic enrichment, homework, lessons, or supervised athletic activities.

Ordinary Japanese adults and parents, as well as teachers and educators, are caught between two conflicting views of summer vacation and life for children. On the one hand, education is seen as crucially important for the success of individuals and the nation. There is so much to learn and so little time, that vacation is an unwelcome intrusion into a serious business. Teachers feel this way about all children; individual parents feel that because everyone else is working full time, vacation or not, their children must work equally hard not to miss out and fall behind the competition.

On the other hand, childhood is fleeting, and not everything can be learned in school; surely this constant supervision and adult agenda setting will make children more dependent, less able to act on their own initiative, less healthy, less able to develop and rely on their own inner resources. Neither of these conflicting views has been totally victorious in the battlefield of summer vacation, but it's my impression that the "formal education is important" position is gaining the upper hand.

Sam and Ellen had just completed a school year before we came to Japan and definitely felt they had a school vacation coming to them. They felt the homework was too much—not too difficult, just too much. They liked the increasing feeling of competence that learning to read the syllabary gave them, and they liked the swimming lessons. They read (in English) with more pleasure than usual, and more than usual, in part because they had fewer friends than at home and television was not so attractive. They liked the fireworks, riding their bicycles, and the trip to Nagano. They liked not having a bedtime or a set time to get up. They liked the less regimented, less scheduled life.

I liked all these things, too, and would have enjoyed them even more if I hadn't felt compelled to urge Sam and Ellen to make a somewhat credible showing in the homework assignments. They disliked my pushing them to do it and reminding them, and I resented having to do it. Still, taken all in all, those six weeks were a vacation; they gave us the chance to accomplish the second stage of settling into life in a new city and a new country, as well as to have some experiences that were pleasant in themselves.

SPORTS DAY

No sooner had summer vacation ended than the schedule for September was sent home, with the announcement that Sports Day would take place on October 1. Sports Day is a major event in the school year and is the model for similar events held for younger children in preschools and for adults in various organizations, often those connected with employment. These events have been going on for many years, so parents and grandparents all have memories of their own participation in sports days, and many parts of the event have become traditional and unquestioned in format.

Sports Day at Okubo Higashi was set for a Sunday with the expectation that many parents would attend. During the month of September, some time every day at school was spent in preparing for this event, and four full days were scheduled for the whole school to practice together. Throughout September notices came home with more information about the equipment needed by children in different grades, the events they would participate in, lunch and transportation arrangements, the rain date, and the schedule for the day.

Fortunately, Sunday, October 1, was a beautiful day, sunny and just warm enough that jackets were not needed. The walking group from our buildings left at 7:20, because the children were supposed to be at school at 8:00 to get ready for ceremonial events that started at 8:30. The opening ceremonies began as all the students paraded onto the field in front of the school to music provided by the school marching band. Students and audience listened to the principal and several other people give short speeches. Everyone was encouraged to try hard and to be careful. Everyone sang a Sports Day song, and the huge loving cup that is awarded to the winning team was displayed. This ceremony was all orchestrated by a sixth grader who announced each speaker and called the school to stand to attention, bow, stand at ease, and begin the first real event of the day, calisthenics by the whole student body. Following this, the students left the playing field for their assigned seating positions by grade and team color around the field.

For Sports Day the students of the school were divided into four teams: red, blue, green, and yellow. Students wore headbands of their team color on their caps. They were all wearing their physical education uniforms, which have a stripe of their class color and their name written in large characters on the shirt. Except for the first graders, each classroom had members on each team.

The schedule of events was as follows:

1. Calisthenics, whole school
2. Sixty-meter race, third grade
3. Race, first grade
4. Jump-rope dance, second grade
5. Obstacle race, sixth grade
6. Ninety-meter race, fourth grade
7. Pom-pom dance, third grade
8. One-hundred-meter race, fifth grade
9. Fifty-meter race, second grade
10. Animal Land dance, first grade
11. Pulling poles, fourth grade
12. Relay race, sixth grade
13. Horse battle, fifth grade
14. Short race, five-year-olds
15. Teachers' relay-obstacle race
16. Folk dance, whole school
Lunch
17. Cheers and songs for each team
18. Tug of war, PTA
19. Tug of war, third grade
20. Capture the pole, sixth grade

21. Ball in basket, first grade
22. Fireworks dance, fourth grade
23. Big ball relay race, second grade
24. Gymnastics routine, fifth and sixth grades
25. Four-color relay race (batons), third through sixth grades
26. Calisthenics, whole school
Awarding of prize, closing exercises

I looked at this list of events and thought that we'd be there for a long day, but everything ran on schedule, and it was all over at 2:50.

Each child participated in seven of the events (those in the last relay race in eight), and band members also played three times during the day. So although there was a lot of waiting time for each child, there was a lot of doing time, too, and a lot of moving around to get into the right place at the right time for different events.

Everyone participated in several different types of events. One was whole-school activities: opening and closing calisthenics and the folk dance just before lunch. There were also team events for each grade, such as the third-grade tug of war or the horse battle by the fifth graders. In this event the forty-five members of each color team divide themselves into groups of five, four of whom put their arms around each others' shoulders to support a fifth person who sits on their shoulders wearing a paper samurai hat. The point of the game is to protect your own paper hat while trying to capture or dislodge those of other teams. The team with the most of their own hats left at the end wins. Several games such as this one looked potentially dangerous to me and not like activities that schools would encourage. I didn't see anyone get visibly hurt, though.

A third type of event for everyone was a noncompetitive group dance. The first graders did a dance imitating various animals to music, the second graders did a jump-rope routine to music, and the fifth and sixth graders together did a long and impressive gymnastics routine of group balancing and pyramid formations. Some people say that girls like these events but boys don't; I saw no obvious lack of enthusiasm in the boys' performances.

Finally, everyone participated in at least one race, organized by grade level and scored by team color. In this school there are about 1,000 students, about 160 in each grade. Okubo Higashi School knows how you can get 160 children to run a race efficiently. First, all of them are lined up by height, girls in one line and boys in another. Then each line is divided into groups of six, which run the specified distance against each other. They line up at the starting line, are set off by a racing pistol shot, and run to the finish line. At the finish line, a group of monitors wearing vests numbered from one to six are waiting to escort the runners to areas for the first-place runners, second-place runners, and so forth and to record the teams of the first-, second-, and third-place runners of each group of six. Since the next cohort of runners will start very soon, more than one set of monitors are working. After everyone has run, the first-, second-, and third-place runners of each cohort get a ribbon to wear on their wrist, and the scores for the four color teams are announced. There is no runoff or other recognition of individual performances. All this moves very quickly—it took less than ten minutes, from entering the field to leaving it, to run twenty-four cohorts of third graders through a sixty-meter race and announce the results.

Children seem to run very hard in these races, the girls as enthusiastically and skillfully as the boys. ("Did you see those big girls running?" asked Ellen that night. "Their boobs bounced. I'm not going to run like that when I'm big.") All the race events were done to music—very lively Western classical music: Rimsky-Korsakov, or the Lone Ranger overture, or a very fast rendition of Beethoven's "Ode to Joy." It must improve performance, as well as add to the general air of excitement and liveliness. As each cohort runs, a loudspeaker encourages the last-place runner, calling him by team color—"Red team, keep trying!"

The last race of the day was the only one involving selected participants. This was run as a relay race among the four color teams, and the contestants were the fastest runners of the third through sixth grades; only about 20 of the 160 or more students in each grade were chosen. The level of excitement and competition was very high during this race. It seemed like the high point of the day, but no recognition was given to any individual runners, and it's hard to discern individual performances in such a long relay race. Sam was able to talk that night about several boys he knew and how they did in this race, though.

Some of the events of the day were not for students. There was a relay race for the teachers, and all of them participated. One of the obstacles they each had to overcome in the race was determined by throwing a big die, introducing an element of chance that was not present in any other event. There was a tug of war for parents, with one team from each of the four named neighborhoods that send children to this school, and there was a race for five-year-olds who would be coming to the school the next year. They hadn't been coached for this event and seemed very unsure of how to do it or what the point was, but they were guided through the procedure by the principal and the first-grade teachers.

At the end of the day there were more short speeches. The highlight was the announcement of the official scores for the four teams, with the first- and second-place teams giving themselves big cheers, the winning team accepting the trophy for the year. In the closing speech appreciation was expressed for everyone's efforts, each grade's dance was acknowledged, and the day was declared a success.

The major impression created by Sports Day was the sense of lively, enthusiastic, competitive participation, culminating in the color teams' relay race near the end. Children are assigned to the different teams by their teachers, who attempt to make all the teams equal in ability. Children are not on the same color team every year, so these Sports Day teams are ones pulled together only for this one day, not ongoing groups. Each team has designated cheerleaders, both boys and girls, a set of cheers, and a team song. The cheerleaders were pretty active all day long during the competitive events. Score keeping for these events was treated quite seriously. Under a tent awning a team of adults were the official score keepers; they kept a running total of the scores for each team, relayed to a group of students on the second-floor balcony who posted large signs there throughout the day so that everyone knew how the scores stood as the meet progressed. Winning the prize for the team was clearly an incentive. The silver-colored loving cup is about three feet high, adorned with ribbons from previous years' winning teams. It is displayed throughout Sports Day, and for the rest of the year it is placed in a cabinet near the formal entrance to the school.

But there are also some curious features about the competitiveness involved in Sports Day. For one thing, as explained in the description of the races, there is never an individual winner identified. Second, there is no weighting of points for different events, so that the most skilled performances are not rewarded more. It felt to me that a great level of competitiveness was stirred up by the cheering, the music, and the vigorous participation, and then just fizzled out. No winners, and no resolution of the contests. Some individual students and some groups of students did do much better than others in all of these events, but there was no time at which their accomplishments were openly recognized. For races, for instance, there were no runoffs to determine who actually ran fastest in the fifth-grade race. These would have been easy enough to organize, but the possibility was just ignored. During later discussions at home, it became clear that somehow or other Ellen knew she was the fastest runner in her class, and Sam thought he was number three or four in the fifth grade. I asked many adults later why children worked so hard in these events when there were no prizes and no recognition for individuals. This question was greeted with looks of amusement and the counterquestion, "Why not?"

During calisthenics and other activities the general impression is that everyone is participating actively and correctly, but on closer inspection it can be seen that it's a little ragged (compared to the dances we saw five- and six-year-olds in China doing, for instance, not compared to grade school performances in the United States). No one gives the appearance of actively resisting any particular activity, and most students do most activities enthusiastically most of the time, but if there's some calisthenic exercise you don't much like doing, and you sort of go through the motions, no one will stop the group activities to make you do it right. If your shoe comes untied, you stop to fix it. If you trip in the jump-rope exercise, you just get untangled and go on. The whole set of activities moves along at a very brisk pace, and 100 percent compliance or participation or enthusiasm doesn't seem to be enforced. One result is that there's a lot of activity packed into short periods of time and relatively little time spent waiting by the more compliant or more organized pupils for the slower ones to be ready.

Even during the sixth-grade obstacle race, some kinds of noncompliance were tolerated. The last obstacle was to jump onto and over a fairly high set of wooden boxes. Some children didn't make it, but they and their teams were not penalized for failing to do it—everyone made some attempt. On the other hand, one boy forgot the somersault at the middle obstacle and went back to do that. In general those who made mistakes—missed a step in a dance, for instance—appeared to pick up and go on with equanimity and were certainly not singled out. The only exception may have been the encouraging remarks offered over the loudspeaker to the last-place runner in the races—I think I would have been embarrassed by them, but they may be felt as encouraging and helpful rather than derogatory. Overall, neither unusually good nor bad performances were overtly commented on.

I was very struck by how well organized everything was and how little teachers and adults seemed to be involved in running things. Early in the morning, students from the fifth and sixth grades were in charge of getting the physical apparatus set up—the score board, the goal posts, the entrance and exit gates from the field, the awnings and tables for the judges, the equipment for the different events. They stayed behind to put everything away at the end. The leaders of the opening and closing exercises were students, the people who fired the pistols for the races were students, the monitors who assigned places in the races were students. Except for the first and second grades, teachers did not take responsibility for getting groups of children into the right places at the right times for different events, and because each child participated in seven or more different events taking place at different times and in different group organizations, there was a lot of moving around "offstage." This all went very smoothly and unobtrusively. When children were waiting for their various turns, they sat in or near assigned seating areas, but they played together and sometimes went quietly to the sides of the playground to play in small groups. No one seemed to think this was amiss, and I didn't see any problems develop.

Teachers and schools have several objectives they want to accomplish through Sports Day besides having fun, a major and legitimate purpose, too. They want children to experience and practice cooperating in groups organized for specific endeavors. For this reason the teams involved in Sports Day do not correspond to other groups the students are used to working in, such as classroom groups. The students are prepared to run the day through long hours of practice, but then they are really left alone to do it in public. The teachers did not do a lot of coaching and prompting from the sidelines to be sure things ran smoothly. A whole month of preparation in school was spent to insure a day that was fun, was run by children, brought forth enthusiasm and effort from everyone, and recognized only group performances, not individuals, honoring only groups that would never operate again.

Sam and Ellen thought the day was fun and interesting, that the preparation was hard work, and that some events were challenging or even painful, such as being on the bottom of a pyramid in gymnastics, as Sam was.

THE TRIP TO AKAGI

September's big event was Sports Day, and October's was clearly going to be the fifth-grade trip to the Akagi Youth Nature Center. Akagi is a town in the mountains of Gunma prefecture about three and a half hours from Urawa by bus, where the Urawa board of education has established a nature study center. Sam's class, with the other four fifth-grade classes from Okubo Higashi, was going to spend two nights and three days there.

This trip gave us a chance to observe how 196 students with their chaperons prepare for an event like this—and to puzzle about the point of it all. My initial reaction was that there was a lot of work and preparation put into an event that turned out to have very little educational impact. I was probably wrong, as usual: a lot of effort was put into an event that had a different sort of educational import than I was expecting.

The first preparations for the children began in the home economics and practical arts class held twice a week. The project was to sew a knapsack to use while hiking at Akagi. Everyone purchased a kit from the school containing a printed quilted cloth, cord and fasteners, bias tape and needle and thread—everything needed for the project. The knapsacks were sewn by hand. They have a drawstring opening, finished seams on the inside, and binding on the open edges, with the drawstring also serving as shoulder straps. Sam's was light green with a print of cartoon dinosaurs. Years later it is still in use in our family for picnics and sleepovers, and it has stood up well; Sam did a good job of making it.

Everyone who travels in Japan carries some kind of pack or container for things one can't leave home without. For children this is an outlet for the expression of cuteness. Their backpacks or knapsacks are often in the form of animals or cartoon characters or decorated with elaborate appliqués. They can be bought but are also a favorite home sewing project for mothers, and sometimes a project of the mothers' group in preschools or elementary schools.

I have seen classes of two- to four-year-olds walking from a day care center to the local park for an hour's play, every child equipped with a cute knapsack. When children travel with adults on trains or buses, even one-year-olds often have a pack. I don't know what's in these all the time, but I do know what went to Akagi, because the directions about what to put in were included in the instructions for the trip.

For parents the first official preparations were at a meeting for parents (mothers) held at school during the day. Since all fifth graders in Urawa make this field trip each year, everyone knows that this will be on the agenda sometime during the year, and probably everyone but me had heard about trips made by other children. Mothers who attended the meeting signed in on a class sheet. (I was interested to see that it was a sheet for the whole year and there were spaces to record attendance for a number of events.) The principal and each of the four fifth-grade teachers spoke about the arrangements and purposes of the trip. I should have paid more attention to the announced purposes, because they turned out to be the real ones, too. They were reiterated in the written materials we were given.

The stated purposes of this trip were (1) to experience with one's own eyes and ears the natural beauty of Akagi and to see the plains below the mountains, (2) to strengthen body and soul by being in the mountains, and (3) by working and playing together, indoors and out, to experience the joy and importance of group living. In their talks, the teachers also stressed that for many children this would be an important experience in independence from their families. For many children, including Sam, it would be their first experience away from home with a big group for so long.

Mothers were asked to help prepare their children for the experience by making sure they could make decisions by themselves about what clothes to wear, according to activities and weather, that they could determine by themselves whether or not they were sick, that they could handle their own bedding, and (especially for girls) that they could do their own hair. A week before the trip each child had to take a stool sample to school for some kind of a health check; I never figured out what. We were also supposed to keep daily records of our child's temperature and send those to school a couple of days before the trip. Later we were told that the students were supposed to take a thermometer with them and take and record their temperatures seven times during the three days! All the food for the trip would be provided except a box lunch for the bus trip there, which children were to bring from home. The only written instructions about the lunch were that no cans or bottles were allowed.

During the question period, almost every question asked was about this box lunch. My puzzlement about this preoccupation with the lunch lasted for years, until I read Lois Peak's *Learning to Go to School in Japan,* where she discusses the role of the lunch from home at school (1991:90–94). She proposes that the home-packed lunch is a symbol of *amae* in an environment where *amae* conflicts with values of group participation. Because it is the focus of two conflicting sets of values, it is the topic of intense concern and much discussion. I think her analysis also sheds light on other topics that were more salient for Urawa mothers and teachers than I anticipated, for example, the concern with decisions about clothes and sickness, especially knowing whether or not you are sick.

In order to understand the importance of a lunch brought from home, it is helpful to consider the differences between home and school, a part of the world outside. According to Peak and other observers of Japanese childhood and domestic life, home and school are two very different kinds of places in Japan. Home is not a miniature society, and school is not a place for indulgent individualism. At home two important kinds of emotion and behavior are expected. One is *amae* and the other is "skinship." *Amae* is the feelings and behaviors appropriate between people who have a relationship of loving dependence based on an intense individual hierarchic bond between them.

Japanese do not think that infants are born knowing how to be loving dependents; teaching them this is the family's, especially the mother's, most important job. Usually, emphasis is put on the dependence of the child in this relationship, but I believe the mother becomes almost equally dependent for emotional support and validation on the child she teaches to feel and behave this way.

"Skinship" is a set of behaviors that enables people to feel *amae*. It refers to skin-to-skin contact, the close, intimate physical contact that is a feature of Japanese child rearing and family life. "Skinship" includes, for example, bathing together and sleeping close together. Practicing these behaviors in effect almost erases the skin barrier between isolated individuals such as a mother and her infant. What one body feels becomes accessible to the other. Thus, the ability of Japanese mothers to toilet train their children very early is partly a matter of being so tuned in to body cues from the child that the mother knows when the child is ready to urinate or defecate and so is able to hold an infant over the toilet to do it. Similarly, mothers' use of a hissing-sounding word to stimulate children to urinate means that the child is accepting and acting on the mother's perception of its physical needs. Mothers and children spend a lot of time in physical contact, sleeping together, bathing together, and nursing. Mothers seldom use child restraint devices such as infant seats, high chairs, or playpens, instead carrying their babies on their backs as they do housework. Even outdoors, strollers are less commonly used than in the United States. One of my favorite articles of Japanese material culture is the winter coat that fits over both mother and baby. When women carrying babies on their backs talk with one another, they always position themselves so that the babies are participants in the conversations. In the Japanese view of child rearing, the mother's job is to erase the gap between the infant and herself that exists at birth and to draw the child into a social relationship so rewarding that it will encourage the child to want the other social relationships that are the defining features of a truly human life.

Among the things that mothers (and other caretakers to a lesser extent) do for children to increase "skin" contact, is to dress and undress them, to wash them, to comb their hair, and to check on their body state and health, for example their temperature, fairly constantly. But the approved *amae* behavior of letting your mother decide whether you are hot or cold, tired or hungry or sick, is impossible if you're away on a school trip. Teachers are not substitute mothers; the responsibility for making and acting on such decisions must be passed to the children, not the teachers.

The box lunch is a bridge from home and *amae* to school and group life. Box lunches prepared by mothers are expected to be individual, appealing to the child, elaborately prepared, and presented as a symbol of the mother's attention to her own child. Box lunches are usually complicated affairs by American standards. They include rice and four to six other items of food, for example a bit of pickled vegetable, a slice of hard-boiled egg, two or three bites of vegetables boiled in soy sauce, and one or two bites of fried chicken or fish. There is usually some decoration included, a flower or a pretty leaf, or a design drawn on the rice with sesame seeds. One can buy magazines illustrating how to make nutritious, appealing box lunches for young children; they sell well. The magazines and other "authorities" on rearing children say that the lunch should contain food cooked especially for the occasion, not a collection of leftovers.

Food that children get at school lacks these qualities. It is the same for each child, and starting in preschool the child is expected to eat everything, without regard for individual likes and dislikes. In preschool children are encouraged/forced to eat everything their mothers send, and mothers are encouraged to include some problematic items in their lunch boxes. (The year Sam was in kindergarten in Japan, he and I both scored a lot of points because I included raw carrots in his lunch, and he ate them. This is the least favorite food of Japanese children and many adults.) In elementary school, the school kitchen prepares the food, and children are encouraged/forced to eat everything.

The mothers' emotional concern with the box lunch for the first day, revealed in the number of questions at the preparation meeting, was in effect a concern for the degree to which they would be allowed to indulge their children at the beginning of this period of group life, life with no *amae*.

Other behaviors, health monitoring and dressing children properly, are also part of *amae*. In order to enable mothers to participate, if only by preparations and vicariously, in keeping their children clothed and well, detailed information about the weather at Akagi was included in the booklets for parents—a chart of the monthly average high and low temperatures and the average number of days of sunshine, cloudy weather, rainfall, and snow, to be compared with the information given for Urawa. The thermometer that children took along and the chart for keeping track of their temperatures were also, I think, meant to be reassuring to parents, to make them feel that children had the needed information to gauge their own state of health.

I think this symbolism accurately reflects Japanese feelings and pre-occupations, but in practice, by the time children are in fifth grade their mothers are no longer routinely dressing them, washing them, and making all the decisions about their feelings of health. It seemed to me that children had great freedom to make such decisions them-selves without parental nagging. At the time I didn't believe that mothers could still be combing their fifth-grade daughters' hair either, but later, as the mother of a fifth-grade daughter, I did it, for exactly the same reasons Japanese mothers do. It's legitimate, intimate body contact; neither of us was anxious to give it up, though by sixth grade Ellen refused to let me do it anymore. Sam also recalls that neither he nor anyone else in his sleeping room ever took their temperature and that teachers did sometimes make people dress sensibly. So the differ-ences in practices between home and school were not quite so extreme as the symbolism.

There was a symbolic bridge at the other end of the trip, too. The ¥9,000 each child paid for this trip included charges for transportation, food, and lodging, as might be expected, but also ¥1,000 for souvenirs. There was a shop at the nature center for buying these, and children used the allotted money to remember as many relatives as necessary. Sam brought home thoughtful gifts for each of us.

The purposes of the trip outlined for the mothers at their meeting, to enjoy nature, to strengthen body and soul, and to enjoy group life, determined the kinds of preparations that preceded it. The pleasure and the experience were the point of the expedition. There was no need to justify the trip by making it a means to do science experiments, for instance, or by requiring children to write compositions about it, or other activities that often accompany American field trips. The trip was an end, not a means to some other end.

Since the experience itself was important as a positive group life experience, tremendous preparation went into these aspects of the trip. Everything that was not individual was planned in advance, written down, and predictable. Written materials distributed to parents and children enabled everyone to carry out the necessary activities with no surprises or unpredictable demands. There were three lists of things to take in three printed pamphlets of information, one from school and two from the nature center. The list from school included P.E. hat, school name tag, free choice of clothes (suggested wear was jeans or long pants and long-sleeved shirts), a jacket, comfortable shoes, rain gear, the knapsack, five or six plastic sacks, something to sit on, towel, toilet paper (the standard little packages of Kleenex), gloves, pajamas, bellyband (optional), two sets of underwear, more than three pairs of socks, a towel, a toothbrush, toothpaste, soap, a comb (put these small things in a little bag), a sweater, a pack for carrying all this, the guide book for Akagi, a thermometer, pencils, an eraser, a pocket songbook, handkerchiefs, medicines one might need, such as antihistamines or dramamine, shoes for inside the building, a kerchief to wear while cleaning, a cleaning rag, an apron, a hat and a mask for those serving food, and the box lunch for the first day (no cans or bottles)—*name on everything*. Additions from the other lists: a notebook, newspaper, a water bottle, a warning about warm enough clothes, a hat, earmuffs, ski gloves, a flashlight, hand towels, colored pencils, a sketch book, postcards, a book, games.

Bringing all these things would assure that nearly any emergency could be met and that leisure moments could be filled by activities that students were equipped to carry out. We managed to get together all but a few items from these lists, and Sam carried it all in a large backpack we borrowed from friends. It added up to quite a few pounds of belongings in bulky packs and containers that the children had to handle alone. They had to walk to school the day of departure with all of it and manage it by themselves on the bus and at the center. The luggage compartment was used only for the teachers' gear. Most children carried everything themselves, but a few mothers came running after with some forgotten item, usually the water bottle.

The buses were scheduled to leave at 8:30, and the children were to be at school at 8:00 to get ready. At that time there was a brief meeting to introduce the college students who were going to help chaperon and to get everyone lined up, and so on. About a third of the children's mothers had come along to see them off; the principal was there, too, being helpful, pointing out that bicycles should be moved out of the path of the buses, for example. The buses pulled away from the school at 8:31.

Both students and parents had detailed schedules for each day's activities. The second day's schedule is given below, translated from the one in Sam's guidebook.

DAY 2

6:30	get up
	wash
	put away bedding
7:00	cleaning assignments
	take temperature
7:30	morning meeting
8:00	breakfast

         pick up box lunches
         outside play
9:00   hiking—a choice of several trails; what to put in the knap-
         sack: towel, jacket, rain gear, lunch, water bottle, snack,
         gloves, something to sit on, garbage container, toilet paper;
         in case of rain: activities at the center
3:30   return to Nature Center
         milk and snack
5:00   evening meeting
         flag lowering
5:30   supper
6:30   study meeting
8:00   baths
         journal
         letters
9:00   get ready for bed
9:30   go to bed
10:00 lights out

This schedule doesn't begin to reveal just how much was preplanned. The booklet that each child had also listed which children would sleep in each room, what duties they were assigned, when they would bathe, where they would sit in the dining hall, where they would sit on the bus and at the first evening's campfire meeting, when they were expected to be on duty to do their assigned chores (for example, the food helpers were to clean the water bottles at 8:00 P.M. on day two), and full menus for each meal.

This seemed to me like overkill, but it did mean that teachers didn't have to keep reminding people of what came next, what they should be getting ready for. Maybe it was reassuring for children to have this much predictability. Several years later our family took a long trip to Australia with a complicated itinerary. Sam and Ellen asked me questions a dozen times a day about where we were going, when we would change planes, where we would sleep. I finally remembered the trip to Akagi and prepared for each of them a schedule of everything I knew about flights, stopovers, hotel names, and so on. They kept them in their packs, consulted them often, and stopped bothering me.

Each child at Akagi was assigned to a work group, and each group had specified duties. For some groups, such as those responsible for helping with food, the recorded duties were no more detailed than that. There is such a group at school too, and by fifth grade everyone understands what jobs must be accomplished by this group and can easily organize themselves to get them done. For others, such as the recreation group, much more specific assignments were included in the guidebook. Who would lead the songs at the morning and evening meetings, who would think up games for the bus, who would play the part of the fire spirit at the campfire: all these were individually assigned to recreation group members.

As a result of this organization and planning, the purposes of the trip were accomplished. Because many things were decided in advance, precious time at Akagi did not have to be spent on organizational matters. Everyone could experience the beauty of the natural setting undistracted by figuring out who was going to do what next. Equally important, each child made a clear contribution to the group living experience and benefited in visible ways from everyone else's contributions. Everyone gave, everyone received. Teachers were able to remain in their preferred background role, available but seemingly no more central than any other group member. They weren't needed to give orders or make moment-by-moment decisions about children's activities, and they didn't have to do a lot of heavy-handed disciplining. Everyone, children and teachers alike, was able "by working and playing together, indoors and out, to experience the joy and importance of group living." Did it work? Sam reported that they had a good time, nothing went wrong, the teachers didn't get mad at anyone, and they didn't feel oversupervised—no one enforced the lights out, for instance. It was fun. Everyone got a picture of the group as a souvenir.

6

The Three R's, Japanese Style

In Japan as in most countries, reading, writing, and arithmetic form the academic core of elementary school, along with science and social studies. It would be hard to tell that from the textbooks, however. On the first day, when Sam and Ellen received their books, we were surprised by the number of textbooks given to them and also by their appearance.

We were used to having no texts for subjects like art and physical education and having textbooks for the basic subjects that in their size and weight seem to embody physically the importance of their subject matter. American textbooks tend to be hardcover, thick, large-format books intended to last for several years. They do not belong to students in our children's schools but to the school; they are loaned to the children, who are supposed to return them in pristine condition.

The Japanese texts are thin, small paperbacks, nicely printed on good paper, which belong to students. The texts for reading, writing, and arithmetic are no larger or thicker than those for art, home economics, and physical education. My initial reaction was that there just wasn't enough material in these texts to keep a class occupied for a whole year. In fact, for reading and arithmetic there are two text volumes for each year, but they still add up to a very modest number of pages, compared to American textbooks. It seemed that teachers would have to do a lot of extra work to stretch these texts into a year's worth of work.

As I thought about American textbooks and reflected on conversations I had had with curriculum developers in the United States, especially some people involved with the New Math and the Basic Course in Biological Science curricula, each intended to introduce sweeping changes in the way these subjects were taught in U.S. schools, I remembered a basic distrust of the classroom teacher that pervaded those conversations. I think the elaborate textbooks of American publishers are designed to be teacher-proof: to have so much material, so many teaching aids, so many different exercises and problems, that even a bad teacher can't distort the material being presented. Because the understanding and teaching skills of the classroom teacher can't be relied on, the textbooks have to provide all the material, to be almost self-teaching, programmed instruction materials. (Incidentally, since these textbooks free students' learning from dependence on the teacher, they also free learning from classroom interaction and make learning a solitary, individual activity. This conception is basically opposed to Japanese notions of where and how learning best takes place.)

From watching classes and from talking with teachers and parents, I learned that Japanese elementary school classes in the basic academic subjects are very much textbook centered and that using the textbook constitutes a good part of every day's class in these subjects. I decided to look at the books to see just what was in them that could absorb so much time.

READING

Learning to read and write is the foundation for all other academic skills, and learning to read Japanese is not easy. (See the appendix for an explanation of what is involved.) Reading as a mechanical process is very difficult because of the Japanese writing system, and learning to read as an intellectual process extending beyond the mechanics is as difficult as in any other language. Because of the writing system, writing in the sense of being able to inscribe words on paper, on the conceptual level of penmanship and spelling, is also difficult and requires effort throughout the elementary school years. Writing in the sense of composition of effective communication in various formats is also learned in Japanese schools, starting in first grade, and is as difficult as writing in this sense in English or other languages.

All these skills are encompassed in the subject known as *kokugo,* "national language." This name derives from the historical period when standardization of the writing system and spread of a standard Tokyo-based dialect were aims of the education system. Now that these objectives have been accomplished, the name remains and may have some overtones that emphasize the uniqueness of the Japanese people and the Japanese language.

For first graders there are two textbook readers, two writing workbooks, one calligraphy text, and two workbooks that provide the basic material for reading and writing for the year. For Ellen's class there was also a drill book that the teacher had students purchase each term and exercise books for homework.

The first-grade text stories range in length from the first of 30 words in nine sentences, to one of the last, which is 425 words long. Most are fiction, but there are some poetry and nonfiction entries. Each story is followed by discussion questions and exercises. Many of the exercises deal with Japanese grammar, and especially the formation of the full-sentence forms appropriate for written Japanese as opposed to the more elliptical forms used in much of spoken Japanese. Children begin writing "compositions" using these sentence formulas from the beginning of first grade.

During class time major emphasis is placed on reading aloud, and the whole class in unison or in small groups or as individuals read the text out loud over and over. Not only is the accurate pronunciation of written words a goal, but reading in a fluent and expressive style is emphasized also. Children are not considered to have learned to read a story until they can do a polished performance of it.

The never-changing homework for *kokugo* in Ellen's class was daily reading aloud at home. The teacher prepared a special checkoff sheet for each story of the text. Spaces were provided on the sheet for an older person at home to grade each day's reading on the following factors:

1. not mumbling, clear words, to the end
2. using a clear voice that can be heard throughout the room
3. separating words correctly, leaving pauses in between
4. using a speed for easy comprehension
5. using appropriate expression for people and animals in stories.

The parent, grandparent, or older sibling who helped with this homework each day was supposed to mark each day's grades with a stamp (equivalent to a signature); the teacher also marked each day's entry with her stamp to indicate she had seen it. In addition, she sent home to the student and the helper complimentary, encouraging, or scolding notes on effort and perseverance.

First grade incorporates a lot of practice of the mechanics of writing. The required calligraphy and reading workbooks give children exercises and repetitive practice in writing, of both the syllabic characters and of *kanji* (ideographs). In many cases children are expected to do ten to thirty repetitions of the same symbol. There is strong emphasis on standard form, not merely on intelligibility. The space in which a symbol is to be written is divided into four quadrants, for instance, and the same proportions of length, curve, and so forth are to be copied and maintained in each repetition of the symbol.

Until the advent of word processors, all Japanese was either printed at printing presses or hand written, and a standard penmanship, one that did not encompass vagaries of personality or personal style, was important. Even now, I think, Japanese would regard idiosyncratic handwriting as a sign of rampant, "selfish" individualism in its pejorative sense—unless, of course, calligraphy as an art form is involved. Here, the expression of individuality and personality is entirely appropriate—so appropriate that many Japanese cannot read what is written in this "art form." The writing done at school is not meant to be like this.

For first graders, another daily practice in writing is the preparation of the *renrakucho*. This is a book in which children write their daily assignments and other information that the teacher wants to reach each home: notes about plans for future projects, equipment, or money required, for instance, or exhortations about getting to school *wasuremono nai yo ni,* "without any forgotten things." (I thought this was only our problem for a long time, but I've come to think it was a problem in many homes, and not just in first grade.) The teacher's message amounts to two or three sentences a day copied from the board, where the teacher writes it at a pace a quick student could keep up with. The fact that this information is needed at home means that parents join in the pressure to produce intelligible writing. Parents must stamp the message each day and can use the booklet to send messages back to the teacher. She also stamps it each day to indicate she has seen it.

Ellen also brought home many drawings that, like the drawings in the reading text, included writing on the same page. Her writings here were more than just captions, often several sentences, and by the end of her time in Japan, the writing was exclusively in Japanese. (She continued to answer some questions in English in her homework book and other contexts.) In the third term of first grade students were required to make and keep a book of reflections on school life, which they handed in periodically and which the teacher reviewed.

Both Sam and Ellen seemed to enjoy writing and the calligraphy classes in school. They seemed especially proud of the writing they did at *kakizome*. *Kakizome* is a ceremony held just after New Year's in which writing is done "for the first time" that year. The emperor invites noted calligraphers and authors to a party for this activity, and their "writings" as well as the emperor's are published in newspapers and shown on television news reports. Schoolchildren are assigned a phrase or a passage to practice for their own ceremonial "first writing" at school after the New Year's vacation. Children all gather in the school gymnasium for this school activity, and their writings are exhibited in the school hallways during January. Ellen and Sam worked on their calligraphy over the vacation and produced quite respectable writings for *kakizome*.

All the writing that first graders do, and most of their reading, is in the vertical format, with lines running from top to bottom of the page, the first line at the right-hand side of the page. Some texts, science and social studies, have horizontal writing in a Western format. In my experience it is not trivial to change from one of these formats to the other, in terms of eye movements and patterns of grouping word or phrase units together for fluent comprehension. Though Japanese students learn to handle both from the beginning of first grade, they are given more practice in the vertical format.

In reading classes, even through the sixth-grade level, reading of the assigned text out loud is an important and standard part of class time. This is because, as explained in the appendix on the writing system, the relationship between the symbols of Japanese writing and the sounds of words of Japanese is far from straightforward. Repetition and practice are necessary to make these connections easy for learners. It's possible to skip this step, so some incentive to include it is necessary for learners. What I mean is that it is possible in the Japanese writing system to move directly from the written symbol to the meaning, without knowing the actual spoken "word" that the symbol stands for. *Kanji* are identical in form and meaning to Chinese ideographs in many cases. I studied Chinese before learning Japanese, and there are many situations in which I can figure out what some written Japanese means without being able to read most of it out loud. Japanese children, however, are expected to be able to associate spoken words with symbols, and reading aloud provides the practice for doing this.

A student taking a turn at reading is expected to stand beside the desk, adopt a formal posture, and read in a loud, clear, expressive voice. This was more likely to be accomplished after a period of work on the story; it was not done so well on the first days of a unit, when just getting through the sentences with correct pronunciation of the words written in *kanji* was difficult for many students. One sixth-grade teacher did not insist that students stand for reading aloud on the first day of a unit that I observed.

This teacher introduced the new unit by asking those students who had not read ahead to think about the title of the story and the pictures in the text and speculate on what the story would be like. He was insistent that only students who had not already read the story should respond; the effect, it seemed to me, was to disparage the initiative of the students who had gone ahead of the class rather than reading the story with everyone else. Students seemed reluctant to give responses to this questioning. Partly, the teacher said later, that was because of my presence, but also because the older students are always more shy than the younger ones. Gaining a sense of reserve is seen as a sign of maturity in Japan, so while teachers may enjoy the enthusiasm of younger students, they expect and do not disapprove of more restrained response from the older ones.

Although this was the first day of a new unit, and the mechanics of reading the story absorbed much of the energy of the class, the teacher's discussion beforehand pointed out some aspects of the structure of the story, that it was a "story within a story" and that observing the transitions from one part to the next was crucial, as was the question of how much of the inner story should be considered fantasy. Other activities I observed in reading classes included discussions of the characters, the situations, the students' reactions, and the literary structure of the story. Sometimes the teacher asked specific content questions about the story.

By fifth and sixth grades many American students are reading relatively long books that could be considered "literature" rather than texts. The transition from short pieces mostly read aloud to long works read silently and individually takes place around fourth grade in many American schools. After this, only poetry and plays are read aloud. In Japan, even in the upper grades stories in the texts continue to be relatively short units that can be approached in such a way as to become polished, read-aloud performances. By third grade the reading texts are written without divisions between words, as are texts for adults, giving an added complication to smooth comprehension in reading silently or aloud. It seems that comprehension is judged by how well that comprehension can be orally communicated to others. Some poems in the fifth-grade text are marked with suggestions for reading—where to increase or decrease volume, where to speed up or slow down, and tones of voice to incorporate. Even prose descriptive passages are to be read "so that the mood and description of the place are clearly conveyed to the listener."

All classes included some reading aloud, but in classes that came at later points in a unit, other analysis was more emphasized. One lesson for sixth graders near the end of a unit was focused on outlining the story, a biography. Here the class was notable for the small amount of time spent reading aloud and the large amount of time spent silently with each person working on an outline, under the general guidance of the teacher. His talk was repetitious, emphasizing the major headings of an outline of this story, pointing out what was overtly mentioned in the text and what had to be deduced. He left large stretches of time for students to work in their notebooks on an outline, but he also wrote on the board and ended up with an elaborate, elegant outline in four colors of chalk.

Fifth and sixth graders, too, have workbooks and drill books for writing practice. For them the emphasis is on the new *kanji* they are learning, but repetition and careful following of a standard writing pattern is just as important as in first grade. A weekly lesson in calligraphy, using a brush to write *kanji,* is also part of the curriculum at this level. This is the first step to calligraphy as an art form, but there are also social contexts in Japanese life in which writing with a pencil or pen would be inappropriate—only brush writing will do.

They also practice composition in various formats: book reports, expository writing, preparing reports in science or social studies, and writing letters and essays. As noted elsewhere, many classes end with students writing a summary or a reflection on the material of the class. These are often read aloud to the whole class.

Elaine Gerbert (1993) has written a content analysis of Japanese *kokugo* textbooks that emphasizes the differences between them and current American texts. She also notes the sheer volume of materials in the American texts, which are two to three times as long as their Japanese counterparts. Often American teachers do not use all the material in a text but choose to omit certain parts. In Japan all the material in a text is used because the required curriculum will not be covered if parts are omitted. In Japan the content of the texts remains relatively constant, so that a college student working with me who saw a second-grade text story said, "Oh, I remember that story." Some shifts in focus have taken place in Japanese texts, but not to the extent that American texts have been overhauled in recent years.

Gerbert sees an important source of variety in the American texts in the many literary forms that are included. A Japanese text for fourth graders incorporates seventeen units in eight genres, ranging from poetry through stories and biography to a report on an experiment. A fourth-grade text for Americans contains forty-nine units in eighteen genres, including autobiography, a photo essay, and a play, for instance.

American texts emphasize the diversity of peoples in the United States and the diversity of their conditions. Such variation is treated as valuable in and of itself, as well as worthwhile because it portrays challenges and opportunities for individuals in American society. The appreciation of individuality in diverse and difficult situations is a major theme in these texts, Gerbert says. (My reading of some texts confirms this; it would appear from the textbooks that there are no nonhyphenated, white children without handicaps living in intact employed families in America.) Life as presented in these texts is fairly dramatic—important events spur people on to major changes in life; introspection and quiet reflection are rare events. History is presented as full of conflict, and moral evaluations of historical events and movements is overt, as is principled moral evaluation of actions in other stories. Stories about nature either anthropomorphize animals or present humans intervening to conquer or improve nature. Activities associated with the reading texts ask students to develop analytical skills—to understand and evaluate the structure of arguments; to distinguish among fact, fiction, opinion, and fantasy; to discuss hypothetical situations; and to make overt judgments of literary and moral merit.

In the Japanese texts nearly all situations presented are familiar, comforting, safe situations. The interior life of the characters in the story, often rather generic narrators, is emphasized more than events in the social or real world in which the characters live. A fifth-grade story about a boy's birthday talks about his anticipation of the day and his excitement, but the focal event turns out to be his watching a single perfect leaf falling from a tree, an event he observes in solitude. Stories with more distant settings in time and space are most often inspirational biographies.

A significant number of units deal with a close, empathetic observation and understanding of familiar natural phenomena. Human action seldom intrudes in these observations, and the atmosphere is not one that emphasizes the mystery or awe of Nature, but the intimacy of humans and natural events. There seems to be a preference for observations of small things, insects and small plants, for instance, rather than of larger or more sweeping aspects of nature. Both a conventionalized and a real appreciation of immediate natural phenomena is an important part of the Japanese literary tradition and of modern everyday writing. All letters, newsletters, announcements, and so forth make an initial reference to the season of the communication by mentioning plants and animals and natural events that are thought to characterize the time of year.

Some potentially salient characteristics of characters or narrators in these *kokugo* text units are nearly completely ignored. Differences between people based on social categories, such as occupation, region, income, gender, religion, age, disabilities, or even talents, are not presented as background or made the focus of situations in the stories. These are the characteristics that are made central in stories in the American texts.

Gerbert does not mention one of the striking features of the Japanese texts. In those books illustrated with drawings rather than photographs, the children and adults depicted do not look physically Japanese. This occurs not just once in a while but very consistently. Most noticeably, the coloring of their hair does not match the range of black and near-black hues found in Japan. Instead, most people, both adults and children, are shown with brown, light brown, and even almost blond hair. Eyes are drawn in a way to de-emphasize the epicanthic fold, which is nearly universal in Japan. These illustrations occur with stories that are set in Japan and are about Japanese characters. If photographs are used, they are accurate, showing black-haired children with a variety of eye shapes, nose shapes, and face shapes.

The producers of children's literature in America have felt it was important for children to find people "like themselves" in the illustrations. Perhaps as an American observer of that emphasis, I am overly sensitive to the anomaly of textbooks that systematically portray Asians as though they were Caucasians. Illustrations of stories set in historical times consistently show people with stronger Japanese coloring.

Japanese to whom I have mentioned this observation do not seem to find the phenomenon interesting, saying only that it makes for "prettier" or "more interesting" illustrations. I don't think the Japanese suffer from an unhealthy desire to be physically different than they are, but this style of portrayal is too widespread to be accidental or to be ignored.

The same pattern can be found in children's books that are not schoolbooks, but it is much stronger in the textbooks. When it is found in advertisements, the usual interpretation is that the use of Western or Western-looking models imparts an air of modernity and glamour to a product. Could this be an attempt to make Japanese textbooks more "international" by understating physical differences between Japanese and other nationalities?

The Ministry of Education controls the textbooks used in public schools, not just for reading but for all subjects. The ministry publishes a detailed national curriculum for each grade and each subject, and texts must cover all the material prescribed by the ministry. Textbooks prepared by about six publishing companies are submitted for approval by the ministry, which controls the format and the content of the texts. Local school boards at the prefectural or city level then choose among the approved text series for a set of texts to be used in that jurisdiction.

There is almost no educational or political objection to this system of text control. The only area in which there are political objections is in the treatment of Japanese history in high school texts, in the sections dealing with the history of Japan in the decades of military and colonial expansion and with the actions of Japan during the Second World War. Protests against a presentation of events in those years that is seen as denying, mitigating, or excusing Japan's actions come from the political left in Japan and equally from the governments of nations that were occupied or conquered by Japan. These textbooks have become a political issue both domestically and internationally. But at the elementary school level the texts are not controversial and seem to inspire little or no discussion.

ARITHMETIC

Here, surely, the textbooks must be really different from American ones—everyone knows that Japanese students are the most proficient in the world at mathematics. But no, these too are soft, friendly-looking little paperbacks.

The first-grade text is 109 pages for the whole year. There are seventeen units and four review sections for the forty weeks of school. A unit on telling time by the hour and the half hour contains only two pages of text, though as I remember it, Ellen's class spent several days on this topic. The unit on adding single digits with a sum greater than ten is eight pages long and contains only fifty-eight practice problems to solve. This unit involves learning thirty-six arithmetic "facts" (for example, $7 + 8 = 15$), and students were expected to be able to explain a procedure for the addition and produce quick memorized answers for these problems. Fifty-eight practice problems won't produce world-class proficiency. These problems are used in class with physical counters to illustrate the procedure of the addition and to check answers by counting. A lot of time is taken up by the actual manipulation of the objects and counting. The learning that goes on in class is both concrete, because of the visual and tactile stimuli involved, and abstract, because of the generalized procedure for understanding that is used.

Though little class time is spent in practice, there are several devices to encourage it. First, a number of games involving practice can be done in class: cards with problems are laid out on a table for a group of children, and they take turns answering them, scoring points for correct problems. Other games with dice also are suggested. For practice at home, each child has a set of flash cards for addition and another for subtraction and work books that are purchased at bookstores. The first-grade workbook for addition offers twenty-four pages of practice problems for this unit, totaling more than three hundred problems. A prize of a colored sticker is provided for each page that is perfectly solved; no time limit is given. This workbook is not homework, taken to school to be presented to the teacher; it is a study aid for home. At school, however, teachers quiz students at odd times, while they are getting ready to go home, for instance, so that children know they are expected to gain quick mastery of the "facts," as well as of the principles that are the focus of teaching time. American observers of Japanese mathematics classes have often commented on the time teachers are willing to give to concrete physical operations that clarify mathematical operations and concepts. Much more emphasis in class is placed on this than on getting through a large number of problems. As reported by Stevenson and Stigler (1992:192f.) and other observers, mistakes are treated as teaching opportunities, not ignored or passed over quickly. Since teachers place an emphasis on finding as many ways to solve a problem as possible, classes often consider several strategies. The teaching style suggests that knowing why a suggestion that turns out not to work didn't work is as important as memorizing a procedure that is correct. Again, Lewis (1995) reports on an incident that illustrates both the social and the academic approaches to mathematics learning in elementary schools.

A second-grade class was working on ways to solve the following problem: seven children were riding in a train car; two got off, and then three more got on. How many children were then riding on the train? Equations to represent the problem, not the "answer," were what students were expected to give. Among the equations offered were one boy's set, $3 - 2 = 1$ and $1 + 7 = 8$. When he was asked to explain his thinking, however, he tried for several minutes but couldn't. The teacher asked if other children could figure out what he was thinking about as he wrote these, but no one could, and the general feeling was that the equations were wrong. After giving the boy another chance to explain, the teacher suggested that he touch her hand to transfer his power of thinking to her, so that she could explain. She did so, leading the class through the reasoning that makes these equations a correct statement of the problem, although they were not the only correct solution and not the only one dealt with during the class. At the end of class she asked the boy how he felt when everyone thought his answer was wrong. He replied, "I didn't feel good." "I think he was very brave to try to explain when everyone disagreed," said the teacher. Brave enough that the whole class, agreeing, applauded him (Lewis 1995:169–71).

In general, Japanese students think math is hard, taking a lot of work and study, but they feel confident of their ability to learn it. Adults agree with children—that the learning is demanding but within their reach. By the end of first grade, children have learned cardinal and ordinal numbers through one hundred, can add and subtract numbers up to one hundred without borrowing or carrying, can tell time, can do simple measurements and comparisons of length, and can name several geometric figures.

In fifth grade the emphasis continues to be on a few examples, worked out in the most concrete way possible, and a few practice problems offered in the text. A unit on measuring the volume of rectangular solids, for instance, includes eleven pages of text, nine examples fully worked out in the text, and about fifteen practice problems. In the last set of problems, students are asked to deal with displacement measurement of an egg, and the problem is followed by a page explaining Archimedes' discovery of this principle of measurement. A class would spend about two weeks on this unit. More problems, to offer practice in the principles emphasized in the text materials, can be found in the drill books that students purchase to accompany the text. The time in class is devoted to discussion of ways to solve the problems and analysis of the errors in thinking in possible solutions that turn out not to work.

Harold W. Stevenson and James W. Stigler (1992; Stigler et al. 1987) have conducted several studies to analyze differences in teaching styles between Japan and the United States, including differences in ways of teaching mathematics, where the divergence in test results between the two countries is the most striking. Among the consistent differences they report are greater coherence, greater concreteness, and more thoroughness of the Japanese teacher's lessons. A fifth-grade class they report on (1992:177–78), for instance, was designed to teach the use of bar graphs in analyzing data. It began with the teacher bringing into class six different containers, including a pitcher, a vase, and a beer bottle (much laughter), and wondering aloud which would hold the most. Animated class discussion led pupils to decide they had to fill the different containers with water, using a common drinking cup as the standard measure. A bucket of water from the wash basins outside was brought in, and each *han* group was given one of the containers to fill with measured water. The teacher wrote the names of the containers on the blackboard in a column and a scale of cup measurements across the width of the blackboard. She then asked each group how many drinking cups of water their container held and drew lines to the appropriate place on the scale. Again she asked, "Which one holds the most water?" and led the class to arrange the containers in rank order, relating this to the bar graph. After leading the class in a review of the procedure they had used to solve the problem, she mentioned the specific terms that are used for the vertical and horizontal axes of the graph. It was a lesson in drawing graphs, but the emphasis was on using one to solve a problem, not on abstract discussion of the properties of graphs—and even for fifth graders, humor and water play were part of the lesson.

Stevenson and Stigler's extensive observations showed that Japanese teachers usually begin lessons with practical problems to be solved, that they are often willing to give an entire class to working on one problem, and that they shape coherence through the problems and explicit summaries of what principles have been used to solve them. Merely getting through a lot of problems to correct answers is not part of the classroom program of teaching mathematics.

Again, the picture I expected of docile, quiet Japanese students plodding through reams of repetitive problems, becoming computational wizards with no notion of the meaning of the problems they were dealing with, turned out to be a fiction dispelled by seeing what goes on in Japanese classrooms and by looking at the teaching materials Japanese children are exposed to. Sam and Ellen found mathematics hard. Sam had trouble following the discussions that led to understanding in his classes because of the language problem, and he wasn't accustomed to depending on us for help with schoolwork. The pace of material was difficult for Ellen. It was too easy not to do the drill work at home that led to computational proficiency. Ellen's mother did not learn until the year was almost over that her job included coaxing and participating in practice activities to solidify the understanding of mathematics that comes in the classroom.

Japanese students consider math hard, too. In their case there is nearly always a mother at home who went through Japanese schools herself and who knows what kind of studying it takes to keep up with the curriculum, who reinforces the importance of doing so, and who expects to be a mathematics coach during after-school hours—or who sends her children to a private tutor or *juku* for help and drilling.

In spite of the school principal's advice to us that he did not think a tutor in Japanese for Sam and Ellen would be necessary, in retrospect I think we should have hired a college student to help Sam with his schoolwork, and I should have spent more time with Ellen on her work. But I felt pretty sorry for Sam and Ellen, who were already spending forty hours a week or more in school, and was reluctant to increase their burden. I usually didn't feel like doing homework in the evenings myself, either.

SOCIAL STUDIES

Social Studies is one of the most ideological subjects in the curriculum of modern nations. Here, the educators of all countries agree, children learn "facts" not only about their own social world, but about the social worlds of people in other times and places. The history children learn about their own country and others is a story that places social facts in a framework for interpretation, and both governments and families care deeply about the interpretation presented to children and absorbed in this subject at school.

That being the case, it was instructive to see the materials that are used in Japanese social studies classes and texts and to compare those with the corresponding American materials. The first-grade curriculum is organized around the theme of the social life of the school. School does become for Japanese children a social life nearly complete in itself and thus is a social world in microcosm in ways it probably is not for American students. The textbook is a large picture book with very little text, and the captions for pictures are phrased as comments that seem to come from children looking at the pictures. The illustrations are both drawings and photographs, sometimes mixed on the same page.

The introductory unit is "New Friends" and features drawings of first graders in several school settings: on the playground, entering the classroom, and presenting their self-portraits to be hung on the bulletin board. The pictures include teachers, but children are more central. The physical features of the classroom and school yard are prominent. Like the curriculum, these are nearly uniform for the whole country of Japan.

Unit 1, "Our School," moves in pictures through activities that the whole school participates in, such as school assembly, to specialized activities and their spaces—the orchestra room, the library, the teachers' room, and others. There is a picture to stimulate discussion on school equipment that everyone shares and school equipment that is the same for everyone but is individually owned. A second unit, "School Workers," illustrates the roles of teachers, the school nurse, the kitchen workers, and the maintenance men.

The third unit, entitled "Summer Has Come," marks the end of the first third of the school year and discusses the special activities of summer and its special foods and clothing. It emphasizes the contrasts between summer and winter. The fourth unit is about a neighborhood park, picturing the many activities that take place there, the facilities that are there to be shared, and the many different kinds of people who use the park. There seems to be a parallel drawn between the school world presented in the first unit, with its varied public and private facets, and the public park.

The next unit, "Roads to School," looks at other features of the surrounding neighborhood. The pictures are rich in detail (and Japanese towns all look enough alike that they will be familiar to everyone), and the artistic perspectives that are used to portray the scenes are complicated, sometimes overhead looking down, viewpoints that seem to be designed to lead into map making—and that is the activity of the first graders shown on the last page of the unit, construction of a large map on the floor of the classroom. Traffic safety in traveling through the neighborhood is also emphasized.

A unit called "Work at Home" presents a fairly sexist view of the division of labor in a "typical" family: an employed father, a mother apparently not employed outside the home (though about half the mothers of elementary school children are employed [Japan Institute of Labour 1989:72]), a grandmother, and two children. Some attempt to step outside the usual sex role typing of household jobs can be seen, as when the father and the son dry the dishes the mother is washing, or when the father hands a plate of food to someone, but generally, the mother's work is housework and the father's work is invisibly somewhere else.

Ellen said that when this unit was going on, each *han* group constituted itself as a family—she was the little sister—and acted out many different activities. I remember being irritated at the requests for household equipment to be sent to school: a vacuum cleaner, a mop, a pail and rags, dishes, and pots and pans. They even did laundry at school for this unit, including ironing and folding clothes. Talking about household tasks is not as good a learning tool as doing them, in the view of the Japanese teachers. A notion made explicit in this unit is that school is the work of children. Just as their mothers cook, shop, and clean, and their fathers go to work and fix things around the house, children go to school and study. The end of the second term comes at the beginning of winter, and the unit "Seasons and Life" is another opportunity to stress the changing activities correlated with the seasons of the year.

The last long unit of the year is entitled "Since I Was Born . . ." and talks about the changes in physical and social abilities that each child has experienced since birth. Pictures of children at different ages are brought from home for posters, along with clothes, toys, and family reminiscences, to make concrete the changes that have taken place. Into this schema are put all the many experiences of the first grade that have contributed to children's growing up, things like Sports Day, the school excursion, the entering ceremony, and swimming lessons. The conclusion points out that "Soon We'll Be Second Graders." Like the seeds of morning glories, first graders have grown and changed, and they are about to enter a new stage of life as second graders.

Several standard American social studies curricula also take as their starting points the social life of school, the family as a social unit, and the personal development of children from birth to first grade. But the American curriculum for the year also includes a number of other topics—a little history, usually related to holidays like Thanksgiving and Martin Luther King, Jr., Day, and definitions of basic human needs and wants, explicit consideration of rules that characterize families, schools, and neighborhoods, and pictures of unifying places and symbols for the whole nation: the Capitol, the White House, the Statue of Liberty, Mount Rushmore. In all of this there is an overt emphasis on variety of people and forms for living in groups. Each unit, on housing for instance, or meals, gives pictures of scenes from other countries (Japan, Norway, India, and Nigeria in one text series).

Within the United States the variety of physical types, ethnic backgrounds, family forms, and individuality are emphasized. Differences in living patterns in cities, suburbs, and rural areas are pointed out, and the fact that the food in the local store comes from many different places. It looks as though conscious effort has gone into choosing pictures that break possible stereotypes about gender, race, and ethnic patterns in occupations and activities and that show people with disabilities doing possibly unexpected things.

Perhaps because the United States is more varied than Japan in terms of geography, settlement patterns, and architectural environment, the pictures in the U.S. texts seem more abstract and less realistic than those in Japanese texts, where for an American reader at least, part of the delight in looking at the pictures comes from recognizing features one has seen in one's own neighborhood and all over Japan. I've traveled all over the United States, too, and the drawings in the American texts look like no places I've ever seen, in contrast to the photos, which are readily identifiable.

American children are presented in the first-grade curriculum in social studies with a world that has greater time depth, more connection with the world outside, and more variety and complex structures within their own country than the world shown to Japanese children. The text is much more verbal, with significant written passages that seem to be beyond the reading level of many or most first graders. The text and other material are more complex and difficult than the materials for Japanese first graders; they are noticeably more abstract, less connected with daily life and personal experience.

In Japan fifth graders study Japan, and in the United States many fifth graders study the United States. In Japan the two small fifth-grade texts for the year are supplemented with a glossy, handsome atlas full of maps, charts, and graphs and a grim, gray study guide. Five units for the year cover agriculture, fisheries, manufacturing and traditional crafts in Japan, and the land forms and climatic patterns of Japan. The written material in the textbooks is quite informal in style, and the meat of the content seems to be in the many visual presentations of data in the atlas. Only in the section on agriculture is any historical perspective given. In this unit changes in the last forty years as Japanese agriculture has become more mechanized are highlighted.

Family sketches of the activities and income of both a full-time farming household and a part-time farming household are presented. What is striking about these sketches is how full of quantitative data they are. Not only does the text say that transplanting rice seedlings used to be more time-consuming, but it also specifies that forty years ago it took five people ten days and now it takes one person one day. Charts, graphs, and pictures make more quantitative comparisons having to do with plowing, harvesting, and other activities.

The feelings and atmosphere of farm life are also presented, however, in terms of the things farmers worry about—the weather, mainly, and whether they have made the right decisions about seed variety, fertilizer, and timing. The anxiety of having all one's efforts and income dependent on one harvest, which is affected by many factors farmers can't control, is discussed. The section on agriculture is the only one presented in such human detail, however; the sections on fisheries and manufactures don't have this kind of humanized approach.

Possibly this is because Japan was only recently a country where most people were engaged in agriculture. In 1960 almost a third of all Japanese households were engaged in agriculture, full or part time. Add to this Japanese with relatives who are farmers, and a large part of the total population is included. The number of people in agriculture is steadily declining, but farmers remain an important political and cultural force in Japan.

The atlas used by fifth graders is notable for the quality of the printing and production, the lavish use of color and color photography, and mostly for the sheer amount of data that is presented in chart and graph form. Being able to digest and comprehend data presented in this way is a sophisticated accomplishment.

A general overall impression of the text materials for Americans and Japanese in social studies is that the American material is mostly words, with a few charts and pictures, and the Japanese material is much more heavily visual, with data presented in charts and graphs, some quite complicated, rather than in prose. A lot of interpretation is necessary, and is discussed in class, to make these charts and graphs meaningful. A great deal of information is packed into this mode of presentation, an overwhelming amount, it seems to me.

What the words of the American fifth-grade texts talk about is the history of the United States. The time period dealt with is from 40,000 years ago through the Cold War, the first landing on the moon, Martin Luther King, Jr., the Civil Rights movement, the Cuban Missile crisis, and the Vietnam War. (Experience suggests that most classes don't get through all this material, and it's the modern period that is usually omitted.) Though the text does not go into vivid detail, there is continuous reference to the conflicts between groups and interests that have characterized American history. Separate sections, nearly a half of the text, deal with the geography of regions of the United States. Also included are chapters on the history and geography of Mexico and Canada.

The American material is much broader in historical and social scope than the Japanese fifth-grade material; the Japanese material is much more thorough and analytical. The American material is more overtly ideological, in that it presents a view of America that emphasizes a particular interpretation of American history and resources, specifically, an interpretation that promotes patriotism and identification with a set of social and political goals for the United States. No such material is found in the Japanese text.

In both countries the materials in social studies curricula are potentially politically contentious, but the policy in America has been to recognize the importance of this part of school for citizenship learning and to present a consensus view of the United States. In Japan the response has been to eliminate the overt political content and present more "factual" material, with little or no social or political interpretation.

Other areas of political socialization are handled differently in the two countries, too. The ritual of saying the Pledge of Allegiance to the flag is a normal part of American school life, and its purpose, to make children feel like united American citizens, is recognized and accepted.

Patriotic songs, such as "The Star-Spangled Banner," "America the Beautiful," and "My Country, 'Tis of Thee," are used in U.S. schools with no protest. The national flag is displayed prominently in several locations in schools both public and private, and no one seems to think this is inappropriate.

In Japan, however, where since the end of the Second World War teachers have been a leftish political group and opposed to many policies of the rightish Ministry of Education, the display of the national flag in schools has been opposed and minimized; many teachers refuse to teach or sing the national anthem (actually a song to the emperor that is not quite the official anthem but the closest thing to it Japan has) or other patriotic music. School texts do not present material related to the national holidays of Japan, some of which have political significance. Among these are the Emperor's Birthday, Constitution Day, and Accession Day, which commemorates the first (mythical) Japanese emperor.

Religion, religious symbols and holidays, prayer, and moral values that many Americans identify with religion are perennial sources of contention in American schools and on both the local and national political scene. Nationalism in the schools is an issue that emerges only sporadically, as when high school students in the late 1960s wore black armbands to protest the Vietnam war, or when some students on religious grounds decline to say the Pledge of Allegiance. Nationalism in Japanese schools is an ongoing political issue in Japan, but religion is not. The social studies curriculum in each country reflects that country's orientations to social problems. The curriculum of American schools is overtly political and religiously "neutral." The curriculum of Japanese schools is politically "neutral" on the issue of nationalism and less indoctrinating than the U.S. curriculum.

7

The Rest of the Day

LESSONS AT LUNCH

It's not a hard and fast rule, but Japanese elementary school teachers seem to prefer to schedule the "heavy" academic subjects for before lunchtime, since lunch and the activities that go with it break up the concentration that the long morning provides; it also makes children and teachers a little more lethargic. In this book, too, lunch will provide a break in the academic discussions. Lunch takes a major chunk of the school day in Japan, however, and it's a mistake to think of it only as a distraction and not part of the curriculum.

A question we encountered over and over from Japanese during our time in Japan was, "Can you eat Japanese food?" At first we thought this was a way of asking whether we could use chopsticks, so we answered that Chinese restaurants in America had taught us to cope with that problem. But that's not what the question was about, nor was it about a specific issue like eating raw fish, which all Japanese know is not a Western custom.

The question really arises from the Japanese feeling that their food is a unique cuisine, part of their national character, so that non-Japanese are not expected to be able to eat it, let alone enjoy it. Japanese cuisine taken as a whole, the range and combinations of ingredients, tastes, and textures and the patterns of combining them in a meal, is unique, sharing very little in character with other Asian food patterns. Unlike the French or the Chinese, who assume that everyone will adore their cuisine once exposed to it because it is simply the universal best, Japanese feel that their food is not something others will take to, and they're not at all sure that they want others to be able to eat and enjoy it.

Having encountered this question often and having experienced the frequent newsletters and discussions about lunch at Sam's preschool, I didn't find it too surprising that both the school board officials and the principal of Okubo Higashi raised the question of school lunch as a possible stumbling block to having Sam and Ellen attend this school. They seemed very insistent, however, and I thought it curious that such a minor point would be raised more than once. But I hate packing school lunches, so I wasn't about to suggest to anyone, child or adult, that such an alternative might be available.

Sam and Ellen didn't say much about it, but they were understandably a little anxious about this issue, too. Japanese cuisine is about as different from American as it could get, and they have been expected to put up with a lot of very weird food in travels with their parents. (And at home, too, to hear them tell it.) When they came home from school their first day, the first topic of conversation was the food at lunch—how good it had been, and what was it anyway? (A fish and vegetable stew, Sam said, and Ellen resolved never to eat anything unidentified again, since she "hates fish.") On the day the rice, usually a reliable friend, turned out to be mixed with one-inch long, skinny silver fish with bright blue eyes, there were some comments at home, too. Gradually we picked up more tidbits of talk and comments about lunch and learned why lunch is part of the curriculum, how it fits into a sense of Japanese identity, and why when a group of Japanese go to a restaurant they all order the same thing.

Every month a detailed plan is sent home, giving the menus for lunch each day at school. It lists the dishes for the day and tells whether it is a bread-, rice-, or noodle-centered meal; also provided is a breakdown of the ingredients used into four categories—bodybuilding foods, heat- and energy-giving foods, body harmony-regulating foods, and seasonings. The first three seem to parallel American categories of proteins, carbohydrates, and fruits and vegetables. Milk is given to children every day, but they get no desserts except fruit, included about half the time.

A sample menu based on bread might include a meat stew, a cucumber salad, a roll, milk, and fruit; or chicken with lemon sauce, potato salad, a slice of bread, and fruit. A meal centered on rice might include *oyako donburi*, a dish of seasoned chicken meat and egg on top of a bowl of rice, a slice of pumpkin fried with sesame seeds, mixed pickled vegetables, and milk. Chopsticks are used for some meals, but a spoon-fork is used for the more Western meals.

Each month's menu plan also illustrates foods in season and discusses healthful eating. In October the importance of calcium and fiber were highlighted, a number of foods containing them were shown, and the consequences of a shortage (cavities and unhealthy gums) were pointed out. In February the danger of the month was not getting enough exercise: people have a tendency to stay in their warm rooms, huddled around the heaters and getting fat, during this coldest part of the year. For March, the last month of the school year, children are given a checklist of healthful diet habits and offered the opportunity to score themselves. The guidelines suggest that they should eat 80 percent foods they like and 20 percent ones they don't care for and that they should drink milk and eat soybean products every day, not eat too much meat and fish, remember to eat green vegetables, and avoid drinking juice and the like. "The like," I think, includes soft drinks and coffee, sold in the same kinds of cans as juice.

Most of the menus seem nutritionally in line with American thinking on good eating habits, and most of the advice sounds a lot like what we hear in the United States. The major difference is in the classification of fruit and the effects of sweet foods. Fruit is considered a sweet and therefore both fattening and debilitating, since sweet things cause lethargy and listlessness, not, as in the United States, a sugar high. Pregnant women avoid fruits for this reason, and when I included apple juice and a banana in the lunch for my children on Sports Day, I was seen as sabotaging their efforts. (The peanut butter sandwich made it even worse.) A sweet tooth is considered a stereotypically feminine, childish characteristic, and I expect that older boys in elementary school are moving away from liking sweet things.

Nutrition and health are major focuses of the school lunch program, and the history of the program is rooted in these concerns. It began during the American occupation as a way of improving the diet of children in the war-impoverished country; American surplus foods supplemented what was available in Japan. The inclusion of milk as an ordinary beverage for children in the Japanese diet dates from this period, as do meals without rice.

The contemporary importance of school lunch is not nutrition, however; it is the social role of eating together *and all eating the same thing*. When teachers and administrators talk about lunch, this is what they emphasize. When children and parents talk about lunch, this is what they talk about, too. The Japanese recognize that individuals have different food preferences, and they recognize that there are certain foods children typically don't like—carrots, for one example, and things that require a lot of chewing, for another. At home the general expectation is that these preferences will be catered to, and many mothers do prepare different dishes, or entirely different menus, for different members of the family. But in the context of a group, such insistence on individualism is not only a nuisance but also disruptive and destructive. One ought to be willing to subordinate one's own tastes in that situation. This is a hard lesson for Japanese children to learn, but one that adults feel very strongly about. It doesn't seem obvious to Japanese children that this aspect of self is one that needs to be given up. To behave properly, it is not enough not to insist on foods one is fond of; it is required that one eat foods that are disliked. Health may be improved by this, but moral character definitely is—selfishness rooted out, sincerity and cooperation exhibited and attained.

By the time they are adults, Japanese have learned this lesson so well, and have come to feel so strongly that the camaraderie of eating in a group includes eating the same foods, that they naturally place identical orders in restaurants. When groups travel and eat in hotels or inns, the same meal is served to everyone, ordered by the host or the most senior person present. At weddings or memorial rites the same meal is given to all participants. When families dine out together, the same unanimity of choice is not necessarily seen. Most family restaurants have children's menus, and in family groups people may order individually.

School lunch is important because it is a lesson in group life, in learning to like putting aside one's own preferences in order to appear and feel more like a part of the group. It is a lesson that takes several years to learn fully. Ellen's teacher was strict about trying everything, and Sam's was less so. Overall, they both complained less about school lunch than they do in the United States.

In a different way, too, lunch is part of the moral curriculum. It is served by students, in the classroom, and students are responsible for cleaning up afterward. It's not so easy to look at a cauldron of rice or stew and dish it up so that all forty students get helpings that they like, but starting in first grade this responsibility is left to children. Because food is served by children to other children, there is also some room for negotiation with the servers for smaller or larger helpings of particular foods. Your friends may help you out as a friend, or they may be less accommodating and become part of the peer group pressure to conform to the approved group eating behavior. Children who spill or make messes cause work either for themselves or the cleanup crew, who will not be shy about showing their displeasure. Everyone takes a turn at the lunch chores; they are neither reward nor punishment.

Pleasing and being fair to everyone, taking turns at responsibility and not causing trouble for others, enjoying the sociability of eating together, finding a sense of community in shared activities and shared food—all these are things to be learned while eating a nutritious lunch.

The issue of school lunch as a distinctively Japanese activity has also recently come to the foreground of public attention. The many families returning from overseas bring with them stories of how different lunch is in foreign settings, and their stories reconfirm the social learning that goes on. When Japanese children in the United States speak of what they miss about Japan, school lunch is often on the list, and when Japanese adults talk about the differences between U.S. and Japanese schools, lunch is a topic usually raised. School lunch is about learning to be a social human, specifically a Japanese human.

In part because of this, and also because of a generally increasing concern about what it is to be Japanese, the actual foods served at lunch have come under scrutiny. As mentioned before, this program started under occupation forces initiative and with American foods as an important element in the menus. Now there is some impetus for getting rid of the "foreign" elements in the food. This has been expressed in the sentiment that modern Japanese children are not becoming skillful enough in the use of chopsticks and that the schools should assist in passing on this skill by serving more meals that require chopsticks. Taken at face value, this criticism of the younger generation is not very credible. The Japanese diet has changed and become more cosmopolitan recently, but Western food and Western eating implements have by no means supplanted Japanese customs at home. Children use chopsticks routinely and often at home. Nor has it ever in the past been part of the school's task to teach children to use chopsticks. Only as another assertion of "Japanese-ness" does this make sense. It could be interpreted by Japanese of some liberal political persuasions as another move on the part of the Ministry of Education, or the education establishment generally, to reestablish the inculcation of patriotism and Japanese identity as part of the legitimate function of public schools, a function that has been vigorously contested since the end of the Second World War. Okubo Higashi served chopstick meals about 40 percent of the time.

PHYSICAL EDUCATION

Japanese schools have large playgrounds and athletic fields. These spaces contrast with the congested buildings around them and in most neighborhoods are the only open areas. They almost always seem to be filled with boys and girls in physical education uniforms, all of them active. I had been more or less prepared for a strong academic program in Japanese elementary schools, but I was surprised at the emphasis placed on physical education and other nonacademic subjects, such as art and music. Japanese education has taken to heart the notion of educating the whole child.

Japanese schools approach physical education as an educationally important subject that should be fun. Children should learn skills, strength, and endurance, taught through a sound pedagogy and lots of practice. Everyone, not just those with athletic ability, can become physically proficient and have fun. Physical education is one of the subjects the national Ministry of Education requires and provides a curriculum for. Not only are there detailed guides for teachers, but there are also specified numbers of hours of physical education classes each year (three periods per week), and there is a textbook for each grade. It had never occurred to anyone in our family that there could be such a thing. There's homework, too!

Children and teachers always change into their physical education uniforms in the classroom. Classes are usually held outdoors on the playground, and the equipment there is used in the curriculum— it's the same in nearly every school in Japan. Each school also has a gymnasium and a swimming pool for use in the physical education program. The regular classroom teacher also teaches physical education, wearing a track suit for these classes and participating vigorously in demonstrations. Some are known to be better at this that others; Sam's teacher was considered a very athletic woman who had no trouble keeping up with the fifth-grade boys, and this was worthy of comment.

Children seem to enjoy these classes, and the general philosophy that everyone can do everything, with effort and practice, is in full play here. Competition between individuals is consistently minimized; even team activities are mostly of the kind in which any one individual's efforts are submerged in the group's efforts, so that praise or blame are not easily attached to specific people. But the skills that each child is expected to learn are quite challenging, and there are definite standards for achievement.

The physical education curriculum and style of presenting new material shares some general features with the pedagogical style found in other subjects. Each stage starts with instructions in how to do something everyone can already do and moves on to things that are new. These are presented in the same format as the ones already mastered. The effect seems to be to entice kids into new competencies with minimal anxiety, a sort of "Well, I did the last step, so I guess I can do the next one, too" attitude. (I can't help thinking that an equally plausible reaction would be "It can't be very serious if they're teaching me stuff I already know," but I didn't see any signs that Japanese react that way.)

In keeping with this strategy, the first-grade textbook for physical education opens by showing pictures of how to use the playground equipment to play. There are pictures of children climbing the jungle gym, jumping over the tire hurdles, and swinging from the monkey bars. This same equipment is found in public playgrounds and preschools, and everyone knows how to use it. Most American children figure out what to do with a jungle gym without any instruction; so do Japanese kids.

The next page shows diagrams of how to run a simple relay race and of three versions of tag, again games children are very familiar with. Then there are some pictures of things to do on the stationary bars, such as skinning the cat, several mounts, and turns or somersaults, which are not necessarily familiar. Other pictures on this page show first graders on low balance beams. Depicting several children on one beam at once is not just for economy of illustration; it's part of the lesson, mentioned in the box at the top of the page. If several children can use a piece of equipment at the same time, no one will have to spend much time waiting for a turn, and everyone will get more practice and play time.

On this page for the first time is a little chart for grading one's own performance. Most succeeding sections of the textbook include such a chart. Several questions about the activities of the unit are asked, and children are asked whether they could do these things very well, well, or if they needed improvement. But the questions, to my surprise, are not focused on objective or competitive measures of competence. Every set of questions includes the word *tanoshii*, "enjoyable, pleasant." It's the word teachers and parents use to entice children into doing something. "Try it, it will be fun." Or, "Did you have fun?" Children are really directed to ask themselves, "Did I succeed in having fun doing these activities?" Hidden in these questions is an assumption that skill brings pleasure, that being able to do something makes that activity enjoyable, that the way to have fun is to become skillful, and that one ought to evaluate this aspect of one's own participation. Failing to have fun in required activities is a failure, too, one that can be measured only by self-evaluation, not by grades.

The questions also focus on doing activities according to the rules, safely and cooperatively. By fifth grade the questions are also asking whether one has really tried and has set goals for learning new skills or improving one's performance. The fifth-grade text also has numerous charts of national performance averages and provides places to calculate class averages as well as to record one's own achievements. Competition and measuring oneself against others comes into play here, but the competition is not directly against classmates so much as contributing to the class's record compared with other classes.

Each year's textbook includes a wide range of activities: lots of gymnastics, swimming, field events, racing and relay races, basketball, soccer and softball, calisthenics, and dancing. These are all profusely illustrated. There are also yearly fitness tests with national standards given for children to meet.

The textbooks for physical education are not just for show. In Ellen's class each physical education period was preceded by looking at the textbook to study the day's activities. At this level there are many pictures and not much text. Many of the pictures are series photographs or drawings showing how a game should be played, a relay race run, or a gymnastics move attempted. The class changed clothes and moved to the playground and, after short reminders about what they were to do, started the active part of the class. Usually the beginning of class included a demonstration of the activity, done by a student or the teacher. Sam reported that the fifth-grade procedure was about the same but with less use of the textbook. Probably other students read the text for homework, but Sam was unable to do this.

I attended part of Sam's physical education class on one of the parents' visiting days. The students in their uniforms were standing loosely around the gym at the beginning of class, ignoring the visiting mothers. They were wearing headbands in four different colors. The class began as the daily monitors looked around at their classmates, announced it was time to begin, gave the signal for everyone to bow to the teacher, and intoned the usual opening formula, "*Sensei, onegai shimasu,*" "Teacher, please teach us."

The first activity was warm-up calisthenics led by the teacher with a whistle. The routine seemed familiar to everyone. Even though some students were not very enthusiastic about doing these, no one stopped to scold them, and no child refused altogether to participate. Next they quickly divided into groups of five for some gymnastics, again done by whistle and command. These involved various balancing routines that would show up in the Sports Day performances later. Again, everyone seemed to have them pretty well under control, but occasional mistakes passed without comment and were self-corrected. All of these activities moved along quickly and more or less in unison but certainly did not look militaristic. They would have seemed rather sloppy if military appearance had been the goal. But if the goal was for everyone to proceed at a quick but individual pace, and for everyone to do everything, then it was well done. Next they lined up by height and divided into groups to do basketball drills. I heard from Sam later that after the drills they played a "game" of basketball. The part I watched took about twenty minutes of a forty-five-minute period.

Textbooks give a good indication of what goes on in school but not a total picture. However, during summer vacation all children attended school swimming classes, and because these were held outdoors, it was easy for me to sit under a nearby tree and see how things proceeded. On various visits to the school, I watched other physical education classes outdoors as well, and Sports Day is a showcase for what children do in physical education.

On the first day of swimming classes for Ellen's group, about eighty students and only six or seven mothers were present. Each child brought a uniform swimming suit, with a large name label on it, a swimming cap, green for first graders, and a health check card. This card is to be shown before each swimming lesson. You're supposed to take your child's temperature in the morning and record it, along with comments on their health that day. A teacher checks the card for each child and stamps it. One boy who didn't have the card was sent in to telephone home. His mother came and looked through his pack for the card and couldn't find it. She had to acquire a new one from the office and say he was okay. Then he was allowed in.

The students were divided into four groups, though these didn't seem to be ability groups. There were two classroom teachers in charge of getting the pool ready, checking cards, and checking the water temperature and purity, and there was one teacher who did the swimming instruction. The first routine was stretching exercises. (The boy who came in late because he didn't have his card was taken through these separately before he joined the group.) All the children seemed pleased to be doing these and cooperated. In this, as in the other joint activities that followed, though the teachers clearly expected everyone to be doing them together, they were not willing to take the time to get 100 percent attention—85 to 90 percent seemed to be sufficient for them to move on. There was no one who was totally uncooperative; they all joined in before the activity was over.

After the stretching there were a few sentences of talk, and then the first half of the students got into the water, on a shallow ledge at the edge, and proceeded to splash themselves gently in the tummy, then turn around and splash each other's back. Then the second group got in to do the same thing. Ellen was in this group, and it was 10:00 exactly when she got in the water for the first time, thirty minutes after the beginning of class. The next step was for the first group to do this all over again and also to walk over to the center of the pool and back. Then the second group. Then the first group did it again, walking to the center and going underwater. Then the second group. I left at this point and didn't get back till the lesson was over at 10:45. Talking to Ellen, I sympathized that there wasn't much swimming time and not much time for play. She seemed surprised and insisted it had been fun.

In other classes I watched, I could see that there was a great deal of variation in swimming ability at the beginning of these lessons. Many first graders have taken swimming lessons; others are beginners. The teachers largely ignored this disparity. Children with greater swimming skills were not held back or discouraged from swimming as well as they could, but they were not praised for this either, and they were not separated from less skillful children for different instruction. Nor were there any steps in the procedures that they skipped. Less able swimmers were matter-of-factly instructed, and their efforts were noted. The emphasis was on having everyone reach the goals for first graders set by the curriculum. Since not everyone attended every swimming class, it was hard to tell about the achievement of every child, but at the last class I watched, every first grader managed to swim twenty-five meters, and this was recorded on a certificate.

During the winter term of our year in Urawa, everyone in school was given an inexpensive jump rope and a program for using it. Each grade had a list of goals, including several styles of jumping, such as forward, backward, on one foot, and with arms crossed and the number of times you should be able to jump in each style. There was also a goal for the number of consecutive minutes of jumping, which increased yearly. These goals were not impossible, but they were not easy for Sam and Ellen to achieve. Although classes at school gave children an opportunity to practice, they also brought their ropes home, and both Sam and Ellen needed the "homework" practice to reach the goals for their grade. I don't think it's accidental that this was scheduled for the winter term, a time when children might be inclined to be less physically active.

The routines of daily life for Japanese children also encourage physical activity, as they do to a lesser degree for adults. Children all walk to school and home, up to a mile each way, carrying heavy backpacks. Most families use public transportation most of the time; this always entails a walk to a bus stop or a train station and climbing stairs through the station at each end and at each change. Even though the public transportation system is efficient and easily accessible (unless you're physically handicapped in any way), using it still entails more walking and carrying than using a family car. Women do most of their daily errands walking or on bicycles, including grocery shopping, and men who commute to work nearly always use public transportation. Many children play outdoors during free time, riding bicycles or playing soccer or baseball, and many are enrolled in activity classes. The most popular are probably swimming, gymnastics, ballet, and Japanese martial arts such as judo or kendo.

In addition to the sections devoted to physical skills in the textbooks, short sections on growth and development are included each year, and each child's height and weight are recorded several times a year. For the fifth graders this section also discusses the social and physical changes that are associated with approaching puberty. Among the physical changes mentioned are a general toughening of body for boys and a rounding and softening for girls, deepening voices for boys and first menstruation and breast development for girls, and more body hair for both. The book emphasizes that the timing of these physical changes varies greatly; charts show the range of ages at which Japanese boys experience the appearance of pubic hair and deepening of their voices and the range of ages at which Japanese girls develop breasts and begin menstruating.

Both sexes are said to be becoming more mature, with better judgment, greater physical and mental competence, increased capacities to persist and endure hardship, more ability to control the expression of emotion, and improved competence with words. This is shown by a chart indicating the growth of vocabulary during this period and by illustrations of disputes that they can now handle verbally. The text also points out that whereas boys and girls played together as young children, during third and fourth grades they formed separate play groups; but starting sometime in the period of fifth grade through junior high school, they can expect to become more interested in the opposite sex. Boys will become stronger and more manly; girls will become gentler, more thoughtful of other people, and more womanly.

On reflection, back in America with an adolescent and a preadolescent in the house, I am struck by the positive view of this period of life articulated in the text. There are no warnings about stormy emotional times ahead, about conflicts with parents and teachers, about new temptations and distractions that may appear. Instead of talking about troubles, this text emphasizes the new and greater powers of self-control and restraint that come with this stage of life—not a view of teenagers widespread in the United States.

Finally, there are several sections in the text that deal with safety concerns, especially those involved in streets and roads for pedestrians and bicyclists. In fact, Saitama prefecture supplements these sections with additional small textbooks devoted solely to safety, mostly concerned with traffic and roads, the setting of most injuries to children.

Children in America often dislike physical education for various reasons. Those who are physically proficient view it as additional playtime hampered by the interference of adults, while those who are not proficient feel that they are not "taught," that the classes do not give them new skills or competencies but simply highlight their inabilities vis-à-vis more athletic classmates. The range of activities in Japanese physical education classes is wide, very little of it is competitive, and there is an emphasis on learning skills. After all, this is another area in which native talent is thought to play only a very small role; everyone needs to learn and practice, and ability follows. Even the best students are thus willing to do drills and accept instruction, making their activities in class not so different from those of other students. It turns out to be true that almost everyone can become competent at these activities and improve performance to acceptable and enjoyable levels. For, though students do not compete directly with each other, there are many activities in which they try to reach or exceed standards set from outside by the Ministry of Education, which determines how far first graders should be able to throw a softball and how many seconds fifth-grade girls should take to run fifty meters. When I watched children during physical education classes, I noticed that most of them seemed happy, all of them were active almost all of the time (no waiting passively in line for one's turn), and their activity was focused, not just horsing around.

ART AND MUSIC

When friends in Japan needed to explain a word to me, or ask for a word in English, they often drew a picture. I can't draw, so I was denied this useful technique. Addresses in Japan only get you to the general neighborhood, so people draw maps to help one another quite frequently. I was always impressed with their neatness, accuracy, and pleasant appearance. I myself could barely produce an intelligible map of how to get to our house from the train station. At some point I began to wonder why everyone in Japan could draw and I couldn't. Of course, I'd known since about second grade that I wasn't good at art, and I hadn't drawn anything since then. I had only vague memories of any art classes in school, though I enjoyed wood carving, weaving, and some other crafts in seventh grade.

When I started reading about the Japanese philosophy of education, the "anyone can do anything" school of thought, I wondered how teachers could sustain this attitude in the face of what seemed to me to be overwhelming evidence of natural differences in talents and inclinations, especially in the arts. But not being able to draw bothered me more and more as I reflected on my friends' competence and comfort in drawing. Surely not all 120 million Japanese could be more talented than I.

I finally decided that I would make a private test of the Japanese approach, and I signed up for beginners' drawing lessons at a local museum. I learned that I could learn to draw. I still think I have no talent, and it would take more than eight Sunday afternoons to become competent, but I'm sure I could do it. Drawing is a very physical skill, I was somehow surprised to discover, and practice pays off, just as it does in music. The confidence those eight afternoons gave me enabled me to avoid quitting in panic when I discovered that my flower arranging lessons in Japan included making a drawing of my finished arrangement at the end of each class. Teachers and fellow students were polite enough not to comment.

In the United States Sam and Ellen had both had art as a regularly scheduled subject with specialist teachers. Sam had brought home some art projects that seemed interesting and good to us, usually constructed, three-dimensional things rather than drawings. Ellen has always been considered the one in our family who is "good at art," the kind of child who always carries around a notebook and pencils or crayons to fall back on during boring times, like car trips or religious services.

I was really looking forward to seeing how art and music would be handled in elementary school in Japan, and I was sure the lessons would incorporate the idea that everyone, not just specially talented people, could do these things. I was able to watch some classes in these subjects, see the things children produced and listen to their performances, listen to my children talk about them, and study the textbooks.

To me the most surprising thing about the first-grade art projects was how many of them were cooperative efforts. Even drawings, such as murals for the classroom wall or huge drawings made with chalk on the school playground, were joint productions. Large sand sculptures in the school sand box, as well as snowmen and snow buildings, were part of art class, and the text shows pictures of a group of children using newspapers on the gym floor to lay out a human figure big enough for everyone to lie down on. Sometimes individual children made parts for a larger construction such as a mobile or a display of many clay figures all arranged on the seat, the back, and the legs and rungs of a chair.

Sometimes children did individual drawings on suggested topics: something nice that happened at school today, a picture to tell *sensei* a story, a picture to show a friend. Several projects called for making toys, puppets, or props for playing house, or floating toys for a bathtub or pond.

Art is scheduled for a double class period, so children have at least ninety minutes for each art lesson. Some of the projects are quite elaborate and require several steps. "How good it'll feel when we're finished!" seems an appropriate comment in the text.

The fifth-grade art curriculum continues the emphasis on using a wide range of media and on persistence in carrying out a project. Like the first-grade text, the fifth-grade one is illustrated mostly with things made by fifth graders, but some illustrations of artworks by both Japanese and Western artists are also used, in contexts that make them seem like achievable models.

Fifth graders continue to do drawings on assigned topics, such as "A Day to Remember," but more technical advice is now offered. Planning is emphasized: what shape to use, choosing a viewpoint, the emotions conveyed by color choices, how to frame a picture with one's hands to compose it, choosing what to foreground and what to exclude. A lesson on watercolor landscapes teaches various approaches to representing the sky. Explicit approaches to figure drawing and perspective are included in the text. One lesson on illustrating a folktale suggests choosing the three most important elements of the story and somehow incorporating all of them in the illustration, as well as including other supporting elements. Six examples of this for one story are shown.

One of the big projects of this year, which took several art periods, was making an illustrated storybook for a younger child. This meant choosing the story, planning the layout of text and illustrations, writing the text, making the illustrations, mounting them on pages, designing and making a cover, and binding the book. Other projects also took planning and difficult execution with a variety of tools: wood block prints, geometric cardboard boxes decorated with cutouts, a wooden jigsaw puzzle made with a power jigsaw, and fanciful wooden frames for mirrors. Even stone carving is included in the text, though Sam said his class didn't do this. There were still a few class projects, but many fewer than in first grade.

There is a national holiday in October in Japan, Culture Day, and though it is a day off from school, it is celebrated on other days in school. Friends commented to me during the month, "Ellen is in first grade, isn't she? Did she have a chicken at school for Culture Day?" If an activity turns out to be a good idea in Japan, it can turn into a tradition, not a sign of stagnant thinking. Ellen's class did have a chicken, alive and wandering throughout the classroom for Culture Day. The children talked about how it looked, imitated its movements, fed it, watched its activities, and drew it. Ellen came home excited about the day, exclaiming about how hard it was to draw something that didn't hold still. Later I saw the exhibit of all the drawings from the class. The first graders were instructed to "fill the page," and they did (Ellen had to start over to do this), but otherwise there was a great deal of variety and spirit in the many depictions.

Sam's class did what fifth graders and many older children do: they went to a nearby temple to draw and sketch and prepare to do a watercolor to be finished in later art periods. I have often seen groups of children on expeditions like this and have been impressed by several things: their freedom—one teacher taking forty-five seventh graders to a park for the day, when many of them will be out of sight for much of the time?—their high spirits and high jinks, the amount of work they did actually get done, and the variety of the works they were producing. Everyone might be sketching in the same temple grounds, but some were making meticulous drawings of small detail, some focusing on a large landscape of the grounds, others choosing different features of the temple to highlight. Some worked in charcoal, some in pencils, some in crayons, some in watercolors.

Sam made a watercolor of the temple, showing its great looming roof, the delicate wood carving, the bell to summon the gods, the old trees, and the frame for hanging up fortune papers. It's not a masterpiece, but it's pleasant, recognizable, somewhat atmospheric, and shows some control of watercolor techniques. When I asked Sam how he knew how to make it, he said, "Oh, I was mixing the paints with too much water, but the kids showed me how to do it." He didn't mention the drawing style, though it's different from anything I have seen him do before or since.

In music, the major instrument used by first graders is called a *pianika*. It's about twelve inches long, four inches wide, with a piano keyboard of two octaves. But it is a wind instrument with a long plastic tube to blow into. One can rest it on a table, so that it can be played like a small piano—powered by wind—or it can be carried vertically, so that it is played like an accordion keyboard, with the air power coming from the player's breath instead of a bellows. Every child has one of these to be used at school and taken home for practice.

Besides this instrument there is a variety of percussion instruments in the class used during music lessons. Each classroom also has a small electric organ for the teacher. Several teachers told me that the hardest part of their preparation for becoming a teacher was passing the course and examination in music, especially playing the piano or organ.

First graders learn the mechanics of playing a wind instrument with a keyboard, so they have to control both their breath and their hands. By the end of the second third of first grade, students have learned twelve short songs. They are all in the key of C major, but some of the later songs involve a change of hand position during the song, and one involves both an ascending and a descending scale in C major, with thumb-under and finger-over fingering patterns.

First graders have also come a long way in learning to read music by this time. They can read the pitch of tones in the C major scale on the treble clef and they know the solfège names of the notes. They know how to count the beats in a measure, the concept of rests, and the time values of notes. The last third of the year is spent in gradually introducing standard music notation for these concepts. The number of beats in a measure is first introduced simply by writing 2, 3, or 4 on the staff at the beginning of the piece, but in the last third of first grade, this is written in the standard 2 over 4 or 3 over 4 notation on the staff. Time values are introduced by using notes of different shapes, such as half circles for half beats and elongated ovals for long notes, but by the end of the year, quarter, half, and eighth notes are written in the standard forms.

When I went to Ellen's class on the second parents' visiting day, I found we had been invited for a music class. They were working on a song I had heard Ellen practicing at home. They all knew how to sing it and had talked about the solfège pattern of the melody. Today's lesson involved using their *pianika*s to play a part of each line in unison. The teacher played the first part of each line on her organ, and the class, or various portions of it, played the end of the line. She insisted that they come in at the right time, with no break in the timing of the song, all together, and play the right notes. If an individual made a mistake, she usually made the class or the group repeat the line. For variation sometimes a part of the class used bells as percussion accompaniment. After working on the ends of the lines for a while, she got individuals to give her the solfège pattern of the beginning of each line, and they practiced a little bit at playing that with their fingers in the air, as a group. It looked as though the goal of this set of lessons was to be able to sing the song, to play the whole thing correctly on the *pianika,* and to be able to perform it as part of an ensemble that included at least three parts: organ, *pianika,* and percussion.

Ellen as a first grader got in on the beginning of learning to read music and could keep up with what was going on. (I couldn't help feeling sorry for her. Here she was, having just learned to read English, needing to learn to read Japanese, and now music, too. She didn't complain about the music, though, and not even about Japanese after the initial hump during summer vacation.) Sam, though, had not had private music lessons at home and had had only one semester of recorder playing in fourth grade in school. He had to learn to play the recorder, the instrument most used in Japanese fifth grade, and how to read music, fast. His teacher asked me during one visit how it was that he hadn't learned to read music and seemed surprised that not everyone does this in school in the United States. Sam said, though, that he was just given easy parts in the ensemble playing and that he was not left out of the lessons. He did study the fingering for the recorder at home and apparently picked up enough to get by. It didn't seem to surprise him or anyone else that he would or could do this. When the fifth graders gave a performance for their mothers near the end of the year, Sam's group chose to play several musical selections, and Sam participated as everyone else did.

In the apartment building where we lived, there was a piano available in the recreation room, and for about six months Sam and Ellen took piano lessons and practiced there. In retrospect, and as I write this book, I am amazed that we would have thought piano lessons were a good idea at that time. It seems that life and school in Japan, as I report it, would be more than enough to keep everyone busy. In some ways that is true, but Sam and Ellen also found themselves with some leisure time that was hard to fill. After their forty or more hours a week in Japanese-speaking school, even Japanese TV was not too enticing. They watched some, but not very much. They also played with friends after school, but some days they just wanted to escape having to deal with Japanese. I read a lot in the evenings to Ellen; Sam usually listened, and he read more in English than ever before or since. Piano lessons turned out to be an activity that gave them each a feeling of accomplishment that didn't depend on knowing Japanese. Sam said that learning to read music made music in school better too.

The teacher we found was a university music student who also taught the son of some friends. I went along to the lessons, both to help translate and to observe. Much of the lesson procedure was familiar from my childhood piano lessons, but two parts of each lesson were activities I had never done. The first was a dictation: the teacher would play a simple sequence of notes, and Sam or Ellen would have to write them in music notation. She would give them the first note, but after that they could not see what she was doing. They were supposed to get both the rhythm and the notes annotated correctly. This is difficult to do, but its value in learning to listen seemed clear to me, and I wished I had had similar practice.

The second activity is still puzzling to me. Here the student turns away from the piano, and the teacher plays a single note in isolation, which the student then identifies by pitch name. She always used notes in the range of the pieces the children were playing. This seemed very peculiar to me because I associated the ability to do this with "having perfect pitch," something one simply had or didn't have, like blue eyes. When I finally asked the teacher about this part of the lesson, she said it is standard practice in Japanese music lessons, and that everyone who studies music at a university is tested on their ability to identify the absolute pitch of any note in the range of the piano. One can learn "perfect pitch"? Only in Japan. On reflection, and thinking about other abilities humans have in hearing, I can't think of any reason why one can't learn to identify eighty-eight pitches, but the skill isn't one American music lessons typically emphasize.

Some Japanese children take private music lessons. Elementary school is considered the best time for this, because children may have to sacrifice such recreational activities if they are serious about preparing for high school entrance examinations during junior high school. Okubo Higashi school has a marching band, which some children join. For some reason this is a more popular club activity for girls than for boys. Children get some instruction for these instruments and can use instruments owned by the school. The PTA was planning to buy uniforms for them with money raised the year we were there. The band plays for some school assemblies, on Sports Day, and in the city parade held during the Urawa Festival each summer. In comparison with school bands I have heard in the United States, I thought they sounded good.

MORAL EDUCATION

Among the subjects prescribed by the Ministry of Education for study during all nine years of compulsory education is one called "morals," to be studied one hour each week. This is an idea that always startles Westerners, especially Americans with their fixation on separation of church and state. It is also an idea that is the subject of a great deal of anxiety and opposition in Japan. After describing the morals curriculum, I want to show how the basis for support and opposition to the idea and fact of "morals in the schools" is fundamentally different in Japan and in Western countries.

I observed one morals class, and I have carefully studied the textbooks for first and fifth grades and discussed with teachers and parents the nature of these classes. Sam and Ellen are relatively unable to report on their morals classes; their language competence wasn't at a high enough level to do that. The morals textbooks share the style of the other textbooks—they are paperbacks, attractively illustrated and printed, with thirty-eight lessons for the year. The lessons are stories with study questions appended. One difference from other textbooks is the reading difficulty level. In this book alone, *kanji* (Chinese characters) that children might have difficulty with are identified with accompanying syllabic symbols, so that even students who are not up to grade level in reading ability are not deterred from reading the stories. In other words, the emphasis is resolutely on the content, which is not being used to teach "academic" subjects. These books are also among those that open in the Japanese style, "backward," as are the Japanese language and calligraphy texts.

The stories in each text fall into several categories, each represented in each year's book. The first type of story tells about how some individual overcame a real or perceived inferiority, acknowledging the help of others and emphasizing persistence and hard work. A fifth-grade story, for instance, is told by a woman who is the voice of a famous cartoon character known to all Japanese children. It tells how she made a strength of her "strange" voice. It seems important to me that this model woman succeeded not by changing this characteristic but by using her strangeness in a way that was effective. She didn't have to deny her individuality, or hide it, but learned to use it to best advantage.

A second type of story emphasizes the importance of commitments to other people. A first-grade story about the devotion of penguin mothers to their eggs and chicks is in this category, as is a fifth-grade story about an aspiring performer who makes a promise to perform for a sick child, then is offered a chance to appear in a prestigious show but turns it down to keep his promise to the child. Perhaps the story about a little girl who tries to bring her housebound grandmother an apron full of sunshine and whose disappointment is met by her grandmother's statement, "There is sunshine in your eyes," fits in this category, too. The first-grade story about appreciation day for the school kitchen workers, which tells about one girl's recognition of the hardness of this work as shown by the cafeteria workers' hands, is another example. Each individual is valuable, and the sacrifices or efforts people make for one another should not be unacknowledged.

Another set of stories emphasizes the importance of standing up for what is right and defending others against injustice. A fifth-grade story with this moral is set on a train where a man is berating a fellow passenger, a woman who has inadvertently bumped against him. She apologizes, but he refuses to accept her apology, finally suggesting she kneel with her hands on the floor of the train and kowtow to show her sincerity (thus invoking deep-seated notions about the "dirtiness" of any surface that is touched by people's shoes, surfaces both physically and ritually dirty). An elderly woman then intervenes but is shoved aside by the man, who continues to rail at the offending woman. Suddenly, the old woman calls out in a strong voice, "Wait, all of you. Why are you quiet? Why do you overlook this bad conduct? You mean it is okay as long as you yourself are safe?" The narrator of the story then finds himself protesting to the man; he is joined by the other passengers, and the unforgiving man escapes the train at the next station. The elderly woman tells the storyteller not to be afraid any more. The study questions that accompany this story ask students to evaluate the storyteller and to think about whether they have ever behaved bravely in public.

A first-grade story with this theme is set at school, where a boy observes the class rowdy hiding the shoes of another boy, so that he can't find them when it is time to go home. Though he is afraid of the bully, he suggests to him that he should give back the shoes. The bully's response is a glare, and the storyteller, with his heart pounding, stares back. The story ends with no further resolution.

Many of the stories seem to stop without an obvious conclusion. Another example is an incident in which a boy denies responsibility for spilling milk and instead blames the family cat. His mother accepts his story, but he then feels sad. That's the end of the text.

Another set of stories extends the notion of moral behavior to encompass areas of nature, as well as human relations. One way this is done is through focusing on the beauty and intricacies of natural phenomena and pointing out that humans ought not to destroy these, so some stories show children noticing natural things that they could destroy, such as insects laying eggs or flowers blooming in the snow, but leaving them alone. Another is through attributing moral behavior to animals or plants—the dandelion that pushes through asphalt to bloom seems to be meant to express the idea that persistence is a "natural" virtue. The penguin as an exemplary mother also suggests that human behavior and animal behavior have features and motivations in common. There are several reasons for using animals in fables, and Aesop is a favorite source for stories in these texts, but the effect is to make a connection between humans and other living things and to suggest that their realms are not totally distinct. A major motivation in the proliferation of books with only animal characters for preschool children in the United States is the desire to sidestep the problems involved in identifying characters by race, ethnic identity, and sometimes age. If everyone in the book is a dog, or a cat, or a pig, or a dinosaur, you don't have to decide which occupations to assign to different races, for instance. This motivation is not present in Japan, though the desire for cuteness certainly is also present there.

Nationalism or patriotism is a theme presented by retelling stories from Japanese history or folklore and by discussions of Japanese traditional customs. A fifth-grade story, for instance, tells about a boy going with his grandfather to watch the summer fireworks at the Sumida River in Tokyo (a wonderful display, as we can attest). The grandfather tells how he came as a boy and how the festival had to be suspended for many years because the river was so polluted. Both are glad that the river is now clean and the festival has been reinstated. The study questions for this story ask students to think about the grandfather's feelings when the fireworks were resumed. They also ask, "When do you feel happy about living in your local area? When do you feel happy about living in Japan?"

The nationalism in these stories is neatly balanced by internationalism themes. Non-Japanese are regularly offered as models to follow, two heroes from the first-grade text being Florence Nightingale, presented saving an injured puppy, and Lord Byron, shaming a bully and defending a friend at boarding school. A fifth-grade story recounts the ambivalence of a Japanese boy at seeing the splendid artworks from Japan in a museum in Boston. Though he is proud of them, he also regrets that they are no longer in Japan. An American man tells him, "Japan is a small country, but its art is world famous. Don't you feel that Japan has expanded to the world? When we non-Japanese look at Japanese works, we appreciate Japan. These works are so good they should not be confined in Japan. They are treasures of the world and should be shared with the world." A study question after this story asks, "What do you think about foreign cultures and people?" The depth of the Japanese ambivalence about themselves and other cultures is evident, and hardly resolved, in this lesson.

One of the most striking stories, to non-Japanese, is one found in the first-grade text. This story tells how a boy from the first-grade class becomes suddenly ill and is admitted to the hospital. His classmates send a letter exhorting him to try hard to get better, but he dies without ever returning to the class. After the funeral, his best friend keeps a diary of thoughts about the missing classmate and how they can never again meet or play together. The last line from the diary says, "But your friends will never forget you. We will all persevere to make up your part." Several Japanese graduate students in America confirmed this as a good translation of the Japanese. But it was still a puzzling story conclusion, and I had to ask a number of Japanese students to interpret the meaning for me.

Their first reaction usually was, "What's the problem?" I answered that I didn't understand what "making up his part" meant—what was the dead boy's part, and how could other students make it up? Several themes consistently showed up in their attempts to explain this notion, which seemed straightforward to them until they started to explain it to me. First and most consistent was the recognition that the dead boy's life had been unfinished, cut short in a way that meant he would not experience a full human life. Not only did this mean there were certain positive experiences he could never have, but it meant that there were responsibilities he would not be able to fulfill. His death also meant that a group that had once been complete, the first-grade class, now had a missing piece, a hole. His friend's farewell, "But your friends will never forget you. We will persevere to make up your part," emphasizes that the classmates will carry out his responsibilities and repair the completeness of the group by not forgetting him. All the Japanese agreed that the expression of this sentiment was intended to make the dead boy feel better, more than the living one.

When the Japanese students talked about the incompleteness of the dead boy's life, it was the lack of positive experiences, such as graduation and marriage, that they most often mentioned. But the word that I have translated as "persevere", *gambaru,* is one that has a definite sense of taking up a burden as part of its meaning. I think two Japanese ideas are part of the explanation for this choice of words. First is the notion that doing well what one ought to do is a source of pleasure, and thus there is cause for regret that the dead boy will not have the opportunity for these feelings. Second is the notion that a complete and harmonious group is the result of effort by all its members; therefore, the remaining children will have to "repair" the group by making up the work the missing boy would have done.

Finally, there is the notion that there continues to be a connection between the dead boy and his living classmates, one that is nurtured by memory. When I pressed the Japanese students as to how the children might keep alive the memory of their classmate, they suggested things like taking his photograph along on school trips or picnics. They also said, "Of course, we can't really live his life for him. We can't really increase our efforts to make up for his. But we like to think about this." There was some disagreement about whether the dead boy, if he were remembered, would progress through something like an earthly life course, though he is dead. On the one hand, death is final. This does not cause a problem in the case of someone who dies at a ripe old age, his life course run. Those who remember him will remember him at different ages, in different ways; their memories will be of a complete life. But in the case of a young child, those who remember him will also think about the life he would have lived and imagine what his later years would have been. The Japanese students seemed unsure of whether this in effect meant the dead child would in some way move through later life stages. One student mentioned, and others recognized, an unusual custom: living relatives sometimes arrange spirit marriages between young people who have died without having had this life-fulfilling experience.

The last oddity about this story is its extreme unlikeliness in modern Japan. Unlike children in many poor countries, Japanese children have very little experience with death among their contemporaries. Given the long life expectancies in Japan, most of them will be well into their adult years before anyone they know dies. Why, then, include this story in a first-grade text?

It would be wrong to say that this is a story about religion or ancestor worship, and yet it is a story that points up attitudes that underlie those practices, without which they make no sense. First is the idea that the lives of the living are connected to the lives of the dead, and that the dead take an interest in the living (in Japan, a benevolent interest). Second is the idea that not being remembered by the living causes distress to the spirits of the dead and may even make them vindictive in their connection to the living, the premise of most of the many Japanese ghost stories in folklore and literature. And third, there is the theme of the interrelatedness of responsibility and pleasure and their parts in a complete human life. Elements of all these themes and ideas can certainly be found in other views of life and death and religion, but it seems noteworthy to me that this particular conglomeration of ideas and ambiguities should be purposely raised in the context of a first-grade morals class.

There are many other interesting features of these stories as a moral curriculum. First, there is no appeal at all to any god. There is no sacred writing offered as a source of moral guidance, no set of articulated principles, such as the Golden Rule or the Ten Commandments or Buddha's Eightfold Path—even Aesop's fables are given without their tag-line moral. There is no mention of supernatural reward or punishment. But at the same time there is no hint that the lessons are anything but universal in application. They are not specifically Japanese, there is no suggestion that different kinds of people should follow different principles of behavior (men and women, for instance, or people of different status), and the narrators of the first-person stories are left so vague in character that they could stand for any reader.

Conspicuously absent, compared to Jewish or Christian religious/moral education, is any mention of either personal or community charity or help for the unfortunate. In fact, only in stories set in premodern times are there any people who might qualify as the recipients of charity—poor, or crippled, or outcasts of some sort. One might see this as part of the overall attitude of protectiveness toward children found in Japan, or one might read it as part of a government conspiracy to deny any imperfections in modern Japanese society, if one considered the Japanese government to be that sort of government.

There is an interesting set of moral principles being taught and an interesting intertwining of themes. Individuals are clearly held responsible for their actions and decisions in these texts, and the rightness of their actions and decisions is dependent on human, not supernatural, outcomes. Individuals, regardless of station in life, are treated as valued people. Sacrifice, although it may be called for in some cases, is treated as a personal offering, not something demanded by one's position or role. Rulers as well as subjects in the tales from history are presented as constrained by moral standards. The kind of connection and identification of humans with the nonhuman natural world is one that encourages ecological responsibility, not exploitation. Nationalism and internationalism themes seem evenly balanced, and the nationalism is of a fairly benign sort. It certainly does not suggest anything like an ambitious "manifest destiny" role for Japan in the world. It also, however, does not suggest that Japan has major social or political problems at home, such as discrimination against minorities or women, or unjust economic disparities.

Most of these principles of moral behavior are probably ones that would be acceptable to most Westerners, Christian, Jewish, or secular humanist. Religious people would probably feel that the divine basis for the behaviors being promoted is important, but the behaviors themselves are ones most people can agree on, and no one religious base is being presented to the exclusion or denigration of others.

The whole "religion" aspect of morals is omitted in Japan, where morality and religion are largely separate spheres of action and thought anyway (and where sex is a nonissue, for religion and morals). One of the consequences of this separation is that the emotional and sensual aspects of religion do not serve as reinforcers of moral behavior for Japanese children. Because religion and morality *are* seen as connected spheres of thought and behavior in the West, and because religious practices use music, art, special foods, and gatherings of families and communities to mark religious occasions and holidays, those (generally pleasant) customs reinforce ethical behavior. It may be partly because Christmas is the most pleasant of Christian holidays that it is also the time for the greatest offerings of charity. Surely, the music, food, presents, trees, and family gatherings associated with Christmas in the Western world help to make the custom of giving charity at Christmas time a lighter obligation than it would be if presented only as an intellectually derived principle. This morally enjoined behavior is tightly associated with all these other positive things and becomes a part of them; most people feel there is something missing if Christmas, however secular, does not include charity.

Similarly, Western children who are involved in active religious families and churches can have a sense of community about moral behavior that Japanese children may have a hard time gaining. For them this tends to be more a school subject, and their reference group for thinking about these issues is their classmates and, to a lesser degree, their teachers. It does not include people of many different ages, for instance, or those who have family or community connections to themselves.

On the other hand, probably most Western children get a very spotty exposure to religious education, or none at all. In Japan every child has to spend at least forty hours a year more or less thinking about ethical issues broadly defined. That's more than most Western children spend in Sunday school, and in Japan that time is not shared with learning worship customs and Bible history and theology as well as ethics.

Why is it that morals is a subject in the compulsory education of Japanese children, and not a matter to be taught by families or religious institutions or in some other arena? Why is the inclusion of morals in the school curriculum a matter of controversy in Japan, especially opposed by the leaders of the teachers' unions, as well as by some Christians and radical political opponents? The answers to these questions lie in traditional Japanese views of education and the family and in modern Japanese history.

In premodern Japan, certainly throughout the Tokugawa era (1603 to 1868), if not long before, education was primarily conceived as moral education, and the most important beneficiary of education was the state. This set of ideas is broadly identified with Confucianism, a political-moral philosophy borrowed and adapted from China. In China education supported a theoretically meritocratic examination process that prepared men to become part of the ruling elite on the basis of their performance in the national examinations. In Japan education supported the preparation of young men from the ruling classes to take over their fathers' roles as rulers. Because everyone is capable of learning whatever is needed for this role, it was not necessary to find the "right" man for a leadership position; the problem was simply to get the right education to the next generation.

> There is no need to become a scholar widely read and with encyclopaedic knowledge. It is enough to get a thorough grasp of the principles of loyalty, respect, filial piety and trust. Wide learning and literary accomplishments are not necessary. Anyone can manage to get hold of the general principles of the Four Books and the Five Classics by the time he is thirty or forty. It all depends on diligence. Even the dullest of wits can manage it if he applies himself earnestly enough. (Nishi-oji fief school rules, quoted in Dore 1965:181)

In Japan the state sponsored and supported this kind of education. Commoners and those who wanted education that was not geared toward governing could pursue those interests privately. Mathematics, reading and writing in Japanese (instead of Chinese), literature, and science were among the subjects that fell into this optional area, along with all education for girls and women.

Moral education, or education in general, because it was designed to produce effective and legitimate rulers, was primarily concerned with political philosophy and morals as they related to public life. It seemed reasonable that such education should take place in a public, nonfamily setting. Because the ruling class could not always dominate the religious groups or control their teachings, this was also a nonreligious setting. There are elements of social justice even in Japanese Buddhism. In the long run, the secular institutions took over the political role of the religious ones, which retreated to a concentration on "private" concerns, especially ancestor worship, maintaining purity, and fostering a connection with immanent divinity.

In modern Japan the feeling that morals cannot be really experienced or taught at home has become stronger as *amae*, the cultivation of loving dependence among family members, has become the primary force for holding families together, as economic integration and inter-dependence has lessened. *Amae* works best if the unique individuality of the people involved is emphasized, overriding more rule-governed behavior norms. Morals involves the application of general principles to behavior between people, so it needs to be discussed and learned in a context where those principles are applicable, not at home.

For these reasons parents, teachers, and the general public feel that school is the right place to learn these lessons, and they agree that it is important for children to receive instruction in morals, that the continued existence of Japan ("such a poor, crowded country") and a civilized Japanese society depend on imparting these lessons to everyone.

The puzzle is why there is any opposition to morals in the schools, if those attitudes are very widespread. What opposition there is stems from more recent Japanese history, the Second World War and the period preceding it. As Japan pursued its progress toward industrialization and modernization, with the quest for raw materials and markets in the international arena that were required, its foreign policy became more expansionary and aggressive. Both modernization and these foreign ventures led the central government to demand sacrifices from the population of Japan. The school system was one locus in which these practices were justified to the people, and in which their intellectual and emotional commitment to the policies was cultivated (as our school systems emphasize the great benefits gained from the taxes paid by citizens, for example).

One of the major ideological forms that the persuasion effort took was an emphasis on the emperor as a godlike, fatherlike embodiment of Japan as a nation and a people. Schools taught emperor worship, including the beliefs that the emperor was to be unquestioningly obeyed, that he had the right to demand any sacrifice from his subjects, and that he and his images and words were to be treated with many of the same behavior patterns that were used with reference to the gods.

After the defeat of Japan in the Second World War, many Japanese teachers came to feel very strongly that they had been exploited and deceived into teaching this set of ideas to their students, and they felt extremely guilty about their role in helping to create a docile population who followed the military into these foreign adventures that brought such grief and suffering to the Japanese people. Postwar Japanese teachers collectively resolved through their unions not to engage in such immoral teaching again. Emperor worship had been taught under the title of "moral education" in the prewar and war periods; these teachers were opposed to a postwar resumption of "moral education" under the control of the Ministry of Education.

During the occupation period following the war, the American military shared these views and banished moral education from the curriculum. They also tried to weaken the role of the national Ministry of Education so that it could never again have such ideological control over education. The Americans sought to institute local control of education to destroy the power of the central government over education. For many reasons this attempt was not very successful, and it became less so after the occupation troops left Japan. The Ministry of Education was never very effectively "purged" after the war and has been regarded as a conservative and nationalistic ministry during the entire postwar period.

Certainly there is only a tiny minority of Japanese who would wish to repeat the practices that led to Japan's expansionism and defeat in the Second World War; no one wishes for the return of emperor worship in the schools. But the ideas outlined above about the importance of moral education for children and the appropriateness of schools for such instruction have not disappeared. Despite teachers' and parents' legitimate fears of ideological indoctrination in a moral education curriculum, the need for a moral education curriculum in the school setting has been stronger. Moral education has been reinstated as a school subject, and opposition has decreased but not disappeared.

It should not be thought, however, that the curriculum of moral education is predetermined in the Japanese school setting, that it consists of only innocuous Japanese platitudes. The subject matter called morals in Japanese schools is a set of ideas that could be designed much differently than it is, within the framework of Japanese culture. Several ethnographers have given us descriptions of "spiritual training" in other settings in Japan, and the content is quite different from the school curriculum. In particular, the absence of the themes of filial piety and the concept of *on,* obligation that must but cannot be repaid, is striking to those familiar with Japanese culture.

Kondo, in her book *Crafting Selves* (1990), gives us a vivid picture of a self-improvement course, a "spiritual training" course at Rinri Gakuen (Ethics Institute), to which her employer sent his full-time employees for their personal growth and development and to make them better employees. Here the theme of filial piety, of immeasurable gratitude to parents for the gift of life, was one of the major motivating themes, one that elicited strong emotional reactions from participants. The acceptance of life as it is, including existing authority relationships, was also emphasized at Rinri Gakuen; this theme is absent from the school morals curriculum. Rinri Gakuen enforced behavior patterns, such as the rote repetition of verbal formulas and greetings, that were meant to break down the "selfish" insistence on individuality that variations would indicate; this sort of self-denial is also missing in the school curriculum. There is instead an impressive emphasis on individuality, independent judgment, and remaining true to oneself in the school curriculum. In other contexts concerned with morals in Japan, these are generally de-emphasized if not disapproved of altogether.

It will be apparent from other chapters that Japanese schools do not confine their teaching of morals to the one hour a week labeled with that title. Neither the administration, the teachers, nor the parents feel that the rest of the time in school is devoid of moral content. Many policies, such as those seen in the cleaning of the school, the opportunities for group life experiences in school trips and expeditions and for cooperative activities on Sports Day and at other events, and delegating to groups of students the responsibility for running many everyday activities, are quite self-consciously adopted and maintained because of their moral value, not their academic value.

Japanese pedagogical theory stresses the importance of "doing" in learning, rather than talking. If actions are the desired ones, the thoughts that support them will follow. Morals class, once a week, is mostly talking. School life, every day, is the related "doing."

8

Nagging, Preaching and Discussions

Postmodern, deconstructionist anthropology is centrally concerned with the role of symbolic actions in social settings to establish a shared consensus among participants about what is "real" and what is "really" going on. Language is one of the primary forms of symbolic action, and the power of talk to "construct" reality for participants is a point emphasized by such analysts. The European theorists, especially (Bourdieu, Habermas, Foucault, Fairclough, for instance), generally feel that in the situations they are concerned with, including schools, the use of language to construct understandings is nefarious, justifying unjust power inequities. Japanese teachers and schools, clearly not accepting this moral evaluation of their activities, seem to believe wholeheartedly in the power of talk to make reality. They spend what seem like inordinate amounts of time in talk, specifically intended to get children to think about social issues in particular ways. This talk seems to me to come across as exhortation, preaching, persuasion, and nagging.

Let me go back to preschool and Catherine Lewis's writings (1995: 125–26) for a story to illustrate the reality-making power of talk in Japanese schools. Lewis reports that one day at a preschool there was an interaction of several five-year-old boys with the class goldfish.

Their activity consisted of making small clay pellets and dropping them into the tank, calling out "Bombs away!" The teacher several times pointed out that the fish could get hurt this way, that this wasn't a good thing to do. The activity was apparently compelling enough that the boys ignored her objections. She did not insist that they stop. During the end-of-the-day meeting, however, she brought up this incident for discussion. First she described the boys' activity and gave her interpretation of their actions: they really wanted to help the fish, giving them clay pellets that looked like food pellets, and they didn't realize that dropping the pellets could hurt the fish. "What does everybody think about this?" Some children volunteered that it sounded like fun, but most said they didn't want the fish to be hurt. "What should we do about this situation?" After several minutes of discussion, the teacher summarized two themes: nobody should drop things into the fish tank, and if you see someone hurting the fish, you should tell them to stop. She herself suggested that rotating the chore groups would give everyone a chance to share the fun of feeding the fish.

To most non-Japanese, this seems at best a disingenuous reading of the incident in question. The teacher's resolute ignoring of the less admirable motives that some might discern in the "Bombs away!" that accompanied the actions, her apparent refusal to deal with the boys' actions as springing from "bad" motives, is only the most obvious ploy in her reconstruction of the incident for class consideration. She never acknowledged that the clay pellets might look as much like bombs as they looked like food. Children who, during the discussion, mentioned they might also like bombing the fish were not reprimanded, merely ignored, and their comments didn't get mentioned in her summary.

She also fully refrained from any suggestion that the boys had been at fault in disobeying her. Her talk to them during the incident, "That could hurt the fish." "They look like food, but they aren't." "How sad the class will be if the fish get hurt," are all determinedly not directives, not orders to be obeyed or defied, though hints like this are meant to be taken as directives in schools and homes, and children know how to interpret them. By not following the teacher's hints, the boys confirmed her interpretation that they "did not understand," avoiding the necessity of any interpretation of defiance. In the summary of the class discussion, however, members of the class were given the authority to "tell them to stop," an authority the teacher declined to take on herself.

On the other hand, the teacher's formulation of three practical ways of avoiding the problem in the future seems realistic, and her description of what had happened was not so far-fetched as to be ridiculous to five-year-olds. (If it seems that adults are not susceptible to such simple-minded manipulation, I suggest thinking about the efforts of public relations "spin doctors.")

In another class meeting the problem of children who are so busy playing they don't help their *han* accomplish chores was raised. The teacher's molding of the discussion is apparent in her reactions to solutions offered by class members. A suggestion that a couple of children should just do the work themselves prompted the teacher's question, "Do you think that's right?" and gave children a chance to disagree. This supposedly noncommittal question form is one teachers often use to signal that another answer is required. The next suggestion, "We could make the people who aren't helping stand in the hall," elicited another teacher question, "Is it a good situation when people work because they are forced to?" which again signaled that they hadn't quite hit on an approved course of action. (Incorporated in this question is also the presupposition that those children who are doing the work are doing it of their own good will, not because they are being forced. The power of this presupposition may be no less because it is so taken for granted, so casual, so little a focus of overt attention.) After several other suggestions failed to be recognized as satisfactory— not that they were rejected outright by the teacher, just that she kept asking for more suggestions, someone came up with the idea that "the people who are working could get together and call the others in a big voice." This suggestion was promptly accepted by the teacher, who then moved on to another topic.

It is worth speculating why this course of action was considered appropriate, and it is possible to see several advantages of it. First, it is within the capacities of the age group involved and probably has some intrinsic appeal—"getting together and calling in a loud voice" sounds like fun. Second, it requires no teacher action and yet may provide a solution to the problem of noncooperation. Third, it assumes that the delinquents are really good at heart and just need reminding of what to do. This may well be true, and if so, the problem will be solved in a way that confirms the teacher's reading of the motives, the issues, and the best solutions. Notably, no one has been accused of base motives or shirking, no one has been asked to accept an unfair share of the work, and the teacher has avoided being the arbiter, rule maker, and enforcer.

During persistent questioning by Lewis at the end of the goldfish bombing day, the teacher denied that she even privately thought the boys intended to hurt the fish. When children—or adults—understand why actions are wrong, they won't do them. Conversely, if they do wrong actions, that is compelling evidence that they don't understand and that more explanations are in order.

Learning empathy is difficult, and probably it is accomplished best if it is mediated by language. Teachers constantly talk about the feelings that a child's actions will create in others and assume that these feelings act as motives for a child's actions. A child hefting a rock on the playground, looking to a non-Japanese observer as though he is about to throw it at another child, is asked to "lend" the rock to a teacher, who gently touches the back of his head with it, saying, "Someone could get hurt if they got hit with a rock," and hands it back to him (Lewis 1995:132). In the teacher's construction of what was going on, the boy had not thought he might hurt anyone, so she pointed it out to him. Then she acted on the assumption he would not want to hurt anyone and that the realization of how he would feel, brought to his attention by being touched by the rock, was all the motivation needed to refrain from throwing it. Her actions send a powerful message about what was "really going on" to the boy and to others. It seems to me important that she did not take any actions such as keeping the rock or sending the boy to dispose of it safely that might allow for any other understanding of his actions.

If these teachers are using the "every child is a good child" interpretation of behavior as a ploy to get behaviors they approve of, their use of it is enhanced by their own conviction that this is "really" true; for them it is not a tactic, merely an adjustment to reality. The goal is to get good behavior to follow "naturally" from understanding of the consequences of actions in a social setting.

Teachers can be very patient in their pursuit of such a long-term goal. They are willing to tolerate the misbehavior that precedes understanding, while continuing to place their construction of motives and effects on children's behavior in a way that seems to combine unique portions of idealism and realism. If a teacher makes a policy of praising the most disruptive child in the class at least once during each period, in part "to keep his classmates from giving up on him" (Lewis 1995: 135), she is not ignoring the real costs to his classmates of his behavior, but she is acting on a belief that being treated like a good child will lead him to act like a good child and that in the long run this will most effectively make him a constructive, happy student and friend.

In this particular case, the troublesome boy was a first grader whose reputation as a "difficult child" had preceded him to school. He was assigned to the most skilled first-grade teacher and was an active topic of conversation among all the teachers of the first- and second-grade classes. They were aware of the problems he presented, especially since one of the things he did was to yell insults—"Stupid, stupid!"—at the teacher several times a day, in a voice that could be heard in other classrooms. It seems to me that the level of cultural consensus about the best way to treat cases like his is illustrated in the lack of criticism from other teachers about the handling of the case and their tolerance of her tolerance of his behavior, until he could be brought to "understand" better ways to behave. They seemed to think it would take a year or two for him to understand and bring his behavior in line with his understanding.

Fighting is another form of misbehavior that Japanese teachers want to stop in the long run, but as a matter of policy they refrain from stopping fights, not because they don't recognize what's going on, but because they know that fights between children are about real issues and they feel children can learn to handle them only with experience. It is better for children to learn this when they are young and are very unlikely really to hurt each other, than to suppress fighting through adult intervention until they are stronger and more dangerous. Teachers respond to fights in the first instance by encouraging other children to intervene and mediate.

When fights and disputes become the subject of class meetings, as they often do, the details of what went on are not glossed over, but described in full. Efforts by classmates to intervene are talked about, the resolution of the fight is commented on, weak children are described as having become stronger, and aggressive children are cast in disfavor as bullies. I think the realistic description of actions that is encouraged by teachers in these discussions gives more credence to the interpretations of the actions that allow teachers to construct in adult, culturally Japanese terms an understanding of "what really happened," why the outcome was satisfactory or not, and what should be done in another situation.

Often the "satisfactory" solution seems unexpectedly realistic. When Sam took toys from the other children his first day at kindergarten, his desire to have them was treated as legitimate. He was persuaded to ask, and enabled to ask, and in return the other children were expected to honor his cooperativeness. Sam's desires were not suppressed, but the best possible interpretation was placed on them—he wanted to participate. The other children were expected to tolerate his clumsy efforts at interaction until he got to be more proficient. I didn't see it, but I'd be willing to bet that the class meeting at the end of Sam's first day at kindergarten included lots of talk about what his behavior meant, what children could expect of him, and strategies for dealing with him.

In the give and take of school life, Japanese teachers seem to be constructing a kind of psychological tolerance for what are seen as individual differences of skill and temperament. Just as teachers and adults tolerate misbehavior that arises from lack of understanding and skill, so too children must tolerate such behavior from each other. One shouldn't be so touchy that every little thing a classmate does is irritating and cause for discomfort. Others have their limitations, too. Some kinds of physical contact, including hitting, are often seen in Japanese classrooms, and teachers seem to construe this as not serious and discourage children from taking it seriously. Teachers and parents consistently interpret children's hitting them as unskillful but sincere attempts at interaction, and they teach children to take this approach themselves, too. Again, talk in class meetings is involved in creating in children an acceptance of this approach.

Affectionate forms of physical contact, holding hands and arms around shoulders, are common among Japanese children at school, too. It is also true that outside of Japanese schools physical contact is not seen as grounds for complaint. In crowded trains and subways people are jammed together and do not hold their bodies so tightly as Americans to minimize body contact. On busy sidewalks, people are less concerned about keeping their packages and briefcases from touching other people, and they often brush shoulders in passing. Cars, bicycles, and people come much closer to each other on streets than in the United States.

Learning these norms of tolerance for touching makes it very difficult for young Japanese women when they encounter touching behaviors from men in work and public situations. They report feeling that men they work with touch them inappropriately, and they are shamed and resentful when men "feel them up" on crowded trains and subways. They can't think of very effective ways to avoid these encounters, or to pass the blame to the men involved, without embarrassment to themselves.

The Japanese term for this aspect of social life is *butsukariai,* "bumping up against one another." It is inevitable, literally and figuratively, especially since the Japanese see themselves as living in a crowded country populated with unique individuals. Much of the learning of "how to live in a group" that is the business of school is learning to tolerate and appreciate individuals, at the same time learning the limits of individuality that make social living possible. Tolerance in terms of differences associated with ethnic, religious, or cultural groups is not an issue that many Japanese schools are forced to be concerned with, but the problem of weighing tolerance for individuality with the self-effacement needed for living together is a problem at the center of Japanese social life. It is dealt with at school but not solved there; it is not solved anywhere in Japanese life but always remains an issue, as it does in other societies.

Teachers talk at length and repetitiously about how to interpret other people's feelings and actions and about the lessons to be drawn from social interactions. They stress that other people are much like oneself, that they have generally good motives, that one shouldn't do anything to others that would bother oneself, and that everyone has shortcomings. This way of teaching an interpretation of social interaction, of constructing a viable understanding of social experience, depends on an adult ability to create coherent verbal formulations of experience that make sense of what goes on in school.

Some simple emotions may exist and motivate action regardless of cultural labels or rhetoric for discussing them, but many emotional states are so inchoate that a verbal and cultural interpretation of them is necessary before even the person experiencing them is able to know what is being experienced and what implications it has for action and interaction. An example from American culture comes from the frequent occasions when one young child hurts another and caretakers, in talking about the event, stress that the offending child "didn't mean it." Coming to see that the offense "wasn't meant" is supposed to reduce the hurt felt by the injured child and to change the child's understanding of the emotions engendered by the offense. Older children and adults, too, employ this verbal formula to evaluate and clarify reactions to potential offenses. The talk and the actions of teachers create for Japanese children a culturally valid way of understanding motives and feelings, their own and those of others, in the context where they must interact with others.

In Japanese classrooms seemingly endless discussions of events in class interactions and class academic work offer opportunities for teachers to shape children's perceptions of what happened, why, whether the outcomes were satisfactory or not, how improvements can be achieved, and whether others agree with one's own readings of actions and incidents. I think these discussions provide for Japanese children in school settings a "reality check" that is a "culture check" on their experiences of school life.

Another tactic, if that's a good term, that I see in Japanese teachers' efforts to construct reality for children in culturally acceptable ways is, paradoxically, accepting and acting on the power of children in constructing situations. By this I mean that Japanese teachers seem to take children's own readings of what's going on very seriously and refrain from overriding them in authoritarian ways.

William Cummings (1980:118–19) tells the story of a girl who reacted to her classmates' nickname for her, "Piggy," by refusing to go to school. Her mother reported this to the principal, who visited her at home to hear her complaints, then investigated with the classroom teacher, who held intense class meetings to discuss the issue. After several days of discussion, the whole class went to the girl's home to apologize and ask her to forgive them. After two more days she agreed to return to school. It seems to me that parents and teachers showed an unexpected amount of tolerance in their handling of this situation, a tolerance that amounted to giving a child power over her own actions and assigning legitimacy to her feelings to a remarkable extent. They also demonstrated persistence, patience, and realism in getting the classmates to accept responsibility for better behavior. In other situations one could imagine a mother, a principal, or a teacher not taking this complaint seriously and instead forcing a child to go to school. Or the teacher might simply impose punishments on the children who disobeyed her orders to stop the offending behavior.

The verbal exhortations one encounters in Japan seem to us somehow old-fashioned and quaint. We have become so convinced of the power of teaching by action that we ignore even the possibility of teaching through words. Japanese schools, in contrast, are plastered with mottoes and sayings and admonitions and goals and questions to ask oneself and charts for keeping track of achievements and failures. These do not just remain unnoticed on the walls and in the textbooks and notebooks. Teachers constantly talk about them and involve children in creating them. Goals for the year, for the term, for the week, for Sports Day, and for the summer vacation are all discussed in class meetings and recorded for future consideration of whether or not they have been met.

One of the things I notice about these goals is that many of them seem to be things I would expect, such as making an effort not to forget to bring school materials from home, or practicing *kanji* every day. Others seem to be entirely unnecessary. Do children really need to have set as a formal goal "playing energetically during recess" or "answering in a loud voice when you are called on"? Somehow, for Japanese children, the habit of evaluating even actions like these in terms of goals to be met seems to spill over into the habit of evaluating other behaviors in terms of meeting goals, too.

Some are goals for small or large groups. A *han* might set a goal of finishing their chores more speedily or of reducing the number of "forgotten items"; a class might set a goal of not losing sight of the teacher during a field trip or of listening more quietly when classmates are talking. Some are goals for individuals: to learn the multiplication tables, to eat some of everything at lunch, or to use the horizontal bars on the playground.

Nearly all the evaluation of meeting goals is self-evaluation, done publicly. Often charts are made for keeping track of progress in reaching the goals. For group goals, group discussions precede the recording of evaluations. Often a graduated system of score keeping is used. Not only does a group or an individual get a red star for achieving a goal, but they may get a gold star for trying even if they didn't succeed. It is up to the group or the individual to make decisions about this, but they have to announce the decision publicly, in discussions or on a chart. Especially at the youngest ages, other children will not be at all reticent about saying whether these self-judgments are plausible or not.

The practice of continual self-evaluation in public, for academic goals and goals of character development, is either a brilliant tactic for motivating individuals in many areas of life and at many levels of accomplishment, or a nasty, Machiavellian plot to impose the values of the authorities on tender minds. It is, again, through teacher-guided discussion that these goals for the groups and for individuals are set and formulated. Although teachers may adopt verbal strategies for a role in discussions that does not appear dominating, such as sitting in the back during discussions and raising a hand to be recognized by the student meeting leader before speaking, it is still the case that teachers can and do influence the choice and wording of both goals and evaluation criteria. Their changes of wording usually tend to formalize, soften, and generalize the goals. In this sense they are imposing values and conceptions of actions on the thinking of children. One could see their acceptance of goals that children might find attractive—"playing energetically at recess," for example—among the total set of goals to be pursued as a subtle form of coercion, leading children to accept teacher goals, too.

At the most linguistic, grammatical level, the form of talk in discussions is nonauthoritarian and nondirective. Japanese contains linguistic forms that are imperative verbs, best translated as the equivalents of English imperatives, such as "Stop!" "Give it to me!" "Sit down!" "Answer!" or any other direct order. In Japanese conversation these are almost never used, and they are not used in discussions or formulations of goals. Instead, there is widespread usage of a form that is more like the English "Let's" do such and such, and of another form that is explicitly a request for a favor. In English the "let's do such and such" form is usually clearly addressed to a group that includes the speaker and someone else. In Japanese it usually includes the speaker, but it may not, and it usually includes another person, but it may not. In other words, it can be used for "you do such and such," "let's (us) do such and such," or "I'm going to do such and such." It is, as a form, ambiguous among these possibilities, and in group meetings and in setting goals this ambiguity is exploited.

In Japanese sentences the subject is commonly omitted whenever it can be inferred from the context, and the verb is not marked for singular or plural number or for gender. (It is marked for relative hierarchical status, formality, and for in-group versus out-group membership.) In many contexts the subject that can be inferred is thus indeterminate. This feature is used to avoid pointing a finger of blame at anyone (including oneself, whenever useful) or explicitly saying who is responsible for certain acts or who should do certain things. (English uses forms like "My jacket got lost," "There isn't any more dessert," and "Where have my car keys gone?" to accomplish the same purposes.) Thus, even when the topics of discussion are personally threatening, the forms of speech used tend to mitigate the threats.

(To interpose a totally American reaction, I find it irritating enough when at the end of an airplane flight in the United States, an announcement reminds me to "Check the overhead bins and the area around you for any items you may have forgotten." But I dislike it even more when the announcement at every train station in Japan seems to be saying "Let's check carefully and not leave any forgotten belongings." Who are they kidding?)

It is not just in awarding themselves stars on charts that children are involved in self-evaluation. *Hansei* (self-evaluation, reflection), is an activity that applies to many different kinds of actions. This is what classes do when they review their class trip or their preparations for Sports Day, or after reading a story or completing a lesson in social studies or mathematics. As a literary form *hansei* are intended to embrace both emotional reactions and intellectual understandings, which are not nearly so separated as they tend to be in Western literary forms.

In the third term of first grade, Ellen and her classmates began keeping a formal *hansei* notebook containing reflections about school. Ellen's first entries noted what she liked about school and what she found "troublesome."

I like to read.   I don't like lunch.
I like Japanese.   I don't like to carry a heavy backpack.
I like recess and other things.   I don't like to walk to school.
I like phys ed and art.
I like cleaning.
I like to be class leader.
I like my friends.

This notebook was handed in to the teacher, who responded to Ellen with "You like a lot of things. I'm relieved. As for the troublesome things, what can make them better? If you think good thoughts, maybe they'll get better." Later entries still had lunch as a troublesome thing, but by the end she had stopped mentioning it, whereas the list of things she liked had expanded to include the teacher, the backpack, and school in general. The teacher's last comment in reply dealt mostly with a bad spelling mistake Ellen repeated several times. It is not difficult to see some mental coercion here.

In the cases where writing a *hansei* is used as a disciplinary tactic, teachers sometimes reject what is offered and require children to keep rewriting their thoughts until they are acceptable. During discussions, they refuse to end the discussion until a resolution or understanding they find acceptable has been formulated. They are acting as though the power of words to create reality is very strong, perhaps strong enough to overcome dissimulation on the part of students.

9

Enlisting Mothers' Efforts

I can read Japanese but usually with difficulty, so I noticed the volume of communications that came home from school more than I would have had they been in English—it seemed like a lot. There were scheduled publications, such as the monthly newsletter for the whole school, the monthly letter for each grade, and the monthly menus for school lunch. There were also occasional items like advice about summer vacation and glossy printed collections of writings by the children.

From my point of view perhaps the most useful of the school communications was the monthly school newsletter. After struggling through the first few letters from the principal, which make up about a third of the material each month, and finding they were philosophical reflections on holidays or on reaching the current stage of the school year or on the goals of education for life, I stopped making the effort to read them. But I looked at the monthly feature listing the outstanding achievements of individual students in city art exhibitions or sports competitions or science projects for the names of children in Sam's and Ellen's classes or of other people I knew. I learned I had better check out the announcements for daily events, because they included notices about early closing, days with no lunch, class trips, when extra fees were due, meetings for mothers to attend, and in general any events that might involve a change of daily plans. Announcements about when the students' eyesight would be tested didn't require any action on our part but were interesting to know about.

I always felt that our family was just barely coping with life in Japan, and I occasionally took comfort from some of the items in the newsletter. Each family with a child at Okubo Higashi needs to keep an account at one of two local banks; each month on an announced date the school withdraws a certain amount from the account to pay for lunches and extra materials the teacher has purchased for each child (drills and practice tests, usually). The two authorized banks were very small local ones, inconvenient to use for most of our family's banking purposes, and our main account was at another bank. Reading the item explaining the difficulties faced by the school because too many families were not keeping enough money in this account to cover their fees made me realize that I was not the only one who sometimes forgot to deposit money there. I also wondered about what sorts of reciprocal favors were behind the practice of using only these two banks, but I never got around to asking.

Besides the newsletter for the whole school, there was also one for each grade each month—not each homeroom, but each grade, with usually four classes in each grade. As a regular feature, each of these included a brief description of the topics to be covered in each subject, a summary of notices about daily happenings in each grade (this was a repetition from the all-school newsletter, usually), and reports on activities of the grades, such as the swimming levels attained by the fifth graders during the summer vacation lessons or explanations of the grading system for the upcoming report cards.

There were also admonitions from the teachers about what parents should be doing to help their children at home. At New Year's time the fifth-grade teachers reminded us that we should coach our children on the proper forms and etiquette for offering New Year's greetings and help them decide wisely how to use the money they received as gifts. I felt that none of these things were any business of the school and that the teachers were being insulting by telling me my duties as a mother. I am assured by my Japanese friends, however, that this is an unwarranted interpretation. Such messages only express the teachers' concern for the total well-being of their students.

The advantage of these monthly newsletters was that they gave parents advance notice of school activities in a compact form. If your kid could get only two pieces of paper a month home safely, about the extent of what Sam usually bothered with, you would be prepared for whatever was likely to happen at school. There wouldn't be late-night announcements about crucial equipment for a project absolutely needed the next morning. We were told at the beginning of November about the calligraphy supplies needed by the fifth graders for their New Year's writing, and parents were informed about ongoing projects, such as the month of practice needed before the jump-rope test. The disadvantage for me was the feeling that I was being nagged about my own job and getting more advice than I wanted.

I also didn't always interpret correctly what I was supposed to do about some of the information, and sometimes Sam and Ellen suffered because of it. I didn't realize that I should take the announcement about jumping rope as a serious homework project, so I didn't nag Ellen into practicing as a Japanese mother would probably have done, and she did very poorly on the test. When the October fifth-grade newsletter mentioned that the children would be going to the temple to do watercolors, I should have taken that as a signal that Sam would need paints and equipment, and I should have purchased them. (And I would have known what paints and equipment he needed, if I'd had art lessons in school in Japan.) These were symptoms of my failure to realize until late in the year how, as a mother, I was supposed to be active in the school work of my children. Both the children and the school had a right to expect me to live up to this responsibility, and I just didn't sometimes. I knew intellectually that Japanese mothers are more active, more encouraging, more involved, and more necessary than I am in America; it just didn't sink in emotionally and practically.

The most constant form of communication was the *renrakucho* for first graders. Older children did not have a daily *renrakucho*; they are supposed to be more independent and responsible. *Renrakucho* means "communication booklet," and I was familiar with the idea from Sam's and Ellen's previous sojourns in day care and kindergarten. It is a booklet that is read and written in every day by both the teacher and the parent. Both stamp it with a seal every day, and any information that needs to be passed back and forth is included.

In Ellen's day care center, the *renrakucho* included daily notations of bowel movements, sleeping times, and times and amounts of eating, as well as comments on her mood or general well-being. (I think I was supposed to send back similar information about her behavior at home, but I didn't figure this out until near the end of her stay, and I might not have done it anyway.) Any information about schedule changes, medicines, or the like could also be included. When Sam was in kindergarten, his *renrakucho* did not include so much information about physical health, but nearly every day brought comments from the teacher about his activities, ranging from "Today Sam led the class in opening exercises" to "He certainly does like the swings!"

In first grade the *renrakucho* includes not only daily homework assignments and reports on classroom activities but also special announcements or reminders. Ellen's teacher wrote the daily message on the blackboard, and it was copied by each student, so that it was part of the training in handwriting, and so that parents could see the progress their children were making in this area. Ellen's notes became easily legible in about a month. Parents are to stamp the booklet daily, and the teacher also stamps it, to show that she has checked for messages from home.

This stamp, or *hanko*, is a seal with the family name carved on it that is pressed into a block of red ink and then stamped on the document. Signatures are not "legal" in Japan; the family seal or *hanko* is. Families usually have more than one copy of their *hanko*, and it is okay for anyone in the family to use it if the occasion arises—to sign for a delivery, for instance. You can buy a *hanko* for your name if it's a fairly common one in most stationary stores or department stores; otherwise, you have it individually carved. In addition, families have a hand-carved *hanko* registered with city hall for use in the most important transactions such as the sale of real estate. The possibilities for fraud in this situation seem not to be a danger in the thinking of most Japanese, and Ellen absorbed the notion that it was all right for her to sign my initials, which I used instead of a *hanko,* in the *renrakucho.* In Japanese terms, it was.

The *renrakucho* seems an innocuous if effective technique of enlisting home cooperation and involvement in the daily life of school. Its potential power came home to me strikingly in an incident that occurred during the first few weeks that Sam and Ellen were attending Okubo Higashi School. You may remember from the description of school equipment and the material to be carried in the backpack each day that my initial reaction was that this was a burdensome list of duties, one that it would be unreasonable to expect someone of Ellen's age to be able to carry out alone. I took a deep breath, told myself it would be good experience in Japanese mothering techniques, and prepared to take on partial responsibility for seeing that everything needed got taken to school each day.

One day the *renrakucho* came home with a note saying that entirely too many things were being forgotten; we should work hard to improve the situation. At the time I thought this note was unique to Ellen's *renrakucho*; now I think it went home to everyone. My reaction amazed me: I immediately became angry with Ellen. I scolded her and started talking about how getting ready for school really was her responsibility, after all. All this, I think, to avoid a scolding from her teacher aimed at me! I don't like being reprimanded by teachers. If not forgetting things was Ellen's responsibility, not mine, then I wasn't the one getting the scolding. And so I added my pressure for performance of this set of tasks to the school's moral weight, all so I could avoid getting in trouble with the teacher, even though I had decided the job was too onerous for a seven-year-old!

Within a few hours I got over my irritation with Ellen (and offered an apology). I was disappointed in my susceptibility to such underhanded manipulation by the school, or by authorities in general, became indignant at the use of such techniques to enlist home support for school goals, and ended in a reluctant admiration for whoever devised such an effective form of coercion. I decided to keep on helping Ellen, accept my failures, and not take it out on her.

All this emotion engendered by two sentences in a daily communication notebook! Schools send home dozens of notes, newsletters, and announcements during the course of a school year. When I read this note about forgetting things, I knew right away that we were guilty and that it was addressed to us (and at the time it didn't occur to me that other homes were getting the same message). The guilt I felt myself surely added to the intensity of my reaction.

In other situations, when I read advice and reminders about things to do such as making sure that my children gargled each time they came home during the winter, I was able to ignore the instructions with absolutely no emotional reaction. But this business about forgetting school supplies is one that I didn't disagree with the school about; I too think children need to learn to be responsible for their own school activities.

Most of the behaviors and attitudes schools try to instill in children in Japan are ones that find widespread acceptance among Japanese parents, who also largely agree that it is legitimate for schools to teach children these things. The constant reinforcement of these values in school communications and the somewhat admonitory tone of the writing probably is in the long term an effective way of enlisting pressure from home on children to enhance the school's attempts to teach proper behaviors and attitudes. Another way of looking at it is that these communications are ways of reminding mothers that their role as *kyoiku mama*, "education moms," is one the school system counts on, not one that is optional for them. Some mothers find ways to evade some of the tasks schools ask them to carry out, and I am sure all of them do the kind of selecting of important admonitions from the mass of school communications that I did. But I also think that the volume of information and advice and demands resulted in a higher level of cooperation. Maybe every mother could decide to ignore 20 percent of what the school suggested or demanded, but following 80 percent of a hundred directions means that mothers are doing a lot. It also means that mothers are willing to live with a certain amount of guilt from not perfectly fulfilling their role, or at least one perception of their role that gets a hard sell in modern Japanese culture.

It is perhaps too extreme to call the *kyoiku mama* syndrome a problem, but it is something that Japanese often talk about with some ambivalence. Discovering the relationship between mothers and schools in the educational success and childhood experiences of Japanese was one of my goals for this year in Japan, and the attitudes expressed by Japanese about the issue were important elements for the conclusions I drew.

School and home reinforce each other in the messages they send to children, but they do not duplicate each other exactly, I think. Basically, elementary schools operate in terms of motivations for learning that are fundamentally centered in peer groups and social relations. Competition and getting on in the world are relegated to a very subordinate role. Motivations for learning in elementary schools, that is, are organized to exploit children's immediate social appetites (see chapter 10 for more on this topic).

Parents, and particularly mothers, play two different supporting roles to the elementary schools. First, and not at all trivially, mothers facilitate and support their children's participation in school requirements and activities. They do this in a number of ways. They make it possible for their children to meet the simple physical demands of school by providing the children with art equipment when it is needed; clean shoes, gym clothes, and lunch clothes; and materials called for in summer vacation homework. They put school activities ahead of other activities the family might engage in. They provide study time and space; they either arrange for *juku* attendance or do the drilling and tutoring themselves.

They absorb the frustrations and rebellion children sometimes feel about the demands of school, and they do this not by heavy-handed authoritarian methods, which they feel are not successful in the long run, but by sympathy, cajoling, support, and encouragement. By both Japanese and American standards this is hard work, difficult in conception and tedious in execution.

By their own cooperation with the demands that the school places on them and their children, they legitimate the school's demands for their children. In most cases they may indeed agree with the school about the requirements for education, but probably every mother has reservations about some school practices. For me, one that seemed particularly silly was the card Ellen and Sam had to take with them for every swimming lesson, on which I recorded their temperature that morning and indicated that they were not ill. I did not take a stand on this issue, however; I dutifully filled out the card and made sure it was included with swimming suit and towel when they went off to swimming lessons. I didn't even comment about it much. As I remember it, I even went through the ritual of taking their temperature, though sometimes only by feeling their forehead and making up a number for the card.

During summer vacation we went to a local festival with friends who had a son Sam's age. The mother explained the timing of dinner before we went out by saying the school had a rule that children should be home by 9:30 in the evening during vacation, so we had to eat early to get back by then. She said she thought this was really none of the school's business, and not very rational, but it was a rule.

When parents go along with such rules and arrange life to accommodate school rules and regulations, they are sending a powerful message to children that this is the way things are and should be; their behavior validates the notion that schools can impose standards for behavior and performance on children and adults. Thus, schools have their requirements legitimated, not subverted or challenged.

The second way in which school demands are reinforced by parents is not by duplicating school motivations but by adding a second set. This second set is focused more on long-range preparation for life and on competition. Elementary schools certainly see their job as preparing children for life, but they do not expect this motivation to be very strong for children, and they do not rely on it to be the basis for elementary school learning. Parents are the ones who most often and most forcefully articulate the preparing-for-life motivation for children during these years, not necessarily by talking about it, though they do that, too, but by letting it motivate them in their actions. Even if parents feel that school is too demanding, that summer vacation should be free from homework, that going to *juku* after school and on weekends is too much, when they see that other children are doing these things, they feel they cannot let their own children get behind. It takes an exceptionally strong set of parents to resist this desire to "keep up with the Tanakas." Parents feel that this is a competition in which they must not handicap their children. The long-term and competitive nature of learning and learning activities is foremost in their minds and is communicated to their children.

Junior high school and high school will later reinforce these aspects of learning, but they are introduced first in the family, as a different and additional motivational framework for children. It's not a long step for competition between children for long-term success in education to become a competition between mothers for both long- and short-term success of their children in education. It is widely recognized as unhealthy for both mothers and children when mothers end up doing a lot of homework or summer vacation projects and evaluating their success as mothers by the success of their children in school examinations and competitions. Since the help or cooperation of mothers is in fact necessary for the success of children, however, it is difficult for mothers to avoid this trap.

It is also difficult, Japanese say, for a healthy emotional relationship between mothers and children to survive the demands of education. On the one hand, Japanese parents are committed to persuading rather than forcing children to do well in school. (Parents in many countries who have tried forcing children to do well in school have found that the children ultimately have the upper hand in this game, to the detriment of everyone involved.) An emotional tie between mother and child is the primary context for this persuasion. In the *amae* relationship the lack of differentiation between the identity and interests of the two parties, mother and child, is legitimate to some degree. But that lack of differentiation enables mothers to use their own potential shame as a goad to performance by the child. It is, in this dynamic, the mother who will be hurt by a child's poor performance, and the child's unwillingness to hurt the mother means that mothers can use tactics I identify in the United States as emotional blackmail.

Such tactics are likely to increase in high school. One Japanese friend, who recalls his high school years as exciting and rewarding and less difficult than those faced by his own children, told how his mother, to share in the feelings his efforts produced and to help him, took (and carried out) a vow to pray for his success every four hours around the clock during his three years of high school. How could anyone not do his homework while this was going on? He made it into Tokyo University. I have also heard of mothers giving up a favorite food or beverage, such as tea, for the duration of their children's struggles in high school.

On the other hand, many Japanese recognize that this degree of *amae* can and often does lead to a undesirable loss of will and individuality in both the mother and the child. *Kyoiku mama* is a term that recognizes the contributions mothers make to a child's education and development, but it also recognizes the dangers to both mother and child in the process. It is in several ways, as my friend commented, "difficult to be the mother of an elementary school child."

10

Education in
Japanese Society

We have seen how Japanese elementary schools are meant to be, and seem to be, powerful socialization tools—institutions to turn children into Japanese children and later Japanese adults. Japanese elementary schools are a part of the larger society, and it is worthwhile to look at how they fit into the rest of the education system and how that fits into society as a whole.

Since the beginning of the modernization period, Japan has looked at itself as a nation poor in natural resources, with only its people as a major asset. The education system has always been seen as contributing to the national welfare by producing an educated, skilled, productive workforce. A crucial decision was made early on and continues to be in force in recent times about the targets of the education system—who was to be educated and how.

The Japanese decision was to have two tracks, a mass compulsory education level that would reach all children and be gradually extended in number of years, and an elite track that would select children early for preparation to enter the governing elite, both of business and of government. The government took its commitment to universal basic education seriously, and in only a few years after beginning the national system of education in 1872 had reached close to 100 percent enrollment levels. (Handicapped children were exempted—or excluded —from this education.) In the earliest years the biggest change this made was in the education of girls. Many boys had received private schooling in basic literacy before the national system was instituted, but not so many girls. Girls were included in compulsory schooling from the beginning.

Gradually, more public schools were started to provide vocational training for some girls and many boys beyond the compulsory education period. This schooling had clear economic benefits for the children who received it and clear benefits for the modernization efforts of Japan. There was a steady increase in the number of children, both male and female, who received more years of schooling, and the number of years of compulsory schooling was increased also. More children were provided with special education and fewer exempted or excluded from education because of disabilities.

At the same time that education was becoming longer and more encompassing for most children, the government also maintained an elite system of high schools and universities to prepare the next generations of leaders and rulers. Entry to these schools was determined partly by family background and partly by academic achievement. This sector also expanded over the years, and family background became a less important factor in admission.

The elite sector in Japanese education has always been small, its size determined by the government's perception of its need for leaders rather than by the amount of demand for further advanced schooling. The public appetite for schooling beyond the compulsory years has always outstripped the government's ability or willingness to provide more schooling. But various policies of the central government have made it possible for private schools to operate and in large part to meet the demand for schooling, which seems almost insatiable in Japan (James and Benjamin 1988).

Not only have private high schools and universities been established and maintained, but a system of schooling, largely private, for three-, four-, and five-year-olds has also developed, as has a set of supplementary schooling institutions. The supplementary institutions include *juku* and *yobiko*. *Juku* refers to a variety of out-of-school tutoring for children of ages three to eighteen: classes in ballet, swimming, calligraphy, foreign languages, or other activities and subjects not covered in the school curriculum; or tutoring for children who are behind in their school work, need help to keep up, or want to do advanced work. Many children attend one or another of these kinds of classes several times a week after school.

Yobiko refers to another kind of tutoring school specifically geared to helping students prepare for university entrance examinations. Admission to a university depends on performance on an entrance examination, and in competitive fields such as medicine and at competitive schools, including all the public universities, many students do not pass the exams on their first attempt at the end of high school. Large numbers of students then decide to spend a year or more studying and preparing to take the exam again. They become *ronin*, a well-established identity in Japanese society; the term originally referred to unemployed samurai warriors.

It seems apparent that all these private supplementary institutions dealing with education would not appear in a society unless education were an important factor in individuals' life opportunities. It also seems clear that they provide mechanisms for some individuals to avail themselves of advantages not open to all—for socioeconomic background to become a factor in school success.

Three main questions arise about Japanese society and education at this point. First, does educational achievement have a major impact on an individual's position in the society? Second, do other socioeconomic factors affect educational attainment? Third, do Japanese regard the outcomes of the educational system as fair and just?

In order to answer these questions, we need first to establish that education is an important determinant of life conditions for individuals. Then we need to look at the education system as a whole and understand how individual students and their families are confronted with choices and with strategies for negotiating the system. We need to look for conditions that promote or diminish equalities among schools and among students.

In the way Japanese think about their own society, education is seen as the key to personal and family success. No Japanese parents or teachers seem to question the idea that education is crucial for each individual. How could such an idea become so firmly entrenched in a country that at the time of the American Civil War was a feudal society with hereditary classes and occupations? The level of change associated with modernization in Japan is one important contributor to this perception, along with the ideology and practice of the education system and employers. During the last 130 years or so the level of occupational change that Japan has seen has been such that smaller and smaller proportions of young adults have followed the occupations of their fathers and mothers. As inheritance lost its power as the determinant of occupation, something had to take its place, and that something was education. In many other societies other factors, such as ethnic, linguistic, religious, or racial differences, have defined what life paths were open to an individual. Japanese society did not develop cleavages along these lines, however, and these are not salient factors in Japan. (There are two small minority groups whose situation will be mentioned later.)

The assertions above should not be taken to mean that family economic activities either had no effect on occupation during the last century and a half or are not an influence at the present moment. Certainly, a family that owns economic assets, such as a farm or a small business, can plan that the enterprise will pass to a successor. A very high value is placed on such lines of succession in Japanese families. In this case the relevant education for a successor child may not be primarily school education but vocational education received in the family context. Nevertheless, there are severe restrictions on the abilities of families to carry out such a plan. The family enterprise, whether it be farm or business, that provides a living for one family will in Japan usually not provide a living for all the children of the family when they become adults. This was especially the case during the earlier years of this century, when the birth rate in Japan was high. Land reform after the Second World War meant that most farms became too small to support more than one family, and that not very well, compared to the lifestyle of nonfarm families. This leads to a second consequence of modernization: what was a viable family economic enterprise at one point in Japanese history was very likely to become, in a short period of time, irrelevant or infeasible because of changes in technology and marketing. Third, those families who came to depend on wages or salaries, a very high proportion of the workforce in modern Japan, have no economic enterprise to pass on to successor children. What they can give to their children is education. Like parents everywhere, Japanese parents want to ensure the livelihood and success of their children, and elements of the economic, social, and political development of Japan have combined to make education the resource that Japanese parents can use for that end.

Are parents and others correct in their perceptions that education makes a difference in the life outcomes of individuals? The answer here is yes, but with some qualifications. Here we need to look at the Japanese education system in its entirety and the factors affecting individuals' movements within the system.

In practice, Japanese children enter the school system at the age of three, four, or five. This level of school is called *yochien*, a direct translation of the German *kindergarten*. At the present time 95 percent of five-year-olds are enrolled in public or private kindergartens or day care centers, which are very like the kindergartens. According to American observers, there are very few differences in social practices between public and private institutions, though some private ones have a stronger academic orientation. The levels of teacher training, the physical facilities, and the class sizes are quite constant, and spartan by American standards. The costs to parents are not a major factor in choosing a preschool, being subordinate to convenience. Access to public day care centers is controlled by "need," and children there are more likely to have mothers who work. The effect of the preschool system is that nearly all Japanese children are enrolled, and the atmosphere, activities, and equipment they are exposed to are not very different from one school to the next.

Compulsory schooling encompasses grades one through nine, elementary school for six years and three years of junior high school. Considerable thought and effort, as described throughout this book, goes into making the elementary and junior high school experiences of all children in Japan comparable and equal, as nearly as possible the same for everyone. Funding and facilities vary little, the curriculum is a nationally prescribed one, uniform for all schools, there is no tracking within classes or schools, and the Ministry of Education sets the training and certification standards for all public school teachers. One major difference between elementary school and junior high school is that during junior high, teachers, students, and parents are extremely aware of the coming high school entrance examinations, which will separate students for the first time by academic achievement.

High school in Japan is not required, and not free, even in public schools. During the earlier years students attend neighborhood schools. But which high school they attend depends on the child's and the parents' choice and whether the child can successfully pass the entrance examination. For the first time in the education system there is academic tracking, and it is very severe, dividing students into many levels of achievement and funneling students of similar academic abilities into the same school. Within the school there is no tracking, but between schools the differences are strong.

Students and parents must choose a high school. What are their choices, and how do families decide? Less than 5 percent of Japanese students leave school at the end of the compulsory period, and 95 percent of those entering high school go on to graduate. The choice of high school and the strategies to get into the chosen school are issues that confront every family with children.

High schools in Japan can be categorized in several ways. One is by the curriculum offered, which can be college preparatory academic, general academic (not enough foreign language for college entrance), or vocational. The second division is by whether the school is a public, government-supported one or a private one. Public schools are not free, except to students from very poor families, but private schools are about twice as costly as public ones.

Though the hierarchy is complicated in some local situations, there are certain general rules for determining the status of individual high schools. Academic high schools rank above vocational ones, and public ones rank above private ones. In the end, the status of a high school is determined by the college entrance record of its graduates or the kinds of employment they find after graduation. In the short run that is predicted by the scores on the entrance examination of the students admitted.

It is not surprising that a school that admits students in a narrow range of academic achievement at the beginning of tenth grade also produces students with a narrow range of academic achievement at the end of twelfth grade, whether that is high or low. Since colleges also admit students based on entrance test scores, there is a strong correlation between the high school students attend and the colleges they are able to gain admission to. Note an important difference from the U.S. system here, in that it is *getting into* a school that is difficult, not graduating. The ranking of students is done at the beginning of high school or college, not at the end. Teachers to a large extent are relieved of evaluation of their students, since their grades have little importance.

For those students not going on to higher education, employment practices for hiring new graduates reinforce the ranking of high schools. In effect, the most desirable employers of high school graduates confine their hiring to a small number of high schools. That is, a large company in a city or prefecture that hires a certain number of new high school graduates each year usually has a long-standing policy of hiring only students who have graduated from one of a small number of high schools in the area. They also, in effect, use the entrance examinations for high school as a filter for prospective employees—they let the education system choose the initial pool of applicants they will have to consider. The high school one enters thus becomes seen as a crucial hurdle in the quest for further education and for employment.

For students who go on to college, the same employment system among the employers of college graduates means that at entering college, one has a pretty good idea of the employment one will be eligible for at the end. Elite employers choose from elite colleges, using the college entrance examination system as a first filter for their employment decisions.

The high school entrance examination is, and is known to be, important for nearly all students. The pressures in junior high school can seem to amount to a severe initiation rite, or hazing, as children leave childhood and enter puberty and adulthood (Kiefer 1970). Not too surprisingly, junior high schools experience the most "problem" children; in this age group rebellion against the school is strongest. For children and families who aspire to the most elite colleges and universities, the initiation hazing period can last another three to five years, during high school and study as a *ronin*.

It's difficult to convey to Americans the intensity of public concern with the high school and university entrance examinations. David Berman (1990) has written a study of the high school entrance examination process in one prefecture in Japan, and my observations during our stay in Japan and discussions with friends also lent some insight into why it is so compelling an event for Japanese. Since the public high schools and universities are the most desirable schools in Japan (because they have the best employment and higher education records, and because they are cheaper), their exam practices set the pace for other schools. Practices vary slightly from prefecture to prefecture but are basically the same.

The entrance examination for public high schools is set by the prefectural board of education, based on the Ministry of Education national curriculum. (So although local schools are theoretically free to use another curriculum, this is a strong incentive not to do so.) The exam for all public high schools, then, is the same examination; it does not vary from school to school. One might imagine that students who have taken the exam would be placed in a high school, perhaps with some consideration for location, with other students who have made similar scores on the exam. But instead, there is another step in the procedure, which has the effect of giving more responsibility for the outcomes of the exams to families, students, and teachers. (I contend that the undercover purpose of this step is to diffuse criticism of the education system and its severe tracking at this level by introducing this element of family "choice.") The crucial factor in the procedure is this: though the exam is the same for all public schools, and though the schools are known to take students of only certain ranks, each student applies to *one specific public high school,* and the exam is valid only for that school. If a student "fails" to make the required score for admission to the chosen school, then the student will be barred from attending *any* public high school, even though the score would qualify the student for another school.

There are other factors in the high school entrance equation that apparently make this situation tolerable, although stressful. One is the perceived fairness of the elementary and junior high school preparation for the exams—everyone is given the same chance to do well on the examinations; failure to do so is a result of not trying hard enough. Another is the perceived fairness of the examinations themselves. Though each year's examination is closely guarded against cheating, on the day the exam is given it is published in full in the local newspapers, all four to six newspaper pages of it. Untoward deviations from past practice would arouse intense public disfavor. Records of previous examinations are thus available to help in preparation, and there are commercial companies that operate both privately and in conjunction with the schools to give students many practice examinations and tips for study during their junior high school years. Junior high school teachers in particular are expected to use these practice examinations and observation of students to help families make decisions about high school entrance. Such "guidance" is an important consideration for most families.

Another factor making the system apparently tolerable is the existence of the private high school sector. Students who do not gain entrance to their chosen public school can take the exams for one or more private high schools. Alternatively, students and their families can choose to apply to a "safe" high school, one whose required exam score the student is sure to make, even on a bad day. (It's not a good idea to have the flu or a cold on the day of the exam.)

Finally, though there is little discussion of this publicly in Japan, in recent years the public schools seem to have taken on the role of providing schools of last resort to those students who are not admitted to elite public schools or desirable private schools. The status hierarchy of high schools in most areas thus consists of a ranking approximately like this: at the top are the selective public academic high schools, followed by an interwoven mixture of private academic, public vocational, and private vocational schools, with a set of public vocational and part-time schools at the bottom. The perceived advantages of education in Japan are such that even these schools have students, and almost 95 percent of the age cohort ends up graduating from high school.

The college entrance examination system repeats many features of the high school exams. Students apply to a specific faculty in a specific university, public or private, and the responsibility of choosing is up to the student. It is the student who must balance out the costs and benefits of applying to a less elite, "safe" school with those of applying to a better, but less assured, school. The examinations for both public and private schools are coordinated so that they are given on very few days. This effectively limits the number of schools a student can apply to in any one year and groups the most likely choices for any student together, so that only one of the exams for a group of similarly ranked public or private schools can be taken in a given year. Failure to make the cutoff for one's first choice probably means one has given up the chance for the second and third choices for that year, too, unless those are in the other sector, public or private. The fees for taking the entrance exams are steep, a major moneymaker for private schools, so this is a barrier, too.

Is it any wonder that there is public fascination with the students who make their way through this system to entrance into the elite universities? They have in effect been through a grueling preparation, involving intense effort and high moral character, and have emerged as the best of Japanese youth, embodying Japanese ideals. Mass circulation news magazines publish profiles of every one of the three thousand students who are admitted to Tokyo University (the absolute pinnacle of the ranking system) each year, and detailed statistics are given on the entering classes of the other elite universities, most importantly which high schools the students came from. In 1989, 10 high schools produced 29 percent of the entering class of Tokyo University; it took only 102 high schools to account for 75 percent of the entering class, in a country of more than 5,200 public and private high schools (*Shukan Yomiuri*, Apr. 3, 1983).

One major effect of all this is a public awareness of education and rankings, as well as a public knowledge of the difficulties students encounter, that has no counterpart in the United States. While Sam was still in kindergarten, mothers of students in his class told me that from the elementary school he would attend had we stayed in Japan, about three boys each year from a sixth-grade class of about one hundred students would make it into Urawa No. 1 High School, one of the top high schools in the country, from which that year fifty-eight students got into Tokyo University. The SAT exams are a poor substitute for the intensity of the Japanese exams, and the consequences in the United States of where one goes to school are much less, and much less a matter of public concern.

Because the exams are so difficult, they are seen by the Japanese public as fair. No matter how natively bright a student is, and no matter what level of financial, cultural, and emotional support a family can provide, those who succeed are seen as having come through an ordeal that requires the qualities most admired in individuals, those of hard work, dedication, zeal, unbending commitment, and concentration. It seems right to most Japanese that those individuals should be allocated the most rewarding positions in Japanese society.

We began this section by asking whether education matters to Japanese individuals, whether socioeconomic factors affect educational success, and whether Japanese regard the system as fair. Perhaps surprisingly, the answer to all three questions is yes. Education does in most cases have a substantial effect on the quality of life that Japanese individuals can attain, and those who come from higher socioeconomic levels are more likely to attain high educational levels. However, since even for individuals with all possible advantages, the course to educational success is seen as so difficult, requiring such personal virtue, anyone who succeeds in the trials of the education competition is seen as worthy and deserving of success.

In the total framework of the educational system in Japan, the years of compulsory schooling, and particularly elementary schooling, are seen as the years that should, must, and can provide the level playing field for later competition. Competition is largely excluded from the institutional arrangements of elementary school, though it is still present in the surrounding atmosphere of family, *juku,* and society. In elementary school the emphasis is on full preparation of each individual, with little or no ranking in the school context. Equal—nearly identical—funding, facilities, curriculum, teachers, and experiences for all students gives each a fair chance when they are faced with a competitive world. Schooling is seen as the responsibility of the schools, and family background of students doesn't relieve schools and teachers of their duty to prepare students for later stages of education. There are always enough stories of individual students from disadvantaged backgrounds who do achieve great personal success in education to keep alive the notion that it is possible to succeed regardless of obstacles.

This ideology seems to be very much alive in Japanese culture, in spite of strong evidence that some children face more obstacles than others and that those are seldom the children of families at the top of the socioeconomic order. I think that because the socioeconomic order has been experienced by Japanese as being so fluid for the last century or so, the perception of the children of people at the top usually ending up at the top has been blunted. The top has changed and has grown, so that it appears to be more open than it really is, and the standard of living has risen so rapidly that even if individuals or families have not changed their relative standing in the Japanese social order, they feel they have attained levels of comfort and security beyond what they could have imagined from their parents' or grandparents' lives.

Observers of the Japanese social and political scene are quick to produce dire predictions of what will happen to people's perceptions of the openness and fairness of Japanese society as economic expansion slows down and as room at the top becomes more restricted. As in other countries, upward mobility may have painful consequences for individuals and families, but downward mobility is much more painful, and there are indications that families at the top are making efforts to avoid it. These include new categories of admission to colleges, so that some students are admitted on other criteria than their examination scores—personal recommendations, special talents, contributions to the university from the family, or sports ability. These individualistic criteria are applied to about 2 percent of the incoming students at elite schools and up to 50 percent at lower ranked schools, which find themselves competing for students from the shrinking pool of possible college students (Amano 1988:195). Whether this practice will expand, and whether the whole educational tracking system will become the focus of discontent with the inequities of Japanese society is not yet apparent. It has not happened to a significant degree yet.

DISADVANTAGED STUDENTS

Sociologists have established beyond doubt that in Japan those who succeed best in this system are those with substantial family resources, both cultural and financial. Taken as a whole, from kindergarten through university, the educational system does not provide totally equal opportunities for all children, though it comes closer than those of many other countries. On the other hand, there is both public and scholarly recognition that for some students even high levels of educational achievement will not lead to prized positions after school. Females are the largest group in this situation. Because females are categorically excluded from the most rewarding positions in Japanese society, in spite of public policy pronouncements to the contrary, they are also less likely to put forth the effort to make the highest educational rankings and less likely to receive public and family support for doing so. It is not that no girls are admitted to Tokyo University or other elite schools, but that more of them are discouraged from making the effort to attain admission. A woman's educational level affects her marriage chances, however, and thus has an impact on her life. It is generally regarded as suitable for a woman to have an educational level somewhat less than her husband's. For families dependent on wages and salaries, her ability to support the educational efforts of the children of the marriage is seen as one of the most important assets she brings to the marriage. There are stories circulating in Japan—one hopes untrue ones—that some very selective kindergartens in Tokyo give IQ and achievement tests to the mothers of prospective students.

Other groups that typically have lower educational achievement levels are students who come from Korean ethnic backgrounds and those who come from *burakumin* backgrounds. These two groups together account for approximately 2 percent of the population of Japan, and both groups are concentrated in the Kansai region centered around Kyoto-Osaka. Neither group is racially distinct from other Japanese; they cannot be identified by appearance unless they choose to wear clothing or other badges that label them. There is disagreement about the extent of cultural difference between them and other Japanese.

Korean ethnics in Japan are the families and descendants of Korean laborers brought to Japan during the 1920s, 1930s, and 1940s. These laborers, whose conditions of employment were close to slavery, and their descendants have been denied Japanese citizenship; they are an alien population within Japan by decree of the Japanese government. They speak Japanese as their native language; few of them can speak Korean, and their cultural ties with Korea are not very strong. As aliens they are denied many forms of employment, either by law or by practice. (Aliens of any sort, for example, cannot be school teachers in Japan.) If they marry Japanese citizens, there are often problems concerning the rights and citizenship status of their children.

The other large minority group that suffers discrimination in Japan are those who are descended from a category of people known as *burakumin* in earlier Japan. This was a legal classification and status of people that was officially abolished when other hereditary classifications, such as peasant and samurai, were done away with; legally there are no *burakumin* in modern Japan, just as there are no samurai. However, there are many people known to have come from those backgrounds or whose descent from *burakumin* can be deduced from information such as occupation or address. These people are systematically excluded from many occupations and from marriage with other Japanese, although there is no legal basis for such discrimination. Like many women and ethnic Koreans, people in this category often choose to opt out of the educational competition.

It has been difficult, in a modern Japan intensely concerned with its cultural identity, cultural uniqueness, and cultural unity, for educational policy to face up to the notions that students from Korean and *burakumin* cultural backgrounds are distinctive and that an education system that does not recognize that difference does not do them justice. Schools and school districts where such students are enrolled have begun to take action to acknowledge the needs of these two groups of students. There is ambiguity about the aims of educational programs directed at these students, whether the goal is to legitimate the differences between individuals in these categories and other Japanese, or whether the goal is to integrate them more fully into Japanese society (Kobayashi and Ebuchi 1993).

CRITICISMS OF JAPANESE SCHOOLS

What are the issues about schools that bother the Japanese? What problems do they see with their own system? The difficulty of the curriculum, "diploma disease," creativity, the unnecessary suppression of individuality, bullying, truancy, and competition leading to immoral selfishness are recurring themes in Japanese public and private discourse about the education of their children. In spite of outside evaluations of their education system as effective and humane, at least at the lower levels, the Japanese are not complacent about their school system, and suggestions for ways to improve it are reliably popular topics of discussion in magazines and on radio and television. Japanese society and culture are no more lacking in inconsistency and internal conflicts than other cultures. Some of the problems Japanese perceive in their education system reveal these internal oppositions in their lives.

School Is Too Hard

Criticism of the difficulty of the curriculum prescribed by the Ministry of Education is offered in terms of the 7–5–3 phenomenon. *Shichi-go-san*, "7–5–3," is the name of a religious holiday that celebrates the reaching of the ages of three and seven by boys and age five for girls. In earlier times of high infant mortality, it marked a child's attainment of ages at which mortality rates dropped noticeably, and thus of a child's firmer place in the social order. It is still celebrated by taking children of these ages, dressed in elaborate traditional finery, to shrines to offer thanksgiving and to receive a blessing. With regard to education, 7–5–3 means that in elementary school 70 percent of the children can fully master the material presented, in junior high school 50 percent can, and in high school only 30 percent of the students can really follow the ministry's syllabus. Some critics, including many teachers, say that a curriculum that is too difficult for this many students should be made simpler. Perhaps not all high school students need to learn calculus; perhaps not everyone needs six years of a foreign language.

Diploma Disease

"Diploma disease" refers to the possibly unhealthy reliance on academic schooling to allocate opportunities and rewards in Japan. Many Japanese critics of Japan have suggested that other kinds of education, learning, and experience have been too much ignored by a society that allocates its most visible and important rewards to those who accumulate the most prestigious diplomas. Their feeling is that talents other than those leading to success in school are denigrated and lost to society by patterns of jobs and earnings that offer the most to those with good diplomas.

This criticism is undoubtedly valid to some degree, but attempts to cure "diploma disease" run up against the question of what other reward system would better meet modern Japanese criteria for fairness and equality of opportunity. Although nepotism, favoritism, "connections," and other social ties play a role in Japan as they do in all other modern societies, nevertheless there is in Japan a strong belief that such factors are not the best way for a democratic society to operate. Japan is not alone in facing this particular dilemma.

Creativity

The Japanese sometimes refer to themselves as a "vacuum cleaner culture," a culture that is ingenious in borrowing from other cultures, China in the past and the West in modern times, but a culture that lacks real creativity in itself. Most social scientists would scoff at this pop culture denigration of Japan by Japanese, but it has some popular

appeal. The school system is pointed to as an institution that either sti-
fles or does nothing to promote creativity.

I don't think the Japanese are any clearer than Western educators or
psychologists about what might constitute creativity or about what
schools could do to foster it. In both contexts it's seen as a Good
Thing, but in neither context is it understood very well. The number
of Nobel Prize winners coming from Japan or other countries doesn't
seem a very good measure, though it's one cited by Japanese on some
occasions. I and many other observers in Japanese preschools and elementary schools have been very favorably impressed with the creativity
of children in their school activities and work in Japan. Very little
school time is spent in filling in the blanks of worksheets, and a lot of
time is spent on compositions, artwork, science projects, discussions,
and problem solving, which are far removed from rote learning or
memorization. If Japanese culture is not creative, it's difficult to lay
the blame on modern education for young children, at least as far as
any Western observers can see.

Conformity and School Rules

Japanese schools, especially at the junior high and high school levels,
formulate and enforce rules for their students, rules that apply to
behavior both in school and out of school. Rules prescribe the uniform
clothing that should be worn, sometimes down to the color of underwear, the hairstyles that are acceptable, the kinds of leisure activities
that students are supposed to avoid during nonschool hours, the times
they should be home at night, and so on. Students sometimes rebel
against the rules, flagrantly or covertly, and adults are often sympa-
thetic to their chafing against these restraints. The number and scope
of "school rules" seems to embody an unnecessary suppression of individuality in school contexts. The crux of the issue is in the determina-
tion of what and how much is unnecessary. In Japan and in all societies
socialization does mean that individual urges are molded into socially

sanctioned patterns. How much of this is necessary, and how much is unhealthful for a society? Is it necessary for all the boys in a junior high school to have the same haircut, or is that too rigid? Does the value of identity with a worthy social role that is symbolized by the identical backpacks worn by Japanese elementary students compensate for the lack of individuality this imposes on everyone? Should everyone have to belong to a school club? Should schools try harder to identify each child's individual talents and concentrate on maximizing them?

These are issues that concern thoughtful Japanese within the education system and throughout the society. They have no easy answers. We, and some Japanese, may not agree with all the choices in this area of controversy that are daily made in the Japanese education system, but I hope it is clear that the motivation for them is not just a rigid, unthinking authoritarianism. Sometimes they come across that way to Japanese children and adults, however, and sometimes the techniques of enforcing the rules smack of intimidation and sanctioned bullying.

The poison gas attacks in the Tokyo subway system, in Matsumoto and in Yokohama in 1995, were unexpected, incomprehensible events in Japan, as they might be in any country. One of the most disturbing aspects of them for many Japanese was the revelation that they were apparently carried out by young people who had attended elite universities and were recognized by their peers and professors as excellent students. How could such young people, among the best and the brightest of their generation, have been so misguided? How could Japanese schools have produced such failures?

Why should Japanese schools be called to account for such criminal behaviors at all? Why should anyone expect that students who excelled at physics, political science, economics, or foreign languages would be immune to whatever forces led them to undertake apparently senseless terrorist acts? Only because of the deep-seated Japanese conviction that education is moral education, that it is the responsibility of schools to produce moral adults, not technocrats. In Japan the discussions of the failures of high schools and universities in the education of these brilliant young people focused on the selfishness engendered in them by the competition for academic success and the collusion of Japanese education and society in this competition.

In other words, the failure of the schools in this case was a failure to induce a moral social conformity—the exact opposite of the previously cited complaint, that Japanese schools force too much conformity on children and young people. The contradiction of these two sets of criticisms is not merely a logical inconsistency: it reflects a tension in Japanese society and in all societies. No simple resolution is available to the Japanese education system, nor to Japanese culture and society as a whole, nor to other societies.

Ijime

One of the most dramatic expressions of the issue of social conformity in Japanese schools is the issue of *ijime*, "bullying." There have been sensational incidents of bullying, when a few students have gone so far as to kill the object of their bullying, or when a victim has retaliated with murder, violence, or suicide. Classroom teachers have very occasionally been implicated in such incidents and in less dramatic or extreme ones. Even a few incidents of this type seem intolerable to Japanese and lead them to question the socialization practices of their schools because they were able to result in such events. Bullying in Japanese schools takes the form of a large group of children, most or all of the class, either tormenting or acquiescing in the tormenting of a single child; it is different from bullying that is carried out by only a few children against a victim. Because so many children are implicated in the bullying behavior, the Japanese have felt that it is difficult to change their actions and that intervention must focus mostly on the victim, on helping the victim fit in. It sometimes becomes a forum for "blaming the victim." As *ijime* is more and more in the arena of public discussion, this viewpoint is coming under attack. In some cities telephone hot lines offer aid to *ijime* victims and books for children and for parents now offer advice on how to deal with *ijime;* perhaps gradually the shame of bullying is shifting from the victims to the bullies. It is difficult to evaluate the statistical frequency of bullying in Japanese schools of different levels; for the Japanese themselves the seriousness of the problem is not only a matter of numbers.

School Refusers

Another focus of discussion about the education system among Japanese is the phenomenon labeled *futokoji,* "school refusers." These are students who are truant from school, who consistently or occasionally refuse to attend school. When their behavior is noticed, teachers and school personnel try to ascertain the reasons for their absences. Explanations are often found in children's reports of being lonely at school, of having no friends there, of being embarrassed about their physical appearance (because of acne or disabilities, for instance), of fear of being bullied (though students may be too ashamed to admit this), or of avoiding school because of a failure to live up to performance expectations expressed by parents (mothers). Again, whatever the numerical extent of the *futokoji* problem, it is taken by Japanese as an indication of systemic problems in education that should be addressed by the society at large.

In Japan, as in all other societies, schools are enmeshed in the cultural premises that pervade peoples' thoughts, judgments, and actions, and in other institutions of the society. No cultures and no societies have yet achieved perfect cohesion and internal consistency, having institutions that never act at cross-purposes to each other. But the specific issues that concern the educational system in Japan, and elementary school as perhaps the central unit in the system, are not the same as the issues that arise to trouble educational systems in other cultures and societies.

11

Themes and Suggestions

The end of an ethnography such as this one calls for a summary of themes and motifs, of general coherence in the cultural phenomena described. If we understand the goals and the constraining environment of Japanese elementary school education, we will be able to understand why certain practices are widespread and effective.

In addition, in an ethnography like this one, undertaken in part to compare the education systems of Japan and the United States, it is appropriate to pull together some comparisons of practices in the two countries with an eye to evaluating possible changes in American practice. Both institutional structures and conceptions of children's motivations for learning are foci for evaluating changes.

We can look at the results of the practices of schools and at the structural and psychological foundations of those practices. It seems to me crucial to understand that in Japan the social practices of schools provide learning for social behaviors that remain useful in adult life and that achievable levels of success in school lead to successful lives after leaving school. The institutional format of uniform national standards for elementary school education, the relationship between teachers and students that follows from that, and the motivations for learning that Japanese teachers assume will operate in children are keys to making sense of the ethnographic detail.

In terms of the daily, yearly experience of being a child at school, I think the Japanese schools provide psychologically supportive, intellectually challenging, socially satisfying environments. Japanese children are happy at school; they learn a lot; they make friends with peers and learn to interact with them in culturally appropriate ways. What they learn at school academically and socially is useful to them in life after school; there are no major contradictions between the lessons of school and those of life in Japan, and they are appropriate at all social and class levels.

Sometimes the close parallels between the behavior patterns Japanese learn at school and the situations they confront as adults seem trivial, sometimes pervasive and profound. Even Sports Day, a school ritual, is often repeated in adult organizations such as companies. The same games and events are found at sports days for adults as at schools, the same patterns of team formation and group competition, the same lack of emphasis on individual winners. The eating patterns symbolizing camaraderie learned at school extend throughout the lives of Japanese. The cooperative cleaning activities children learn in school are found in work groups and religious or spiritual training groups. In this instance schools borrowed a traditional behavior and now reinforce its cultural significance.

Most adult Japanese spend their working lives in the context of large and small groups. The small groups operate in many ways like *han* groups at school, and it is noteworthy that this word was borrowed from the vocabulary of adult work in the first place. In Japanese adult contexts, work is most commonly done by groups of people, with different formal titles and abilities, who are jointly responsible for accomplishing a goal or job of work and who act as though they are all involved in all aspects of the task. Factory workers who expect and are expected to cover for each other's absences, the foreman who takes a place on the line when needed (Kamata 1982; Roberts 1994; Kondo 1990), the bank branch employees who all stay until the last bookkeeping error is found, even those who are not bookkeepers (Rohlen 1974), the worker who feels free to make suggestions about improvements, and the foreman and manager who feel free to consider them (Dore 1987), are all acting in ways consistent with school behavior.

Japanese children learn in school that they can profitably and pleasantly pursue both learning and fun in groups that include people with a wide range of personalities, talents, and disabilities. The ability to do this is as valuable in life after school as it is in the school context. They learn that competition between individuals is not the only road to high achievement. They learn that authority figures need not be automatically resisted or regarded as arbitrary or exploitative.

The expectation that there will be more than one way to solve a problem, that many options should be considered and integrated, is an attitude that outsiders have noticed in many adult contexts: in adaptations of basic research to commercial applications, in strategies for foreign policy and national defense, and in efforts to improve energy conservation. The quest for continual incremental self-improvement also seems to be learned at least in part in school, where self-evaluation and improvement measured against both outside standards and one's own past performance are cultivated.

Schools are psychologically supportive for Japanese children because schools have very self-consciously taken as their role the education of all children. Japanese educators do not feel that they can be effective only with certain kinds of children or with children from only certain kinds of home backgrounds. All children can learn, all should learn the same basic lessons, and the same sets of teaching techniques can be effective with all children. Schools in Japan are given the responsibility and opportunity of controlling a large part of children's lives; they not only have the children for a long school year and a long school day, but they also exercise substantial influence over the out-of-school life of children. Given this opportunity, it is thought that schools or educators should not dodge their duty to teach all children by blaming conditions in families and in society for their failures.

Of course, the conditions outside school are better for nearly all Japanese students than they are for many American students. Family stability and economic security for all families makes a big difference. So too does the basic trust in the values taught by schools that pervades Japanese society, so that many families do not resist the efforts of the schools to teach either subject matter or values. But even in the many parts of America where there is little serious dissension from official school values, American students learn less academically, and many of them find school a psychologically destructive environment because they are cast as failures from an early age and because they learn both in school and outside that the behaviors required in school are not the same as those required after school for success in life.

Japanese children can look forward to a decent life, no matter what their social class. The very low level of unemployment in Japan (around 2 percent) and an income distribution that ensures that even those at the bottom of the economic ladder have access to the means for decent housing, food, medical care, and other necessities give credence to the position that all children are being prepared in school for an acceptable life. Because there are very few families in Japan who have experienced seemingly inescapable, grinding, dehumanizing poverty for several generations, the cultural factors that perpetuate maladaptive educational behavior are not a very strong influence. A number of public policies in Japan, including trade barriers and almost absolute barriers to immigration, have helped Japan achieve this enviable position. But education has played its role, too, through its commitment to providing a good general background in compulsory education and good vocational training in specialized education. Japanese citizens are thus equipped for employment in a modern, increasingly technological world. There is a sort of "truth in education" factor here. Schools and society claim that success in education will qualify all children for a reasonable life, and this pledge is fulfilled in adulthood.

The first of the institutional supports that lead to these results is the uniform national curriculum for elementary schools and the uniform level of resources for schools to implement the curriculum. Japan's Ministry of Education sets a curriculum for all levels of schooling in Japan, and it is not a minimal competency requirement. It is challenging for all students, even those at the top. Teachers are among the loudest critics of it, saying that it is too hard. In the strictest legal sense it is not a required curriculum. Very few schools reject it altogether, however, and most adhere quite closely to its prescriptions. It is only "fair" to children to prepare them to compete with others who follow this curriculum. It may be difficult, but there is general agreement among teachers that it is a good curriculum.

The academic and social effects of this demanding curriculum are not what might be expected. Socially, students are never excluded from their classes because of academic failings: they are always promoted to the next grade, and they are not tracked into special classes or groups or excluded from regular classroom activities or social activities. Academically, the elementary school curriculum is the one most students can master, and failure is in any case a relative term. Mastering 60 percent of a demanding curriculum may lead to higher levels of learning than mastering 100 percent of an easy one. All international comparisons show that Japanese students do attain absolutely high levels of learning, with no more range of variation than in the United States (Lynn 1988:4–17; Stevenson, Azuma, and Hakuta 1986:201–38).

At the elementary level at least, the combination of academic challenge and social inclusiveness seems to be a major element in Japan's strategy for spurring the top academic children to high achievement, pushing all children to do the best they can, and maintaining self-esteem by not making academic achievement a requirement of social acceptability. It is not necessarily the case, then, that a uniform, emanding curriculum must be united with an elite-oriented school system that psychologically punishes and excludes large numbers of students.

In Japan the national uniform curriculum is combined with an evaluation system that removes individual teachers from imposing consequences for academic achievement or lack of it on students. Because the only consequential evaluations are those of the high school entrance examinations, the college entrance examinations, and the employment entrance examinations, teachers' only role with regard to their students is to teach, to prepare them all as well as possible for the examinations, which are not prepared or given by classroom teachers.

If teachers and students measure their performance against demanding but possible standards set from outside, and grades are not used for punitive purposes or to separate children into different tracks of education or activities, then the relationship between teachers and students is inevitably less adversarial and potentially more cooperative. Both teachers and students benefit from this environment. Students need not feel that they are in direct competition with their classmates for a limited supply of good grades, and grades cease to be a bargaining arena for the student-teacher relationship.

The structural constraints of the curriculum, the uniform provision of resources, and the examination system do not operate in a vacuum, but in the context of a motivational structure that teachers attribute to children.

> Reward children for good behavior? I think it's demeaning. In fact, I wouldn't even want to train animals that way. Even for a dog, it's humiliating to do tricks in the hopes of getting something for it.
> —Japanese elementary school teacher (quoted in Lewis 1995:124)

People learn more in their first five years of life than at any later time. They do this, the world around, in the absence of an educational system, without formal schools, without grades or other special systems of rewards and punishments, without much rebellion, and without much thought on the part of either children or adults. The joy children take in their expanding mastery of physical skills, language, social skills, and knowledge of the world is evident to any observer, including adults who delight in their learning and assume that life before school will not involve failure for most children. The question of learning in school might better be phrased, why don't children want to learn at school, when they so manifestly want to do so outside of school?

The incentives for learning that surround Japanese children are different at different ages, I think, but in some ways there is a continuity between the incentives that are effective in early childhood learning and those that are institutionalized in elementary schools. Before they enter school, children are carried along by the utter conviction of adults that they should, can, and will learn to speak their native languages, to control their bodies in socially acceptable ways, and to interact in culturally approved ways with other people. Children find acting in accordance with these expectations satisfying. School learning in elementary schools in Japan is approached by students, teachers, and parents in much the same way.

For adults, the knowledge that what is learned in school is needed and useful in later life, generally enjoyable, and no more problematic than learning to take one's shoes off or exchange greetings or defecate in the proper places makes them powerful persuaders of children to take the same view.

Seeking economic success in adult life is probably not a very compelling motivation for Japanese children, however, any more than they learn to speak Japanese because it will be advantageous to them as adults or learn to ride bicycles because it provides good training for large muscle development. They learn these things because at the time of learning it feels good, both within themselves and in their social relationships with family and others, to gain these skills. Japanese schools seem to be good at transferring this motivation into the school setting. Even if the motivation of the adults is to provide children with future benefits, they seem to instill a motivational structure for children that is not based on future extrinsic rewards.

There is compelling evidence from psychological studies that giving children extrinsic rewards like candy or tokens or grades for doing what they were doing by free choice extinguishes their desire to pursue those activities without rewards, and that learning prompted by the search for extrinsic rewards is less effective than learning prompted by intrinsic rewards (Deci and Ryan 1985:245–72). Japanese elementary schools seem designed to embed academic learning in the same framework—intrinsically satisfying, without extrinsic rewards—that characterizes nonschool learning. When I asked adults, "Why do children run so hard in the races, when there are no winners and no prizes?" their answer, "Why not?" was really saying, "It feels good to do as well as possible; no other incentive is needed."

If these structural features and understandings of motivation are the basis for academically and socially successful Japanese schools, are they aspects of education that could be adopted in Western schools? My answer to this question is mixed, but not totally negative. Schools are not the driving force of economic conditions, and schools can do little directly to affect employment levels and income distribution patterns, societal features that I feel do matter in the Japanese context and in other contexts. However, there are structural features of schools as institutions and a way of thinking about the social context of school learning that could incorporate some Japanese practices, with the expectation that they would make schools more effective. Some of the most striking differences in school structure and teaching styles between the United States and Japan seem to come from divergent, deep-seated cultural differences in understandings about the nature of children and their motivations for learning. Such differences, so deeply ingrained in our worldview that we cannot recognize them as cultural because they are so real to us, often pose insurmountable barriers to transferring behavior patterns from one culture to another. It seems to me highly unlikely that Westerners can adopt a view of children as innately good, having no unworthy motives, needing only to learn to understand the rewards and constraints of social human life, and act toward them consistently in terms of that view. I don't think we're ever going to be able to see a boy weighing a rock in his hand and not suspect he's contemplating damage to someone or something. Some of the behavioral consequences of the Japanese view of the nature of children and social learning, however, are also consequences of more Western ways of looking at children and adults.

Two sociolinguists, Penelope Brown and Stephen Levinson (1987), working from a long-standing Western philosophical background and a social science tradition, have proposed a framework for looking at social interaction that may provide the basis for non-Japanese to consider and adopt some Japanese practices. The framework they offer is one they claim is applicable in all human cultures; they have been criticized for being too bound by the self-interested, individualistic view of human nature that is part of the Western philosophical tradition. If their framework provides a way for us to understand in our terms what practices Japanese schools incorporate, then it may be easier for us to adopt some of Japan's effective actions and social structures.

Brown and Levinson see social interaction and the verbal expression that takes place in interaction as the outcome of two contradictory basic needs of every individual. In their view, all individuals want freedom to pursue their own ends unimpeded by interference from others. At the same time, they equally want to be liked, admired, and found worthy by others. Individuals are dependent on each other for this affirmation, and moreover, the affirmation of one's own self from others is of no value if the others are not valued in turn. Groucho Marx supposedly said that he wouldn't want to be a member of any club that would let him in, but in life we have to be members of groups that will let us in, and we have to value those people in order to get admiration, friendship, acceptance, or respect for ourselves. Japanese teachers exploit the tension between these two desires of children to create an environment conducive to learning.

Acquiring competence is one way to enhance individual independence, to become powerful and able to do what one wants. Japanese teachers are attuned to this aspect of learning and use it to motivate children. They do not expect children to learn because they are given extrinsic rewards for the learning, but because it makes them more powerful. In this context physical education, art, and music are as interesting as reading, math, and science.

Japanese classroom organizations and interactions assume that what really motivates children besides the power of competence is acceptance and esteem from other children. In some contexts of school, the athletically able students acquire esteem for their groups; in other contexts the musically or mathematically able students use their competence to gather esteem within the small group and within the larger group. Because the groups are multipurpose and stable for relatively long periods of time, all the members are able to contribute and receive contributions; the result is mutual esteem that operates in both academic and nonacademic activities. In all these contexts social skills that encourage groups to elicit and make the best use of the aptitudes and preferences of all the group members bring about more positive social rewards for all the group members.

The academic competence children gain is frequently exercised in social interactions in Japanese classrooms. A composition is written and read to classmates. An idea for solving a math problem is shared with the *han,* and with any luck the group will be applauded for coming up with it. Both giving and taking from peers bring rewards. The affirmation of worth socially that comes from the display of academic learning is what makes school learning more compelling for Japanese children than for American ones. It is not that Japanese children find learning the multiplication tables or the capitals of the prefectures less "boring" than Americans find them, but that Japanese schools make these the focus of social interactions that are intrinsically rewarding for children.

Many times American adults marvel at the intense interest in learning "boring" subject matter that children display about nonacademic matters. The capacity of children to learn sports statistics, the complicated interactions of many computer games, the trivia of information about television stars, and the characters of television series that children seem to acquire effortlessly, all attest to the contextual, social definition of what's "boring." Japanese schools make academic learning one of the activities of the same groups that focus on social activities. Learning seems to be easier and less "boring" because it takes place in "interesting" groups.

These social interactions in Japan are primarily with peers, not with teachers, whose policy is to be self-effacing. They are relations within a peer group that is stable enough over a long enough time period that one can and wants to seek self-worth and validation from the group members, and they are varied enough so that most members can make valuable contributions at least some of the time. Over time, in Japanese preschools and elementary schools, teachers entice children into academic activities by exploiting the nonacademic search for mastery and independence on the one hand and the hunger for social self-validation on the other.

There is nothing in Western or American culture that precludes exploiting the same basic needs and desires of children in our schools. We could have larger, more stable classes, less focus on student-teacher interaction, more heterogeneous class groups, more "fun" and more noncompetitive academic learning activities, more time spent at school, more genuine learning in the arts and physical education.

The first structural change that would have to be made in American schools to put this motivational structure into practice would be to move to larger, more heterogeneous classes. Japanese elementary schools operate with large classes. Educators claim this is done not to save money, but because the social atmosphere for learning that is centered in the peer group, not in individual student-teacher relationships, requires a certain critical mass to work. Thirty-five students in grades one through three, forty-five in grades four through six, are currently considered the goals in Japan. Some schools have smaller classes because of lower population densities; they are considered disadvantaged. There is a large body of research on learning levels and class sizes in the United States, but no clear conclusion can be drawn about effective class size. The rationales for small classes in the United States are that teachers cannot be expected to control larger groups and that individual attention to each child is possible only in small classes. The assumption that school learning is based on the student-teacher dyad is very clear here, along with the idea that different children need to be taught differently, and possibly different things.

My observations in Japan, the observations of other Western students of Japanese education, and the record of international comparisons of achievement have led me to believe that the Japanese approach is probably more effective. Making learning primarily a matter of interaction between teacher and student, including the grading aspects of that relationship, seems to be less effective than the Japanese group effort to conquer a syllabus. I and others have seen teachers utilizing a number of teaching strategies in their classrooms, including many recommended for students who have trouble with passive verbal presentations of material. I think classes in the United States should be larger but constant, as suggested above: no special groupings for different subjects, no traveling to different classrooms, no tracking within classes, and both social and academic activities emphasized as endeavors that include everyone.

What are the operational advantages of larger classes? First, they can contain a larger variety of children, so that there are likely to be fewer children who stand out because of some unique characteristic. With a larger number of children, the interests and abilities of any single child are more likely to find at least a partial match in some other child. As the Japanese say, larger classes include "more friends."

Some games and activities require a certain number of participants in order to be carried out or to be effective. Here the constant Japanese use of *han* groups is especially noticeable. If the class contains only enough children for two or three groups, those groups are likely to be very different from each other overall, and they are likely to fall into the disadvantages of unequal competition rather than providing the forum for cooperative-competitive stimulation that is the ideal for the *han* system. Again, with more children of more individual characteristics available, teachers can use a greater variety of grouping criteria to provide more experience in group interaction and different learning environments over the course of a year or two. In larger classes with more groupings possible, teachers have more scope to avoid creating class scapegoats, clowns, and stars. Teachers can defuse antagonisms and possible problems through grouping practices when those groupings are not tracking by academic ability. You need lots of students to have effective groups; you need effective groups for socially motivated academic learning.

Observers agree that Japanese teachers have a strong incentive to teach good behavior patterns to their students because they are going to spend a lot of time with those students, in most cases two full school years, 480 days. From a child's point of view, I think it's easier to learn to get along with one teacher and one set of classmates than with many different ones. I suggest that classrooms should be more nearly self-contained units than is common practice in many schools now. One teacher who teaches all subjects, one group of pupils who do not travel from place to place, teacher to teacher, all day long, all in one room that belongs to them and is their real home. The integration of social and academic activities crucial to this view of education happens most easily in the multipurpose homeroom.

The change of mind I was perhaps most reluctant to have forced on me in this study of Japanese schools was with regard to tracking in schools. But I now feel that academic tracking does not provide the best environment for academic learning for bright, average, or slow students and that it would be better to have a hard curriculum and academically integrated classes with the inclusive social practices used in Japanese classrooms. Academic challenges for able students can still be included, as the Japanese experience shows, and with the right social practices the poorer students need not suffer the loss of face and self-esteem they demonstrably do suffer in American schools when they are separated out and put in the slowest reading group or the "dumb class." Overall, the academic level of the poorest students in Japanese classrooms is higher than the performance of the poorest students in American schools, even when the American students have been given special help. So are the achievement levels of the average students and the best students.

Much tracking in American schools, particularly that which separates children into private, religious, and magnet schools is class, race, and ethnic tracking. Perhaps effective teaching and learning in the schools attended by most students could help alleviate the need parents feel for this kind of segregation.

If schools are going to utilize social learning, social ties, and social motivations for academic (and social) learning, then they probably need to have the children in school for longer school days, encompassing more social activities, and for more days each year. If American children were to spend the forty hours a week in school that Japanese children do, then it is crucial that the extra time *not* be filled with academic classes. I would suggest that the eight hours a day should be apportioned as follows: 5 to 5 1/2 hours of academic instruction, including homework, art, music, and physical education, the rest of the time (2 1/2 to 3 hours) for recess, lunch, cleaning or other public service, snack, class meetings, and club meetings. Children would still have the evenings and weekends free.

Japanese schools and teachers seem not to feel guilty about capitalizing on children's desire to have fun in the effort to reconcile them to discipline and learning. Many activities, from generous recess periods to school trips, are undertaken simply for the purpose of having fun, with the conviction that this makes for an atmosphere conducive for learning. Students are not deprived of these activities as punishment. I think school should be more fun in America. Most of these fun activities turn out to involve a lot of physical activity, an advantage in itself.

Most children do not take easily to long periods of sitting still, and large doses of activity seem to make class time more productive.

Many people feel that teachers are the most important variable in schools and classrooms. Japanese teachers are generally good, and there are a number of reasons for this. One is that they have gone through Japanese schools themselves and have received a good education through university level. Next, teaching is regarded as a good job in terms of status and salary in Japan, and it is still one of the few professions in which women can really make a career, though at elementary school level they are only about 50 percent of the teaching staff. Teaching thus attracts a large and good pool of applicants, and there is stiff competition for teaching jobs. Successful applicants must have completed a university teacher training course and a major in a substantive field. They are then chosen on the basis of an entrance examination.

Schools offer strong support for individual teachers. They are not isolated from fellow teachers, as is often the case in other systems. Their workday at school is structured so that they spend time with others in the teachers' room, and both formally and informally they are encouraged to share experiences and information about students, teaching tactics, problems, and effective techniques. They help each other develop supplementary teaching materials and design together ways to approach the requirements of the curriculum. The most effective, experienced teachers are given the most difficult classes and the most difficult students. Their tales about dealing with them are a continuing topic of informal conversation in the teachers' room.

Going to school is a real job for students, and even more, teaching is a real job for teachers. Teachers are expected to be at school from 8:00 A.M. to 5:00 P.M., five and a half days a week (most Japanese work a full or half day on Saturdays). The long summer vacation for students is not a vacation for teachers, who are required to use the time for study, be present at school on specified days, give swimming lessons, and accompany classes that go on summer field trips. There is thus no sense that teaching is just something women fit in around child rearing, a (false) perception I think persists in the United States. Teachers' earnings are at about the median level for workers with their education levels and age; like other salaries they rise relatively steeply with age throughout a teaching career. It is not necessary to become an administrator to reach high salary levels.

Like American teachers, Japanese teachers say they choose the work because they like children and they like teaching. I think they work in situations that increase these professional satisfactions. Their circumstances enhance their ability to be effective teachers, and their involvement with one class of children in a comprehensive social and academic environment over a two-year period of time maximizes their satisfaction with the impact they can have on children.

Accompanying the structural changes to larger, more heterogeneous, multipurpose classes, longer school hours, and supportive teaching conditions should come a move toward an effective national curriculum, accompanied by an evaluation system that is not dependent on grades given by teachers. The changes in motivational structure for both teachers and students that this entails would change the nature of classroom interactions in the ways detailed throughout this book. Emphasis on teaching, with evaluation assigned to the big, bad, external Examination System, means that teachers and students are engaged in the same cooperative enterprise, not opponents or caught in the web of competition, exploitation, and resistance that relations between the powerful and the powerless always entail.

The last major advantage in structural terms that I think Japanese schools have over American ones is that in Japanese social and cultural terms, schools legitimately have academic, social, civic, and moral teaching responsibilities. In the United States schools also do academic, social, civic, and moral teaching, but not all of these are accepted as part of the function of schools. Every social scientist and educator will agree that schools do teach moral lessons, whether the teachers or the system intend that they do so or not. Some of the most eloquent writing in critical education studies of the last twenty years has documented just how schools teach the lessons of the "hidden curriculum" that reproduce the race, gender, and class inequalities of modern societies, their moral justifications, and the behavior patterns that perpetuate them (Ogbu 1974; Bowles and Gintis 1976; Willis 1981; Cookson and Persell 1985; Sadker and Sadker 1994). The public curriculum of American schools certainly does not articulate these goals, but these are lessons learned and taught, though perhaps not intentionally.

Every mention of morals or ethics or values in the schools in the United States, however, runs immediately into the rock of religion. Commonalities of ethical judgment found among different religions and philosophical outlooks become obscured because of the difference in justification for those judgments that different groups offer. Focus in the United States has historically been on the differences in justifications, not on the commonalities of behavior prescribed. These are emotionally laden issues in the United States, so that people who advocate sexual abstinence for teenagers based on divine commandments feel nothing in common with people who advocate the same sexual abstinence based on the immaturity of teenagers and the importance of social and individual responsibility. Religion, morality, and sex are intimately linked in the United States, though they are not in Japan and in some other cultures.

Because schools are inevitably institutions that impart morals, and because morals are "religious" in the United States, it may be necessary to augment the current version of public schools here with ones based on communities that share a moral universe of discourse. I am suggesting that a set of schools of several varieties of religious-philosophical persuasions, chosen by families, be deliberately and overtly given the responsibility of imparting moral values to students, rather than having values be part of a hidden, covert, illegitimate curriculum. Let schools design their activities to teach values openly.

Finally, in connection with the civic and moral teaching roles of schools, let me offer a few arguments in favor of ritual and continuity and against constant innovation in educational practices. Americans seem to have a fear of ritual and patterned behaviors in many contexts, including schools. In Japanese schools rituals and routines seem to punctuate schooltime; they facilitate transitions between activities and are comforting in their constancy. One of the most striking examples is the procedure for beginning each class, with students calling others to attention and leading them in assuming the proper postures and in turning their attention to the teacher and the class material. The alternation between apparently wild recesses or class breaks and the focused attention of class time is greater than in many U.S. schools, and the short ritual effectively makes the transition. Larger rituals such as Sports Day, ceremonies at the beginning of each term and the end of the year, the weekly assembly, and the weekly class meeting also give children a sense of passing time and changing roles and of stability and constancy.

We have a preoccupation with newness in school activities: new textbooks, new approaches, new projects, new learning activities. Many good ideas and practices get lost in the search for new things, and the ritualized passage of children through socially recognized landmarks of schooling is lost. The learning experience of each child will remain unique and individual, even if others have used and will use the same vehicles for learning, the first-grade morning glory and Culture Day chicken, for example. In Japanese schools teachers help each other a great deal to develop techniques for teaching, sharing ideas and stories about what works and what doesn't work to teach a particular point, about the second and third tactics to try in a class, about approaches to use with difficult students. If each teacher feels that her teaching must reflect only her own individual bent, experience, and talent and that it must be different each year, useful experience is lost, not shared and not made tradition.

Shared experience, across grades, across schools, across generations, was chosen in Japan to impart a sense of national identity during Japan's nation-building days. I think it is foolish of us to deny unifying experiences to our children, when we live in a time of such discord and loss of confidence in our unity as a country. A national curriculum and other experiences that children in the nation, the state, the city, and the school have in common might foster a sense of community that education does not seem to be very effective in conveying these days.

12

Sayonara

We timed our departure from Japan for just after the end of the school year in March. Sam and Ellen both received going-away presents from their classes, very nice photo albums with individual pictures of their classmates and a farewell note from each one. The inevitable hassles and confusions of ending the research we had come to do, of cleaning the apartment, selling household gear, closing bank accounts, and moving a family to the other side of the globe somewhat obscured the meaning and significance of the year for us in terms of our individual and family experiences at the time all this was going on.

Sam and Ellen were anxious to return to Pittsburgh. They had not been happy about moving from Washington, D.C., to Pittsburgh the year before, but the year in Japan made Pittsburgh seem like home. Remembered foods, TV shows, activities, and most importantly friends became common topics of conversation. All of us were looking forward to having a car again and a bigger house. All of us were ready to be back in an English-speaking environment; I feel print-deprived and stupid when I can't read everything around me, and both Dave and I were tired of my being the only one who could ask questions, answer the phone, or read the mail. Dave and I were hoping we would again feel confident about our ability to handle the cultural and practical complexities of daily life. In Japan we had a perpetual impression that we were getting by on good luck and a distinctly below average level of social competence.

We also talked about the experiences we had enjoyed, the New Year's trip to Hong Kong, travels throughout Japan, and especially the volcanoes, beaches, and hot spring baths in Kyushu. Strange foods we had encountered, and foods we would miss, also were remembered. Sam tried to figure out ways to take a lot of fireworks back to Pittsburgh. Ellen wanted to take the posters that helped her learn the syllabary and the first-grade *kanji*. The hardest part of leaving, of course, was parting from friends. Many people had helped us; many people we just enjoyed. Letters have helped us stay in touch, but they're not like being in the same town and meeting casually.

Dave and I are sometimes asked if the year was worth it. Certainly in terms of our research it was fruitful and stimulating. The dynamics of the year together as almost the only Americans in Urawa, in a small apartment and without as many separate activities as we are involved in at home, meant we spent more time together, did more traveling and other activities together, and were more socially necessary to each other than when we are in the States. We both felt then, and now, that the experience of intimate contact with another culture was an invaluable one for our children. Sam, these several years later, seems to share this feeling more than Ellen. I think she was the one who enjoyed the year the least. Ellen and Sam both had conversation lessons with a tutor for two years after we returned, but that gave way to increasing academic and social demands. Sam studied Japanese with a tutor for his high school language requirements and retains some ability to use the language. He also shows a continuing interest in people of other cultural backgrounds and a flair for bringing disparate sorts of friends together.

Would we do it again? Would we recommend the same course to others? Yes.

Appendix

Reading and Writing in Japanese

For children especially, learning to read Japanese is very different from learning to read English, in terms of the rhythm of the process and the rate of gaining a feeling of competence. English is harder at the beginning and easier at the end; Japanese is easy at the beginning but then becomes difficult and remains that way longer. These differences are caused by differences in the writing systems, not in the languages themselves.

Reading in English is difficult at the beginning because we have a very imperfect alphabetic writing system. The theory behind alphabets is that each distinctive sound in the language will be represented by a distinctive symbol, or letter. Standard English spelling, however, departs from this principle in several ways, all encountered by children at the very beginning of the process of learning to read because many of the most common words have "irregular" spellings and must be memorized. Because of historical influences and changes, especially in the vowels of English, there are several ways of spelling any given vowel sound and several ways of pronouncing any given vowel spelling. Even more importantly, English dialects vary most in their vowel systems. A writing system that can be read by Irish, Australian, American, and British speakers has to be one that is not very accurate for any one group—because it's a sloppy fit for each group, they all can use it, but imperfectly. Much useful information about the relationships and histories of different words is embodied in these spellings, and this contributes to the resistance people feel toward spelling reforms.

The result of our imperfect alphabetic spelling, especially in the most common words, is that children have a difficult time acquiring the first levels of competence in reading. Learning the patterns of reading and spelling takes a large part of the time for several years in American and other English-speaking schools. By fourth or fifth grade, however, the mechanics of reading, of transferring written representations into meaning units that can be processed like spoken language, is accomplished for most children. Other aspects of reading may still remain problematical, but the mechanics are in place. By the age of ten or so, children can read most written English materials that they can understand on other grounds—that is, if they can understand the ideas in a newspaper story, they can probably read the story, in the form in which it is written for adults. Before the end of elementary school, then, children who are learning to read English are competent readers of adult materials. (Also like adults, their reading is constrained by their comprehension levels—adults who understand chemistry but not sociology can read different materials than those who understand sociology but not chemistry.)

The Japanese writing system is fundamentally different from the English system, and learning to read it is a different process. Japanese writing has developed under the influence of two diverse factors. First, writing was imported from China along with a great deal of learning and other cultural material, and Chinese writing was adopted as the writing system. Most writing was done in the Chinese language and in Chinese characters at the initial periods of writing in Japan. People soon wanted to write in the Japanese language, however, and here the second factor came into play: Japanese and Chinese are unrelated languages, as different in word structure and syntax as English and Chinese or as English and Japanese. The writing system that is adequate for Chinese just won't work for Japanese. The major problem is that Japanese has inflections, changes in words that reflect grammatical relations, and Chinese doesn't. Most words in Chinese appear as invariant forms, regardless of their grammatical context, whereas all verbs and adjectives in Japanese have varying forms.

Anyone who wants to write Japanese rather than Chinese, then, has to have some way of representing the inflections of Japanese grammar. Over many years a way to represent these inflections, based on sounds, was developed. It was closely related to the alphabetic principle of each sound being represented by a symbol, but the Japanese solution instead represents each *syllable* with a symbol.

This solution wouldn't work in English, which has many different syllables as possibilities, ranging from "I" to "strengths," for example. But in Japanese the possibilities for syllable formation are very limited. A syllable can be a vowel alone, or a consonant followed by a vowel, or a nasal consonant alone. Altogether, 103 symbols, some of them complex, are enough to represent the syllables of Japanese. In contrast, this paragraph alone contains 83 different syllables in English.

Over the course of several centuries, the symbols for representing the syllables of Japanese have been standardized, in modern times under the guidance of the national Ministry of Education. At the same time, especially since the beginning of the modern education system in 1872, dialect variations in Japan have been lessened. There are still areas of Japan, especially in the northeast and the southwest, where natives of the region speak a noticeably different dialect. But schools and the mass media, which penetrate every corner of Japan, use standard Japanese; it is everywhere understood, and nearly everyone can speak it if necessary. Thus, the system of representing the sounds of Japanese by a set of symbols for the syllables of Japanese is a good fit for everyone's use of Japanese and an excellent, easily learned writing system. This kind of writing system is called a syllabary.

It is this set of symbols that children learn first when learning to read; this is what their mothers, older siblings, and grandparents teach them, and most children have mastered them before they reach first grade. Sam and Ellen learned these symbols in about three weeks. Everything in Japanese can be easily and reliably written using this set of symbols.

But Japanese is not normally written using only this set of symbols. Instead, the symbols are used ordinarily only for two categories of material. Most importantly, they are used for writing the inflections that Japanese grammar requires of its words, particularly verbs. Second, they are used for words that are identified as Japanese in origin and not borrowed from Chinese or other foreign languages. This second criterion is not very consistently applied, however. What is used ordinarily to write everything else in Japanese is *kanji*, literally, "Chinese writing." *Kanji* are thus used for the stems of words— nouns, verbs, adjectives, and adverbs.

What kind of writing system do *kanji* represent? Something fundamentally different from alphabets or syllabaries. In the Chinese writing system the symbols stand for words (or meaningful parts of words, morphemes, like the two parts of *breakfast*). There are as many different symbols as there are words or morphemes. The relationship between the symbol and the word it stands for must be considered essentially an arbitrary one. Thus, learning to read means learning a fairly large stock of symbols for words by rote memory. Reading a Chinese newspaper, for instance, requires a reading vocabulary of around 3,000 different symbols.

It is true that historically some of the *kanji* used in both Chinese and Japanese are derived from either pictures or sound correspondences. To use standard examples, the symbol for the word *river* looks like this 川, which can be seen as a drawing of ripples of water. *Sun* 日, *moon* 月, *tree* 木, and *forest* 森 can also be seen as pictures. (It matters that the pictures were drawn with a brush; square shapes are done more accurately with a brush than round ones.) Some words in this sort of writing system are formed by pictures of meaning elements of the word, so that the standard symbol for *man* or *male* is 男,

a drawing of fields divided by irrigation dikes 田, over a drawing of a knife 刀. Men work in fields and use knives or swords.

Some words are formed by elements that may relate to either meaning or sound. Thus, the morpheme that is used in compounds to indicate *language* is pronounced [go]: *nihongo* means "Japanese," *furansugo* means "French," *eigo* means "English." It is written 語, and consists of three identifiable parts. The left-hand side 言, is a picture of sound waves coming out of a mouth and is often used in words having something to do with speech. The top of the right-hand side is the symbol that stands for the number five 五, pronounced [go], and the bottom of the right-hand side is a drawing of a mouth 口. Both meaning and sound elements are contained in this *kanji*. However, the left-hand side of this *kanji* is also found in words meaning "to measure," "to attack," "to be suspicious of," and "the death penalty." Although it sometimes indicates a meaning element of a word, in other instances it doesn't, at least in any transparent way. Sound elements also sometimes seem to contribute clues to the sound of a word and at other times have nothing to do with the pronunciation.

What this means for learners, especially early learners of the Japanese writing system, is that every symbol seems both complicated and arbitrary, with mnemonics that are unreliable.

If this weren't enough of a problem, the same *kanji* are used in Japanese writing with several different pronunciations. (This is not true in Chinese, where the sound attached to a particular symbol does not vary, at least within a single dialect.) Thus, the word *go,* meaning "language" written as above, is also used with the pronunciation [kata] in the words *katamono,* "theme of a narrative," and *katate,* "narrator, speaker."

The meaning element can be considered the same in all these compounds, but the pronunciation reflects the origin of the words, *go* having been borrowed from Chinese and *kata* being a native Japanese word. It's as though English used one symbol for the common meaning in *heart, heartfelt,* and *heartbeat,* and also in words like *cardiac, cardiopulmonary,* and *tachycardia.* Though the same symbol, signifying the same meaning, would be used, the words would be pronounced as they are now, with two pronunciations for the same meaning. People learning to read would have to learn the different contexts and the pronunciations appropriate to them.

This analogy also holds for the relative feeling of formality and technicality that surrounds words with borrowed roots and pronunciations, such as *cardiopulmonary* in English and *gogaku,* "linguistics," in Japanese. Chinese is the source of roots for the formation of technical and learned words in Japanese, as Latin and Greek continue to be in English.

Another example that gives a very realistic conception of the problems facing Japanese children learning to read *kanji* can be found in a common affix like the ones in English meaning NEGATIVE. Suppose English were written with words like *Xlikely, Xpossible, speechX, Xrenewable, Xdecisive, Xacid,* and *Xcommunist.* Someone learning to read English would have to know from context that these words should be pronounced "unlikely," "impossible," "speechless," "nonrenewable," "indecisive," "antacid," and "anticommunist." This is exactly the situation facing a Japanese child learning to read materials written for adults.

The two major problems for reading Japanese that incorporates *kanji,* as most writing does, are what pronunciations to associate with a given occurrence of a *kanji* and how many *kanji* one has to recognize. This number could be quite high, as high as the number of words or morphemes in the language. When the universal education system was instituted in 1872, the Ministry of Education took some steps to alleviate the second problem. It established a set of *kanji* that everyone would be taught and limited the number of *kanji* that could be used in certain contexts, such as government publications, textbooks, and newspapers. Over the years the list has been refined and changed somewhat.

At this time there is a government list of approved *Kanji* for General Use. It contains 881 Essential Characters, which are to be learned during the six years of elementary school. There are also 969 more General Use characters to be learned in junior high school and high school and 92 others that can be used only in proper names. These 1,850 characters, along with those for proper names, constitute the mechanics of reading and writing Japanese along with the use of the syllabary.

But Japanese children are also confronted with two other sets of symbols for reading and writing. Besides the syllabary described above, there is another exactly parallel syllabary. For every symbol of one syllabary, there is another exactly corresponding symbol in the other syllabary. The second set of symbols is used for foreign words, for words of foreign origin, for words that represent animal or natural sounds, and also in advertising and other cases where graphic display is important, somewhat as italics or variations in upper and lower case are used in English. Children learn this second syllabary in first and second grade.

Finally, there is a very good system of writing the sounds of Japanese with the letters used in English and other Western languages. This is the romanized Japanese used for the Japanese words in books like this one, and in Japan for graphic interest. Children learn to read and write in this system in the fourth grade.

Every sentence written in the ordinary Japanese used by adults will contain both *kanji* and symbols from the syllabary, and it is not uncommon in newspapers, advertisements, or magazine articles to encounter sentences using all four writing systems.

Traditionally, Japanese was written from the top of the page to the bottom, in vertical lines, with the first line of the page on the right hand side and the book opening backward, compared to Western books. Now the practice of arranging writing from left to right in horizontal rows that start at the top of the page in books that open

Western style has become common. From the first day of first grade, students deal with material written in both formats. From my own experience, I think that moving horizontally from left to right or right to left (as in Hebrew) takes little adjustment of eye movement, but the patterns needed for taking in chunks of material moving vertically require noticeable adjustment.

How can it be, then, that Japanese seems to be easier to learn at the beginning? This is because there is an immense amount of material published for children that uses only the syllabary, which most children can read at the beginning of first grade. Because any word in Japanese can be fully represented in the syllabary, this material does not have to have carefully controlled vocabulary. Therefore, its interest level can be high. It can also be used both by children and adults in real-life situations like leaving notes or making lists.

This level of competence is easily achieved. But the next levels, involving *kanji*, are harder to attain independently, and children in elementary and junior high school are confined to material written for children, incorporating *kanji* at the rate prescribed by the Ministry of Education's national curriculum. Being able to read newspapers, magazines, or other materials written with adults in mind is an ability that comes to Japanese children later than to Americans.

Adults whose lives involve little reading find *kanji* easy to forget in later life, and many publications use fewer than the approved possibilities, substituting the syllabary for some *kanji*. On the other hand many literary or technical writings use more than the 1,850 on the government list.

A number of ramifications of this writing system are worth spelling out. What about using a dictionary? Looking at a *kanji* gives no reliable information as to its sound; there is no alphabet to organize the listing of entries in a dictionary. There is a system devised in China that involves grouping *kanji* according to parts used in writing them, for instance the 言 used in the *kanji* for *language* illustrated above, and then counting the number of writing strokes needed to complete the *kanji.* There are 214 of these elements, and it's not always easy to decide which one is the right one. It's difficult to learn to use a dictionary or reference work. Many things that are alphabetized in the West, such as phone books, are also arranged by pronunciation in Japan (there are at least two "alphabetical" orders that can be used), and this is effective if you already know the pronunciation of whatever you're looking up. But you can't tell that for an unfamiliar *kanji.*

What about writing? There are no efficient typewriters for Japanese; a machine that contains 1,850 *kanji* plus two syllabaries plus English letters is a printing press, not a typewriter. Accurate and legible handwriting in Japan is not only a matter of art and aesthetics, but also of practical necessity. It's much easier to recognize and read *kanji* than to write them fully and correctly; the vagaries of English spelling are trivial in comparison. Most high school and college students carry little reference cards of the General Use *Kanji,* and use them often. Adults resort to sloppy writing or using the syllabary—but that looks really childish.

There is also the obvious question why, with several good alternatives available, the Japanese continue to use *kanji.* There have been reformers in Japan who advocate changing to a different writing system, for instance English letters, but they have been unsuccessful in getting much support. There are several different reasons that Japanese give for continuing to use *kanji.*

One reason is that if people do not continue to use and learn *kanji,* all the literary and historical material that uses *kanji* will become inaccessible. The loss of tradition and traditional learning would be too high a price to pay for the convenience of an easier system. This seems to be persuasive to most Japanese. Another is that adults claim it is faster and easier to read *kanji* than the writing that represents the sounds of language. They claim that one can in effect skip one step of mental processing in reading, going directly from symbol to meaning, rather than from symbol to sound to meaning. It is difficult for nonnatives to evaluate this claim; it feels to me that it might have some merit.

A third reason is related to the feeling many Japanese have that they would like to preserve their uniqueness in the world as a distinctive people. They feel that because the writing system is so tied up with the history and tradition of Japan and the very nature of the Japanese language, abandoning it would be a major step in abandoning "Japaneseness." From a linguist's point of view, writing systems have little to do with the nature of the languages they transcribe, but on social or psychological grounds it is difficult to dismiss this set of claims. Foreigners have sometimes asserted that maintaining this writing system is a part of the Japanese conspiracy to exclude outsiders from knowledge of Japan and from participation in Japanese organizations as equals. According to this view, the writing system is just another unfair barrier to protect the Japanese from outsiders.

Finally, there is the argument that *kanji*, as difficult as they are, still have the advantage of signaling important historical and morphological information, in addition to simply representing (in an especially difficult way) the pronunciation of a word. An English example is the word *photography*, with a spelling that signals to us the sounds of the word but also tells us about the semantic elements that make up the word and its historical derivation. Literate people are reluctant to give up this richness, even though they will concede that the word is easily recognized when it is spoken, with no visual representation of its semantics, and that children learn the word perfectly well without any reflection on its derivation.

Changing the writing system of Japan would be a political decision with many expected and unexpected side effects. At this time there is no prospect of a political or social consensus that would support such a far-reaching change. Learning to read in Japanese is not likely to become a different process any time soon.

One last digression on the writing system involves computers and word processing systems. Though the Japanese never developed typewriters, they have developed ways to use computers and Japanese word processing programs. To handle the input to a word processing program, a Japanese user uses a keyboard with symbols for the Japanese syllabary or, less commonly, English letters. The word processing program then translates the syllabary input, where appropriate, into *kanji*. Because many different *kanji* have the same pronunciation and therefore look the same in the syllabary, the program uses context to make some choices and also sometimes offers a menu of alternate *kanji* for one pronunciation.

Word processors are becoming inexpensive and readily available to both institutions and individuals in Japan. Two contradictory trends are at work for Japanese who use them. On the one hand their use leads to a greater acceptance of the syllabary in more contexts. Utility bills, for instance, are now computer generated and printed, and they use only the syllabary; and supermarkets that provide receipt tapes often are tied into a computerized inventory and accounting system and use the syllabary. Anyone who does computer input uses the syllabary. In several new and familiar contexts, then, the exclusive use of the syllabary is becoming more common.

On the other hand, the computer word processing program can accurately store many more *kanji* than all but the most erudite humans and can present these as choices on the *kanji* menu for users. *Kanji* are much easier to recognize passively than to use actively in writing, and people report that because the computer will take care of the more difficult memory feats, they are using more *kanji,* and more unusual *kanji,* in their writing than ever before. It is difficult to predict what effects these two trends will have on Japanese reading and writing practices in the future.

References

Amano Ikuo. 1988. "Higher Education and Student Enrollment Selection in Japan." *International Journal of Educational Research* 12:193–201.

Berman, David M. 1990. "Case Study of the High School Entrance Examination in Chiba Prefecture, Japan." *Theory and Research in Social Education* 18:387–404.

Bestor, Theodore C. 1989. *Neighborhood Tokyo*. Stanford, Calif.: Stanford University Press.

Bourdieu, Pierre. 1991. *Language and Symbolic Power*. Cambridge: Polity Press.

Bowles, Samuel, and Herbert Gintis. 1976. *Schooling in Capitalist America*. New York: Basic Books.

Brown, Penelope, and Stephen C. Levinson. 1987. *Politeness: Some Universals in Language Usage*. New York: Cambridge University Press.

Cookson, Peter W., Jr., and Caroline Hodges Persell. 1985. *Preparing for Power*. New York: Basic Books.

Cummings, William. 1980. *Education and Equality in Japan*. Princeton, N.J.: Princeton University Press.

Deci, Edward L., and Richard M. Ryan. 1985. *Intrinsic Motivation and Self-Determination in Human Behavior*. New York: Plenum.

Dore, Ronald. 1965. *Education in Tokugawa Japan*. Berkeley: University of California Press.

———. 1978. *Shinohata: Portrait of a Japanese Village*. New York: Pantheon.

———. 1987. *Taking Japan Seriously*. Stanford, Calif.: Stanford University Press.

Foucault, Michel. 1977. *Discipline and Punish: The Birth of the Prison*. New York: Pantheon.

Gerbert, Elaine. 1993. "Lessons from the *Kokugo* (National Language) Readers." *Comparative Education Review* 37:152–80.

Habermas, Jurgen. 1984. *Theory of Communicative Action*. Boston: Beacon.

James, Estelle, and Gail Benjamin. 1988. *Public Policy and Private Education in Japan*. London: Macmillan.

Japan Institute of Labour. 1989. *Japanese Working Life Profile*. Tokyo: Japan Institute of Labour.

Japan Statistical Yearbook. 1989. Tokyo: Statistics Bureau, Management and Coordination Bureau.

Johnson, Thomas Wayne. 1975. *Shonendan: Adolescent Peer Group Socialization in Rural Japan*. Taipei: Chinese Association for Folklore.

Kamata Satoshi. 1982. *Japan in the Passing Lane: An Insider's Account of Life in a Japanese Auto Factory*. New York: Pantheon.

Kiefer, Christie. 1970. "Psychological Interdependence of Family, School, and Bureaucracy in Japan." *American Anthropologist* 72:66–75.

Kobayashi Tetsuya, and Kazuhiro Ebuchi. 1993. *Tabunka Kyoiku no Hikaku Kenkyu*. Fukuoka, Japan: Kyushu Daigaku, Kyushu Shuppan Kai.

Kondo, Dorinne K. 1990. *Crafting Selves: Power, Gender, and Discourses of Identity in a Japanese Workplace*. Chicago: University of Chicago Press.

Lewis, Catherine C. 1995. *Educating Hearts and Minds*. Cambridge: Cambridge University Press.

Lynn, Richard. 1988. *Educational Achievement in Japan*. Armonk, N.Y.: M. E. Sharpe.

Mouer, Ross E., and Yoshio Sugimoto. 1990. *Images of Japanese Society: A Study in the Structure of Social Reality*. New York: Routledge Chapman and Hall.

Nakane Chie. 1970. *Japanese Society*. Berkeley: University of California Press.

Ogbu, John. 1974. *Next Generation: An Ethnography of Education in an Urban Neighborhood*. New York: Academic Press.

Okano Kaori. 1993. *School to Work Transition in Japan*. Cleveden, England: Multilingual Matters.

Peak, Lois. 1991. *Learning to Go to School in Japan*. Berkeley: University of California Press.

Roberts, Glenda. 1994. *Staying on the Line: Blue-Collar Women in Contemporary Japan*. Honolulu: University of Hawaii Press.

Rohlen, Thomas. 1974. *For Harmony and Strength*. Berkeley: University of California Press.

———. 1983. *Japan's High Schools*. Berkeley: University of California Press.

Sadker, Myra, and David Sadker. 1994. *Failing at Fairness: How Our Schools Cheat Girls*. New York: Simon and Schuster.

Singleton, John. 1967. *Nichu, A Japanese School*. New York: Holt, Rinehart and Winston.

———. 1989. "*Gambaru*: A Japanese Cultural Theory of Learning." In *Japanese Schooling*, edited by James J. Shields, pp. 8–15. University Park: Pennsylvania State University Press.

Stevenson, Harold W., Hiroshi Azuma, and Kenji Hakuta. 1986. *Child Development and Education in Japan*. New York: W. H. Freeman.

Stevenson, Harold W., and James W. Stigler. 1992. *Learning Gap.* New York: Summit Books.

Stigler, J. W., S. Y. Lee, and H. W. Stevenson. 1987. "Mathematics Classrooms in Japan, Taiwan and the United States." *Child Development* 58:1272–85.

Tobin, Joseph J., David Y. H. Wu, and Dana H. Davidson. 1989. *Preschool in Three Cultures: Japan, China, and the United States.* New Haven, Conn.: Yale University Press.

Willis, Paul E. 1981. *Learning to Labour: How Working Class Kids Get Working Class Jobs.* Aldershot, England: Gower.

Woronoff, Jon. 1991. *Japan as—Anything but—Number One.* Armonk, N.Y.: M. E. Sharpe.

———. 1992. *Japanese Management Mystique: The Reality behind the Myth.* Chicago: Probus.

Index

259